BARRON'S
BUSINESS
REVIEW
SERIES

D0770679

MANAGERIAL ECONOMICS

Jae K. Shim, Ph.D.

College of Business Administration
California State University, Long Beach

Joel G. Siegel, Ph.D.

Queens College of the City University of New York

Barron's Educational Series, Inc.

All inquiries should be addressed to:
Barron's Educational Series, Inc.
250 Wireless Boulevard
Hauppauge, New York 11788
http://www.barronseduc.com

Library of Congress Catalog Card No. 98-11942

International Standard Book No. 0-7641-0170-6

Library of Congress Cataloging-in-Publication Data
Shim, Jae K.
    Managerial economics / Jae K. Shim, Joel G. Siegel.
        p.   cm.
    Includes index.
    ISBN 0-7641-0170-6
    1. Managerial economics.   I. Siegel, Joel G.   II. Title.
HD30.22.S52   1998
338.5'024'658—dc21   98-11942
                                                                    CIP

Printed in the United States of America
9 8 7 6 5 4 3 2 1

Contents

PREFACE

This book provides a clear and concise introduction to *managerial economics.* The course *managerial economics* is offered in a variety of titles, including *business economics, economic analysis for business decisions, economics for management decisions,* and so on, at both the undergraduate and graduate levels. This book is an excellent supplement to those courses. It focuses on the fundamentals and essentials needed to understand how business decisions are made and how they are tackled using economics and other quantitative tools. It illustrates decisions with many solved problems to test and help students reinforce their understanding of the subject. Further, many business professionals can benefit from this book. The reader is assumed to have done some introductory-level work in economics. A minimal amount of background in college-level math and statistics is also expected.

This study guide extensively and intensively shows the application of economic theory and concepts to real-life business decisions. Throughout the text, you are advised to use the following ground rules to enhance your benefits:

1. ***Understand the Definitions and Key Points.*** Each chapter begins with *Key Terms* that are discussed throughout the chapter. It is followed, wherever applicable, by *You Should Remember,* which summarizes key points.

2. ***Study Each Example Over and Over Again.*** Be sure to work out each example. This is the key process in learning and understanding the chapter material. Of course, you will be tested with similar problems at the end of each chapter, and you will be provided with suggested solutions so that you can check your answers.

3. ***Do All Problems.*** *Do You Know the Basics* tests your understanding of the main concepts of the chapter. *Practical Applications* test your ability to handle analytical—mostly numerical—problems. Do not fail to do both!

If you stick to this game plan and work at it, you will be assured to enhance your understanding of managerial economics and be successful in the course. By the same token, business professionals will gain a better understanding of the subject and be able to apply the tools to make informed decisions.

Jae K. Shim
Joel G. Siegel

1

THE SCOPE AND METHODOLOGY OF MANAGERIAL ECONOMICS

KEY TERMS

managerial economics branch of economics applied in managerial decision making.

accounting profits difference between the total revenue and the cost of producing goods or services.

economic profits difference between the total revenue and the total opportunity costs.

present value analysis technique used widely to account for the timing of cash inflows and outflows.

profit maximization hypothesis that the goal of a firm is to maximize its profit.

wealth stockholders' value or market value of a firm's stock.

wealth maximization stockholders' value maximization, which is a firm's long-term goal.

value of the firm *present value* of the firm's expected future profits, discounted back to the present at an appropriate interest rate.

marginal revenue (MR) change in total revenue resulting from the sale of an additional unit of output.

marginal cost (MC) cost of the inputs used to make an additional unit of output.

marginal analysis analysis that ensures that for the profit to be maximized, marginal revenues should equal marginal costs.

opportunity costs net benefits forgone by rejecting the next-best use of a resource.

WHAT IS MANAGERIAL ECONOMICS?

Managerial economics is economics applied in decision making. It is a branch of economics that applies economic theory and decision science methodology to solve business and managerial problems. Its objective is to bridge the gap between abstract economic theory and managerial practice. It is the systematic study of how resources should be allocated in such a way to most efficiently achieve a managerial goal.

Economic theory and tools often are not sufficient to tackle all kinds of managerial problems. A variety of techniques and tools from finance, operations research, and other business disciplines are also used. In this sense, economic theory and tools on one hand and business disciplines on the other are blended into the subject.

YOU SHOULD REMEMBER

Managerial economics is often called *business economics, economic analysis for business decisions, economics for management decisions,* and so on. The courses are offered in these titles or variations thereof at both the undergraduate and graduate levels.

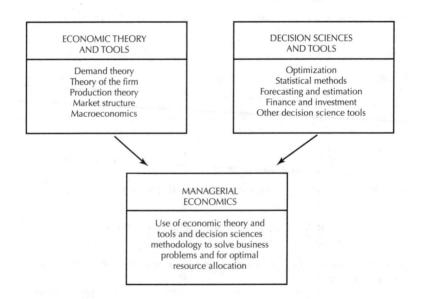

THE MANAGEMENT DECISION-MAKING PROCESS

The basic steps that are taken in any decision process include:

1. Recognize and define the problem. When management concludes that a problem exists, it should prepare a specific definition or exact statement of the problem. For example, how many of what products should the company produce?

2. Select a goal. Is it profit maximizing or cost minimizing?

3. Identify any constraints. Management's choice is always limited to some extent by resources available, law, regulatory action, moral values, or management preferences. Any constraints that might exist need to be identified.

4. Identify alternatives *or* define decision variables a firm is trying to solve for.

5. Select the alternative consistent with the firm's objectives *or* determine the optimal solution (i.e., profit-maximizing or cost-minimizing solution).

PROFITS

A profit is frequently described as a firm's bottom line. What then does the bottom line, ethically and legally produced, do for companies? First, it is a clear message that the company is delivering products or services that people need or want—especially at prices they are willing to pay. Also, a good bottom line means that the company has its costs in line. It also means "efficiency." Why do companies need to produce a good bottom line?

THE ROLE OF PROFITS

A good bottom line allows companies to

1. reward investors for risking their capital,

2. research and develop new and better products or services,

3. add jobs to employees, reward employees, and provide opportunities for employee growth and development, and

4. take pride in efficient performance.

ACCOUNTING VS. ECONOMIC PROFITS

We must differentiate between accounting profits and economic profits. *Accounting profits,* also called *business profits,* are the difference between the total revenue and the cost of producing goods or services. Accounting profits are what shows up on the bottom line of the firm's income statement.

Economic profits, on the other hand, are the difference between the total revenue and the total opportunity costs. The opportunity cost of using a resource results in economic costs that include both the explicit cost of the resource and the implicit cost of forsaking the next-best alternative use of the resource. For this reason, the opportunity cost is generally higher than accounting or bookkeeping costs. For example, the opportunity cost of attending summer school is the cost of tuition and textbooks plus the amount of money you would earn had you decided to work during the summer session.

YOU SHOULD REMEMBER

Throughout the book, when we speak of costs, we always mean economic costs. When we speak of profits, we mean economic profits. Accounting profits tend to overstate your economic profits, because the economic costs are accounting costs plus opportunity costs.

PROFIT MAXIMIZATION AND MARGINAL ANALYSIS

The goal of a firm is to maximize its profit. This is the traditional theory of the firm, which is distinguished from the *behavioral theory of the firm. Marginal analysis* suggests that business decisions should be made and actions taken only when marginal revenues (MR) exceed marginal costs (MC). (MR is the additional revenue resulting from the sale of an additional unit of output, and MC is the cost of the inputs used to make an additional unit of output).

If $MR = MC$, a given decision should maximize the firm's profits.

Unfortunately, the profit-maximization goal, as operationally defined, suffers from some technical flaws: (1) in its practical application, it provides no explicit way of considering the risk associated with alternative decisions, (2) it provides no basis for comparing promising varying flows of revenues and costs over time, and (3) instead of seeking to "maximize" some objective such as profits, the firm

Example 1

Let *TR(Q)* denote the total revenue a firm generates from producing Q units of output and let *TC(Q)* represent the total costs to the firm of producing Q units of output. The profit (π) then is

$$\pi(Q) = TR(Q) - TC(Q)$$

The manager facing a situation like that summarized in columns 1 through 3 in Table 1–1 wishes to determine the output quantity that will maximize its profits.

Table 1–1. Marginal Analysis

Q (1)	TR(Q) (2)	TC(Q) (3)	π(Q) (4) = (2) − (3)	MR	MC	
0	0	0	0	—	—	
1	90	10	80	90	10	MR > MC
2	170	30	140	80	20	
3	240	60	180	70	30	
4	300	100	200	60	40	
5	350	150	200	50	50	MR = MC
6	390	210	180	40	60	
7	420	280	140	30	70	
8	440	360	80	20	80	
9	450	450	0	10	90	
10	450	550	−100	0	100	MR < MC

The profits are given in column 4. Note the following from Table 1–1:

a. So long as *MR* exceeds *MC*, an increase in *Q* adds more to total revenues than it does to total costs.

b. The profits in column 4 are maximized when profits equal $200, which occurs when 5 units of *Q* are chosen by the manager.

c. At the profit maximizing level of *Q* (5 units), *MR* = *MC* (both are equal to $50 in this example).

Note: that the profit is also maximized at 4 units. This situation occurs because we are dealing with *discrete* output units. In a *continuous* case, which we assume throughout the book, the profit is maximized always when *MR* = *MC*.

YOU SHOULD REMEMBER

The concepts of *MR* and *MC* in a *continuous* situation and their relationship to *differential calculus* are discussed in Chapter 2. The marginal decision rule implied by profit maximization provides a strong basis on which many business decisions can be made.

---

is said to *satisfice,* or seek acceptable levels of performance, which is another model of the firm known as the *behavioral theory* of the firm. Furthermore, profit maximization is a short-term goal, which is simply the maximization of profits within a given period of time.

YOU SHOULD REMEMBER

A firm may maximize its short-term profits at the expense of its long-term profitability.

WEALTH MAXIMIZATION

A more operational goal of the firm is wealth maximization (or stockholders' value maximization). It is a long-term goal. Wealth maximization is generally preferred because it considers (1) wealth for the long term, (2) risk or uncertainty, (3) the timing of returns, and (4) the stockholders' return.

The wealth-maximization criterion requires that a firm evaluate the expected profits or cash flows associated with a decision by explicitly accounting for the timing of these flows, as well as the risk associated with them. Timing considerations require that future cash flows be adjusted or discounted by a rate of interest that reflects the "cost" of the funds being used to finance the project. The risk associated with cash flows can be treated in a number of ways, including a way of specifying the probability distribution of the cash flows. The *time value of money* concept and risk factors will be discussed in detail in Chapters 11 and 12.

The behavioral theory of the firm suggests that the firm has multiple goals, such as growth, size, and long-term survival. The growth is frequently measured in terms of increased sales, market share, assets, and/or number of employees. A company's long-term survival is assured only when business decision making is oriented toward the avoidance or minimization of risk rather than the maximization of profits.

RECOGNIZING THE TIME VALUE OF MONEY

A dollar now is worth more than a dollar to be received later. This statement sums up an important principle: money has a time value. The opportunity cost of receiving one dollar in the future is the forgone interest that could be earned on one dollar received today. This opportunity cost reflects the time value of money.

Time value of money is an important consideration in making business decisions. The *present value* (or *discounted cash flow*) *analysis* is used widely to account for the timing of cash inflows and outflows.

• *WHAT IS PRESENT VALUE—HOW MUCH MONEY IS WORTH NOW?*

Present value is the value today of future cash flows. The computation of present values (discounting) is the opposite of determining the compounded future value. The interest rate i is referred to as the *discount rate*.

Therefore,

$$PV = \frac{FV_n}{(1 + i)^n}.$$

EXAMPLE 2

$10,000 you expect to receive six years from now at a 15 percent discount rate would be worth $4,320 today.

$$PV = \$10,000\left(\frac{1}{(1 + 0.15)^6}\right) = \$10,000(0.432) = \$4,320.$$

This means that $4,320 invested today at 15 percent for six years grows to $10,000.

The basic idea of the present value of a future amount can be extended to a series of future cash flows, as shown below.

$$PV = \frac{FV_1}{(1 + i)^1} + \frac{FV_2}{(1 + i)^2} + \frac{FV_n}{(1 + i)^n}$$

$$= \sum_{t=1}^{n} \frac{FV_t}{(1 + i)^t}$$

EXAMPLE 3

You are thinking of starting a new product line that initially costs $32,000. Your annual projected cash inflows are

Year	Cash Inflows
1	$10,000
2	$20,000
3	$5,000

If you must earn a minimum of 10 percent on your investment, should you undertake this new product line?

The present value of this series of mixed streams of cash inflows is calculated as follows:

Year	Cash Inflows	$1/(1+0.10)^t$	Present Value
1	$10,000	0.909	$ 9,090
2	$20,000	0.826	16,520
3	$ 5,000	0.751	3,755
			$29,365

Because the present value of your projected cash inflows is less than the initial investment, you should not undertake this project.

YOU SHOULD REMEMBER

Present value calculations can be done using:

a. financial calculators,

b. present value tables (Tables 3 and 4 in Appendix II)

c. present value function keys in spreadsheet software, such as Excel or Lotus 1-2-3.

Depending on the method you use, rounding errors in answers are unavoidable. Details on *present value analysis* are covered in Chapter 11.

DEFINING THE VALUE OF THE FIRM

The process of determining the value of the firm involves finding the *present value* of the firm's expected future profits (or cash flows), discounted back to the present at an appropriate interest rate. Thus, the basic valuation model can be defined mathematically as follows:

$$V = \sum_{t=1}^{n} \frac{C_t}{(1 + r)^t}$$

where V = present value of the firm
C_t = expected future cash flows or profits in period $t = 1, ..., n$
r = required rate of return

EXAMPLE 4

XYZ company has the following year-end expected profits in each of the next three years: $30,000, $90,000, and $120,000. Then it shut downs. Assuming a 10 percent interest rate, determine the value of the firm.

The present value of this series of profits is calculated as follows:

Year	Cash Inflows	$1/(1+0.10)^n$	Present Value
1	$30,000	0.909	$27,270
2	90,000	0.826	74,340
3	120,000	0.751	90,120
			$191,730

KNOW THE CONCEPTS

TERMS FOR STUDY

accounting profits
economic profits
managerial economics
marginal analysis
optimize
present value analysis

profit maximization
satisfice
time value of money
value of a firm
wealth (shareholder) value maximization

DO YOU KNOW THE BASICS?

1. Define managerial economics.
2. What is the role of a firm? What is the goal of a firm?
3. Differentiate accounting profits from economic profits.
4. What is the value of a firm?
5. Explain marginal analysis.
6. Define opportunity costs.

PRACTICAL APPLICATION

1. You are trying to decide whether to open a new hamburger shop. You presently make $45,000 per year as a freelance consultant and will have to give up this job if you open the shop. If you elect to open the restaurant, it will cost you annually $245,000 per year in rent and other operating expenses.

    a. What are your accounting costs?
    b. What are your opportunity costs?

2. The following table shows year-end expected profits for each firm over the next three years. Interest rates are expected to be stable at 8 percent over the next three years. Determine the value of each firm.

Firm	Profits in Year 1	Profits in Year 2	Profits in Year 3
X	$60,000	$70,000	$80,000
Y	$40,000	$80,000	$100,000

    a. Discuss the differences in the profits associated with each firm.
    b. Which firm has more value?

3. Complete the following table, and answer the accompanying questions:

Q	TR(Q)	TC(Q)	π(Q)	MR	MC
0	0	0		—	—
1	200	10			
2	380	30			
3	540	60			
4	680	100			

continued

Q	TR(Q)	TC(Q)	π(Q)	MR	MC
5	800	150			
6	900	210			
7	970	280			
8	1,040	360			
9	1,080	450			
10	1,100	550			

a. What level of Q maximizes profits?

b. What is the relation between marginal revenue (MR) and marginal cost (MC) at the level of Q?

ANSWERS

DO YOU KNOW THE BASICS?

1. Managerial economics is the systematic study of how resources should be allocated to most efficiently achieve a managerial goal.

2. The role of a firm is to allocate limited resources in an optimal manner and to meet the goals of its owners. The goal of a firm is to maximize profits.

3. Accounting profits, also called business profits, are the difference between the total revenue and the cost of producing goods or services. Accounting profits are what shows up on the bottom line of the firm's income statements. Economic profits, on the other hand, are the difference between the total revenue and the total opportunity costs.

4. The value of a firm is the present worth of the firm's expected future profits, discounted back to the present at an appropriate interest rate.

5. Marginal analysis suggests that business decisions should be made and actions taken only when marginal revenues exceed marginal costs. If this condition exists, a given decision should maximize the firm's profits.

6. Opportunity costs are net benefits forgone by rejecting the next-best use of a resource.

PRACTICAL APPLICATION

1a. Accounting costs are $245,000 per year in rent and other operating expenses.

1b. Opportunity costs are $290,000 per year ($45,000 + $245,000).

2a. Firm X has the higher first year profits, but the lowest second and third year profits, while Firm Y earns less in the first year than X, but more in years two and three.

2b. The present value of this series of profits is calculated as follows:

For Firm X

Year	Cash Inflows	$1/(1+0.08)^n$	Present Value
1	$60,000	0.926	$55,560
2	70,000	0.857	59,990
3	80,000	0.794	63,520
			$ 179,070

For Firm Y

Year	Cash Inflows	$1/(1+0.08)^n$	Present Value
1	$40,000	0.926	$37,040
2	80,000	0.857	68,560
3	100,000	0.794	79,400
			$ 185,000

Firm Y has the higher present value.

3.

Q (1)	$TR(Q)$ (2)	$TC(Q)$ (3)	$\pi(Q)$ (2) − (3)	MR	MC
0	0	0	0	—	—
1	200	10	190	200	10
2	380	30	350	180	20
3	540	60	480	160	30
4	680	100	580	140	40
5	800	150	650	120	50
6	900	210	690	100	60
7	970	280	690	70	70
8	1,030	360	680	60	80
9	1,080	450	630	50	90
10	1,100	550	550	20	100

3a. $Q = 7$ maximizes profits.

3b. $MR = MC = \$70$ at $Q = 7$ units.

2
OPTIMIZATION: PRINCIPLES AND TECHNIQUES

KEY TERMS

optimization maximization or minimization of a special goal.

derivative instantaneous rate of change of a function at a given point or the slope of the function's tangent. It is a specification of the *marginal* relation in economics.

first derivative test test to locate one or more extreme (maximum or minimum) points on a function.

second derivative test test to determine whether an extreme point is either a maximum or a minimum point.

partial derivative derivative with respect to one variable in question, holding the other variables constant.

constrained optimization optimization with the restrictions imposed on the availability of resources and other requirements. Techniques such as linear programming (LP) and the Lagrangean multipliers are used for this purpose.

Lagrangean multiplier measure of the marginal change in the value of the objective function resulting from a one-unit change in the value of the constraint.

USING FUNCTIONS, GRAPHS, AND EQUATIONS

In the field of economics it is often important to talk about relationships between different economic quantities. For example, you will hear that there is a relationship between the price of a good (or service) and the quantity that people will purchase of it. Throughout this book, you will see numerous relationships, such as the production function, cost function, and profit function.

There are two basic types of analysis: mathematical and graphical.

THE CONCEPT OF A FUNCTIONAL RELATIONSHIP

The expression $y = f(x)$ (Read "y is a function of x") means that the value of y depends on the value of x. There is a relationship between these variables. For example, the quantity of a commodity that people will purchase depends upon the price for which the commodity can be purchased. This expression tells us nothing, however, about the nature of the relationship. It can mean that as x increases, y increases; or it can mean that it will decrease. $y = f(x)$ means merely that there is a relationship so that for every value of x, there is a value of y.

If, however, we say, for example:

$$y = 4x + 5$$

we have stated a specific hypothesis or idea—we have given content to that relationship. As the value of x increases by 1, the value of y increases by 4. We can in fact know the value of y for every value of x.

USING GRAPHS

Consider the following functional relationship: $y = 2x + 2$ where x stands for the amount of fertilizer used and y for the amount of the resulting crop. We can make a table or schedule of this relationship showing the value of y for a few values of x.

Each point in Fig. 2–1 (not just the ones emphasized) represents a value of x and a value of y. For example, the point labeled A represents $x = 3$, $y = 8$. To graph this equation, we simply plot several points consistent with the equation on the graph and draw a line through these two points. Each point on the line shows the given value of x (tons of fertilizer) and the corresponding value of y. In mathematics, it is usual to use y as the dependent variable and x as the independent variables and to graph the relationship with x on the horizontal axis and y on the

Table 2–1. Functional Relationship

If $x =$	Then $y =$
0	2
1	4
2	6
3	8
4	10

vertical axis. Not all functions can be represented by a straight line on a graph (Those that can are called *linear*).

YOU SHOULD REMEMBER

Sometimes economists represent the dependent variable on the horizontal axis and the independent variable on the vertical axis. An example of this is in supply and demand analysis for which price (the independent variable) and quantity (the dependent variable) are graphed respectively on the vertical and horizontal axis (See Figure 2–2).

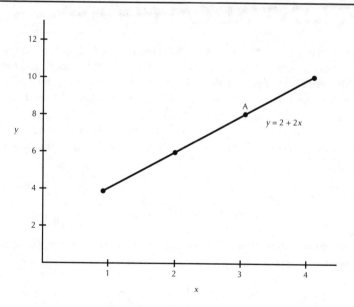

Figure 2–1. Graph of A Function

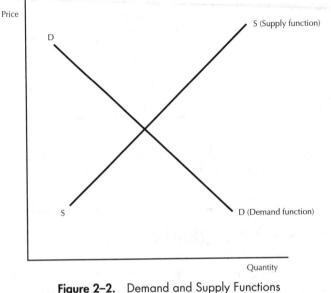

Figure 2-2. Demand and Supply Functions

DIFFERENTIAL CALCULUS

Differential calculus can be used to determine the rate of change in a function relative to a change in the independent variable. In fact, the designation *differential* refers to differences that occur in the value of a function as a result of changes in the independent variable: $\Delta y/\Delta x$ where the change in y, Δy indicates the change in the dependent variable associated with Δx, the change in the value of x.

The main tool provided by differential calculus for the determination of such differences is the *derivative*. The derivative $dy/dx = y' = f'(x)$ of a function $y = f(x)$ at x_0 is defined as

$$\frac{dy}{dx} = \lim_{\Delta x \to 0} \frac{\Delta y}{\Delta x} = \lim_{\Delta x \to 0} \frac{f(x_0 + \Delta x) - f(x_0)}{\Delta x}$$

This means that the derivative $dy/dx = y' = f'(x)$ of a function $y = f(x)$ at x_0 is the limit of the difference quotient $\Delta y/\Delta x$ as the change in x approaches zero.

This section provides the derivatives of various functions. The rules for *differentiation* (the process of obtaining the derivative) provided by differential calculus are as follows:

YOU SHOULD REMEMBER

Simply put, the derivative is the instantaneous rate of change of a function at a point ($x = x_0$), whereas the difference quotient is the average rate of change over some interval (x_0, $x_0 + \Delta x$). They are identical only in a *straight line* case. Graphically, the derivative is the *slope* of the line *tangent* to the curve at some point x_0.

RULES FOR DIFFERENTIATION

RULE 1 (Constant Rule): $y = f(x) = c$, a constant.

The derivative:
$$\frac{dy}{dx} = y' = f'(x) = 0.$$

This rule holds that whenever the function is a constant, the derivative is zero. That is, the rate of change in a constant relative to a change in the independent variable (or any variable, for that matter) is zero.

Example: If $y = 13$, then $\dfrac{dy}{dx} = 0$

RULE 2 (Power Function Rule): $y = f(x) = cx^n$.

The derivative:
$$\frac{dy}{dx} = cnx^{n-1}.$$

Examples: If $y = x^3$, then $\dfrac{dy}{dx} = 3x^2$.

If $y = x$, then $\dfrac{dy}{dx} = 1x^0 = 1$.

RULE 3 (Sum-Difference Rule): $y = f(x) \pm g(x)$.

The derivative: $\dfrac{dy}{dx} = f(x) \pm g'(x)$, where $f'(x) = \dfrac{df(x)}{dx}$ and $g'(x) = \dfrac{dg(x)}{dx}$.

This rule holds that the derivative of the sum of two different functions of the same independent variable is the sum of the two derivatives of the different functions.

Examples: If $y = x^4 + 2x$, $\dfrac{dy}{dx} = 4x^3 + 2$.

If $4x - 5x^2$, then $\dfrac{dy}{dx} = 4 - 10x$.

RULE 4 (Product Rule): $y = f(x)g(x)$.

The derivative: $\dfrac{dy}{dx} = f'(x)g(x) + g'(x)f(x)$.

This rule says that the derivative of the product of two different functions of the same independent variable is the sum of the first function times the derivative of the second function, plus the second function times the derivative of the first.

Example: If $y = x^2(2x - 3)$, then $\dfrac{dy}{dx} = x^2(2 - 0) + (2x - 3)(2x)$

$$= 2x^2 + 4x^2 - 6x = 6x^2 - 6x = 6x(x - 1)$$

RULE 5 (Quotient Rule): $y = f(x)/g(x)$.

The derivative: $\dfrac{dy}{dx} = \dfrac{f'(x)g(x) - g'(x)f(x)}{[g(x)]^2}$

Example: If $y = 5x/(2x + 1)$, then

$$\dfrac{dy}{dx} = \dfrac{5(2x + 1) - 2(5x)}{(2x + 1)^2} = \dfrac{5}{2x + 1}$$

RULE 6 (Chain Rule or Function-of-Function Rule): $y = g(z)$, where $z = f(x)$.

The derivative: $\dfrac{dy}{dx} = \dfrac{dy}{dz}\dfrac{dz}{dx} = g'(z)f'(x)$.

This rule holds that a change in x will produce a change in z, which will, in turn, produce a change in y. Thus, dy/dx, or the rate of change of y with respect to x, is given by the rate of change of z with respect to x, dz/dx, multiplied by the rate of change of y with respect to z, dy/dz.

Example: If $y = 10z - 2z^2 - 3$, where $z = 2x^2 - 1$, then

$$\dfrac{dy}{dx} = (10 - 4z)(4x) = [10 - 4(2x^2 - 1)](4x)$$

$$= (10 - 8x^2 + 4)(4x) = 40x - 32x^2 + 16x = 56x - 32x^2.$$

RULE 7 (Inverse Function Rule): $x = f^{-1}(y)$, where f^{-1} refers to the inverse function, not $1/f(y)$.

The derivative:
$$\frac{dx}{dy} = \frac{1}{dy/dx}.$$

Example: If $y = 5x + 3$, then $x = \frac{1}{5}y - \frac{3}{5}$, and $\frac{dx}{dy} = \frac{1}{5}$.

The following example shows how the derivative can be used to find the rate of change.

EXAMPLE 1

Peruvian Cleaning Supply Company is the exclusive distributor of an important cleaning fluid used by furriers throughout the southeastern U.S. This cleaning fluid is used to prepare fur garments for protective storage in refrigerated vaults during the humid summer season. Peruvian delivers the cleaner in tank trucks, and each customer must take at least 100 gallons. The price is $12 per gallon. A discount of $0.05 per gallon is granted to each customer purchasing in quantities greater than the 100-gallon minimum. This discount applies only to quantities above the minimum; the first 100 gallons are charged at $12 per gallon regardless of the total number of gallons delivered.

Management formulated the following mathematical expression for total revenue (*TR*) per customer on the basis of the information given:

$$TR = \$12(100) + [\$12 - \$0.05(x - 100)](x - 100) = -500 + 22x - 0.05x^2.$$

This is a quadratic function. The derivative formula for this function is:

$$\frac{dTR}{dx} = 22 - 0.10x.$$

This derivative reflects the fact that the rate of change is not constant. That is, the rate of change depends on the value of the variable x, so the rate of change will itself change as the value of g changes. This variability in the rate of change is consistent with the fact that the rate of change of a quadratic function continually varies. To find the rate of change in *TR* when a particular number of gallons is sold to a customer, the number of gallons is substituted for x in the derivative. For example, to find the rate of change (per gallon) in *TR* at 105 gallons, the following calculation is necessary based on the following derivative:

$$22 - 0.10(105) = 22 - 10.50 = 11.50.$$

That is, total revenue is changing by $11.50 at this volume of sales to a particular customer. At sales of 110 gallons, the rate of change is $11, as determined below, again on the basis of the following derivative:

$$22 - 0.10(110) = 22 - 11 = 11.$$

In other words, total revenue is changing at the rate of $11 when sales are 110 gallons in contrast to $11.50 when sales are 105 gallons.

YOU SHOULD REMEMBER

The derivative for the *TR* function gives the marginal revenue (*MR*), i.e., the increase in *TR* resulting from an additional unit of output.

THE EXTREME VALUE OF A FUNCTION AND THE DERIVATIVE TESTS

The extreme value of a function (the maximum or minimum value) that the function can assume is very important in economic decision making. Much of economics deals with optimization, that is the maximization of profit or minimization of costs.

THE FIRST DERIVATIVE TEST

The *first derivative test* (or *first-order condition*) is used to determine extreme points of a function (See Figure 2–3). It states that $dy/dx = y' = f'(x_0) = 0$ at a local maximum or minimum point and x_0 is called an *extreme (critical)* value of the function. It involves three steps: (1) find the derivative, (2) set it equal to zero, and (3) solve for the value of x.

The second derivative is arrived at by applying the rules of differentiation to the first derivative rather than to the original function. That is, the first derivative is itself differentiated, and the result is the second derivative. The second derivative is the derivative of the first derivative, denoted with $d^2y/dx^2 = y'' = f''(x)$.

EXAMPLE 2

Suppose $y = f(x) = 3x^2$. Then, $dy/dx = f'(x) = 6x$. The result, $6x$, is the first derivative. The second derivative $d^2y/dx^2 = y'' = f''(x) = 6$.

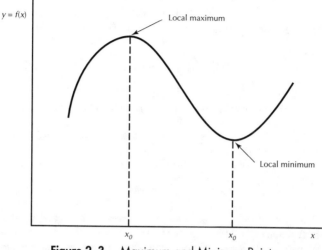

Figure 2–3. Maximum and Minimum Points

YOU SHOULD REMEMBER

The second derivative is the measure of the rate of change of the first derivative. In other words, it measures the rate of change of the slope of the original function f(x).

THE SECOND DERIVATIVE TEST

We need to determine whether the extreme value is a maximum or a minimum. This information can be obtained through the use of the *second derivative test* (or *second-order condition*). The test states that

1. the function $y = f(x)$ reaches a local *maximum* at some point $x = x_0$ if $f'(x_0) = 0$ and $f''(x_0)$ is negative,

2. Similarly, $f(x)$ reaches a local *minimum* at some point x_0 if $f'(x_0) = 0$ and $f''(x_0)$ is positive,

3. the function reaches an *inflection point* rather than a local maximum or minimum at $x = x_0$ if both first and second derivatives are 0, i.e., $f'(x_0) = 0$ and $f''(x_0) = 0$. An example of the function with *no* local maximum or local minimum) is $y = f(x) = x^3$ (See Figure 2–4).

EXAMPLE 3

Recall from Example 1: $TR = -500 + 22x - 0.05x^2$.

$$\frac{dTR}{dx} = 22 - 0.10x = 0$$

We set the first derivative equal to zero and solve for x, as follows:

$$22 - 0.10x = 0,$$

$$-0.10x = -22,$$

$$x = 220.$$

Note that $d^2TR/dx^2 = -0.1$. Since the second derivative is negative, the extreme value of the function ($x^* = 220$) is a maximum.

Substituting $x^* = 220$ for x in the original function we get for the maximum revenue the following:

$$-500 + 22(220) - 0.05(220)^2 = -500 + 4,840 - 0.05(48,400)$$

$$= \$1,920$$

EXAMPLE 4

Given $y = f(x) = x^3 - 12x^2 + 36x + 18$.

To get the critical value we take the first derivative and set it equal to 0:

$$\frac{dy}{dx} = f'(x) = 3x^2 - 24x + 36 = 0$$

$$= (3x - 18)(x - 2) = 0,$$ which indicates there are two roots in this quadratic equation.

The dual roots are: $(3x - 18) = 0$ and $(x - 2) = 0$; therefore, $x_1 = 6$ and $x_2 = 2$.

To determine if they are maximum or minimum points, we need to do the second derivative test, as follows:

$$\frac{d^2y}{dx^2} = f''(x) = 6x - 24$$

At $x_1 = 6, f''(x) = 6(6) - 24 = 8 > 0$, it is a minimum.

At $x_2 = 2, f''(x) = 6(2) - 24 = -12 < 0$, it is a maximum.

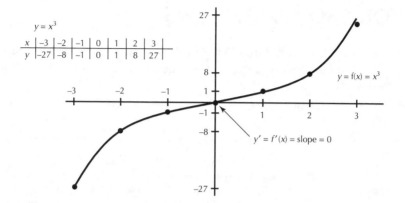

Figure 2–4. Inflection Point.

YOU SHOULD REMEMBER

	First Derivative Test	Second Derivative Test
Maximum	$f'(x_0) = 0$	$f''(x_0) < 0$
Minimum	$f'(x_0) = 0$	$f''(x_0) > 0$

PARTIAL DERIVATIVES AND MULTIVARIATE OPTIMIZATION

Many functions involve multiple independent variables. It is useful to understand the concept of *multivariate optimization,* the process of optimization for equations with multiple decision variables. Total direct labor cost in a manufacturing firm may be used to illustrate a function of two independent variables, namely, (1) the number of direct labor hours worked and (2) the hourly wage rate. As a result, multivariate optimization is employed in the process of optimization.

The process involves *partial differentiation.* Quite often, we wish to know the individual effect that a change in one independent variable [while the other(s) are held constant] will have on the dependent variable. The process is called partial differentiation. This designation refers to the fact that the function is differentiated relative to only a part (specifically, one) of the group of independent variables. The result is called the *partial derivative* denoted with ∂, instead of d.

YOU SHOULD REMEMBER

The rules for partial differentiation are the same with the added stipulation that the independent variables not involved in the differentiation are treated as constants.

EXAMPLE 5

To illustrate, suppose the sales revenue function is $TR = 2x^2y^2z$, where x = advertising expense in the prior period, y = salespersons' travel expense in the prior period, and z = units sold by competitors during the current period. Suppose management needs to know the maximum extent to which revenue is generated by x (advertising expense in the prior period). The procedure for finding the extreme value is as follows:

1. differentiate partially relative to the variable of interest,

2. set the partial derivative equal to zero and solve for the variable of interest, and

3. evaluate the original function at this value to determine the extreme.

Viewing y and z as constants, the full coefficient of x^2 is $2y^2z$. The partial derivative with respect to x, the variable of interest in this example is

$$\frac{\partial TR}{\partial x} = 4xy^2z.$$

Setting the partial derivative equal to zero and solving for x gives the following:

$$4y^2zx = 0$$

$$x = 0.$$

Thus, the revenue function assumes its extreme value when $x = 0$.

In order to interpret this result, it will be helpful to determine whether the extreme is a maximum or a minimum. As explained earlier, the sign of the second derivative (the second partial derivative in the multivariate case) determines this. The second partial derivative is determined as follows:

$$\frac{\partial^2 TR}{\partial x^2} = 4y^2z.$$

Because the second partial derivative is positive, the extreme value of the function is minimal.

The fact that the extreme value of the function results when $x = 0$ may be interpreted to mean that zero advertising expense in the prior period results in the lowest possible contribution of advertising to sales revenue. Furthermore, it is implied that the contribution of advertising expense to sales revenue next period will continue to increase as long as advertising expense continues to increase. This indicates that the firm's advertising expense does have a positive effect on revenue. (Recall that the partial derivative procedure assumes that y and z remain constant, so no inferences are drawn concerning the effect of changes in these variables on the revenue function.)

PROFIT MAXIMIZATION

The goal of a firm is to maximize its profit. The economic theory suggests that business decisions should be made and actions taken only when marginal revenues exceed marginal costs. If this condition exists, a given decision should maximize the firm's profits. To find the profit-maximizing output, we should use differential calculus.

EXAMPLE 6

Consider the following total revenue (TR) and total cost (TC) functions:

$$TR(Q) = \$1,000Q - \$5Q^2 \text{ and } TC(Q) = \$20,000 + \$200Q.$$

The profit function (π) then is:

$$\pi(Q) = TR(Q) - TC(Q) = \$1,000Q - \$5Q^2 - (\$20,000 + \$200Q)$$

$$= \$1,000Q - \$5Q^2 - \$20,000 - \$200Q$$

$$= -\$20,000 + \$800Q - \$5Q^2.$$

Taking $d\pi/dQ = 0$ and solve for Q yields $Q^* = 80$ units, as follows:

$$\frac{d\pi}{dQ} = \$800 - \$10Q = 0; \quad Q^* = 80 \text{ units.}$$

An evaluation of the second derivative of the profit function is

$$\frac{d^2\pi}{dQ^2} = -10 < 0, \text{ which indicates } Q^* = 80 \text{ is a point of profit maximization.}$$

Figure 2–5 presents a graph of (a) the *hypothetical* total revenue, total cost, and profit functions, and (b) the marginal revenue, marginal cost, and marginal profit functions.

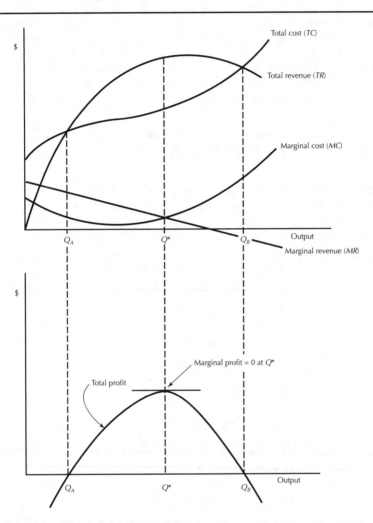

Figure 2–5. Total Revenue, Total Cost, Marginal Revenue, Marginal Cost, and Profit Maximization

CONSTRAINED OPTIMIZATION

Many firms face restrictions imposed on their decision variables. Examples are the limitations imposed by the amount of resources (such as money, facilities, capacity, materials, and personnel) available to the firm. Constrained optimization is maximization of profits with the restrictions imposed on the availability of resources or minimization of costs with minimum requirements needed to be satisfied. Techniques such as the Lagrangean multiplier method and linear programming (to be discussed in Chapter 7) are used for this purpose.

The general problem is that of finding the extreme points of the function $f(x, y)$ subject to equalities of the form $g(x, y) = 0$.

When the constraints take the form of *equalities,* classical optimization procedures can be used to find an optimal solution. Two methods can be used: (1) The substitution method and (2) The Lagrangean multiplier method.

THE SUBSTITUTION METHOD

The substitution method can be used when the objective function is subject to only one constraint equality of a relatively simple nature. By substitution, we reduce the dimension of our objective function. It involves two steps: (1) solve the equation for one of the decision variables and then (2) substitute this expression into the objective function. The procedure transforms the original problem into an *unconstrained* optimization problem so that differential calculus can be applied to obtain the optimal solution.

EXAMPLE 7

Suppose a firm produces its product on two assembly lines and operates with the total cost function, $TC(x, y) = 3x^2 + 6y^2 - xy$, where $x =$ the output produced on one assembly line and $y =$ the output produced on a second assembly line. Management seeks to determine the least-cost combination of x and y, subject to the constraint that total output of the product must be 20 units. The constrained optimization problem can be stated as follows:

minimize $\qquad\qquad TC(x, y) = 3x^2 + 6y^2 - xy,$

subject to $\qquad\qquad x + y = 20.$

First, solve the constraint equation for x, yielding $x = 20 - y$ and plug it into the objective function.

$$TC(x, y) = T(y) = 3(20 - y)^2 + 6y^2 - (20 - y)y = 3(400 - 40y - y^2) + 6y^2 - 20y + y^2,$$
$$1{,}200 - 120y + 3y^2 + 6y^2 - 20y + y^2 = 1{,}200 - 140y + 10y^2.$$

Taking the derivative of this reduced objective function and setting it equal to zero, we obtain

$$\frac{dTC}{dy} = -140 + 20y = 0,$$

$$y = 7 \text{ units.}$$

In turn solving for x yields: $x = 20 - y = 20 - 7 = 13$ units.

Thus, $x = 13$ and $y = 7$ is the optimal solution to the constrained cost-minimization problem.

YOU SHOULD REMEMBER

The limitation of the substitution method is that it works only when there is one constraint equation and it is possible to solve this equation for one of the decision variables. With more than one constraint equation and/or a complicated constraint structure, the Lagrangean multiplier method must be employed.

LAGRANGEAN MULTIPLIER TECHNIQUE

A method of solving *constrained optimization* problems in which the constraint (in a form in which it will equal to zero when it is satisfied) is added to the original objective function. A new, *augmented* objective function is called *Lagrangean function*, which constitutes an unconstrained optimization problem. The function is of the form:

$$L(x, y, \lambda) = f(x, y) + \lambda g(x, y).$$

The coefficient of the constraining equation $g(x, y)$, λ (read as lambda), is termed the *Lagrangean multiplier*. Because the constraining equation is equal to 0, the addition of the term $\lambda g(x, y)$ to the objective function $f(x, y)$ does not change the value of the function.

YOU SHOULD REMEMBER

If a constrained optimization problem has more than one constraint, a separate λ is defined for each constraint and incorporated into the Lagrangean function. The λ values are analogous to the dual variables of *linear programming (LP)* and represent the *shadow prices* of scarce resources. (To be discussed in Chapter 7.)

EXAMPLE 8

From Example 7, our constraint was $x + y = 20$. First, it should be rearranged so as to form an expression equal to zero, $g(x, y) = 0$. That means the constraint $x + y = 20$ is transformed to the expression $20 - x - y = 0$.

Next, we define an artificial variable λ and form the Lagrangean function (L):

$$L(x, y, \lambda) = TC(x, y) + \lambda g(x, y) = 3x^2 + 6y^2 - xy + \lambda(20 - x - y).$$

Note that

1. As long as $g(x, y)$ is maintained equal to zero, the Lagrangean function $L(x, y, \lambda)$ will not differ in value from the original total cost function $TC(x, y)$. Minimizing $L(x, y, \lambda)$ will also minimize $TC(x, y)$.

2. Taking the partial derivative with respect to λ and setting that equal to zero gives you the original constraint.

Since $L(x, y, \lambda)$ is a function of three decision variables, in order to minimize this function, we need to:

1. partially differentiate it with respect to each of the variables;

2. set the partial derivatives equal to zero; and

3. solve the resulting set of equations for the optimal values of x, y, and λ.

The partial derivatives are

$$\frac{\partial L(x, y, \lambda)}{\partial x} = 6x - y - \lambda = 0,$$

$$\frac{\partial L(x, y, \lambda)}{\partial y} = 12y - x - \lambda = 0,$$

$$\frac{\partial L(x, y, \lambda)}{\partial \lambda} = 20 - x - y = 0.$$

Solving three partial derivative equations simultaneously, we obtain $x = 13$, $y = 7$, and $\lambda = 71$.

λ measures the marginal change in the value of the objective function due to a one-unit change in the value of the constraint. In this example, $\lambda = 71$ indicates the costs would be increased by \$71 if one more unit of output is produced; that is, an increase from 20 units to 21.

This artificial variable measures the marginal change in the value of the objective function resulting from a one-unit change in the value of the constraint. The Lagrangean method works when (1) substitution is impractical, and (2) there exist many constraints. Further, it provides interesting economic information. The method is illustrated below using an earlier example.

MARGINAL ANALYSIS VERSUS INCREMENTAL ANALYSIS

Marginal analysis relates to an additional unit of output. Managers at any level who have to make their functional (such as marketing, operational, production, purchasing, financing, investment, and personnel) decisions must always weigh the marginal cost to be incurred against the marginal revenue to be derived from that decision. Many managerial decisions, however, involve a consideration of changes that are much broader in scope. For example, management may wish to investigate the impact on profits of a 20 percent increase in sales or an introduction of a new product line.

Incremental analysis is frequently used in the practical equivalent of marginal analysis. It relates to a specified managerial decision that can involve a choice between two discrete quantities of output (e.g., 10,000 units vs. 15,000 units). It is the process of examining the impact of alternative choice decisions on revenue, cost, or profit. It focuses attention on changes or differences between alternatives. Managers will have to weigh the incremental cost associated with the decision against the incremental revenue. For this reason, marginal analysis is more appropriately called *incremental analysis*.

KNOW THE CONCEPTS

TERMS FOR STUDY

constrained optimization	optimization
cost minimization	partial derivative
derivative	profit maximization
extreme point	second derivative
Lagrangean function	slope
Lagrangean multiplier	

DO YOU KNOW THE BASICS?

1. Define the term *optimization.*

2. Discuss briefly the first and second derivative tests.

3. What is constrained optimization? Give two popular techniques that deal with constrained optimization.

4. Define Lagrangean multiplier. What is it analogous to in linear programming?

5. What is the derivative? What does it try to measure?

6. Distinguish between marginal analysis and incremental analysis.

PRACTICAL APPLICATION

1. ABC Boutique offers all its merchandise for sale at $20 per unit. The total cost of producing Q units is given by $TC = 40 + 4Q + 0.02Q^2$. How many units must be produced to maximize profit? What is the maximum profit at this level?

2. Find the maximum point on the function $y = 75x - 0.25x^2$. Prove that this is a maximum, not a minimum by evaluating the second derivative at the x value.

3. Find the maxima and minima points on the function $y = 1,500 - 600x - 15x^2 + x^3$, and evaluate the second derivative to differentiate between them.

4. Your firm's economic analysis department has estimated your total revenues to be $TR(Q) = 3,200Q - 6Q^2$ and your total costs to be $TC(Q) = 90 + 2Q^2$

  a. What level of Q maximizes profits?

  b. What is marginal revenue at this level of Q?

  c. What is marginal cost at this level of Q?

  d. What is the maximum level of profits?

5. Jon Electronics operates with the following total revenue (TR) and total cost (TC) functions:

$$TR = \$200Q - \$0.5Q^2 \text{ and } TC = \$1,000 - \$40Q + \$0.5Q^2$$

  a. Determine the revenue maximizing Q (the quantity of output).

  b. Determine the cost minimizing Q.

  c. Determine the profit maximizing Q.

  d. Prove that marginal revenue (MR) equals marginal cost (MC) at the profit maximizing Q.

6. The purpose of inventory planning is to develop policies that will achieve an optimal investment in inventory. This objective is achieved by determining the optimal level of inventory necessary to minimize inventory related costs. Annual total inventory costs (TIC) are the sum of carrying cost + ordering cost, i.e., $TIC = C(Q/2) + S(D/Q)$, where C = carrying cost per unit, S = ordering cost per order, D = annual demand (requirements) in units, and Q = order quantity. Develop a formula for determining the economic order quantity $Q*$ (EOQ) by minimizing the TIC.

7. Using the Lagrangean multiplier method, find the extreme point.

Maximize $z = xy$

Subject to $x + y = 6$

8. Suppose that a firm's production function is $Q = M^2 + 5MK + 4K^2$ and that the price of a unit of labor services (M) and the price of a unit of capital services (K) is $5 and $10, and that the cost function is equal to $1,000 per time period.

a. Formulate the problem as a constrained optimization format.

b. Use the substitution method to determine the quantities of K and M that will maximize output (Q).

c. Use the Lagrangean multiplier method to do the same.

d. Give an economic interpretation of the value of λ obtained in **c** above.

9. A firm has the following profit function in which the profit variable Z is a function of the output level of two products x and y: $Z = -60 + 140x + 100y - 10x^2 - 8y^2 - 6xy$. Assume that the firm has the raw materials in short supply, having only 200 units. Products x and y require 20 units and 40 units of the raw materials to produce one unit of output. The firm wishes to determine the profit-maximizing mix of products.

a. Formulate the problem as a constrained optimization format.

b. Use the substitution method to determine the quantities of x and y that will maximize profit (Z).

c. Use the Lagrangean multiplier method to do the same.

d. Give an economic interpretation of the value of λ obtained in **c** above.

10. Given:

Maximize $Y = 10xzw - 3w^2$

Subject to $x + z + w = 12$

                                  $x - w = 2$

Set up the Lagrangean function and develop partial derivatives equations. (Do not solve).

ANSWERS

KNOW THE BASICS

1. Optimization is the maximization or minimization of a specific objective (i.e., profit or costs).

2. The first derivative test is a test to locate one or more extreme (maximum or minimum) points on a function, while the second derivative test is a test to determine whether an extreme point is either a maximum or a minimum point.

3. Constrained optimization is optimization with the restrictions imposed on the availability of resources and other requirements. Techniques such as linear programming (LP) and the Lagrangean multipliers are used to attack this type of problem.

4. The Lagrangean multiplier measures the marginal change in the value of the objective function resulting from a one-unit change in the value on the right-hand side of the equality sign in the constraint. This is analogous to the dual variables of linear programming and represent the shadow price of a given scarce resource.

5. The derivative dy/dx measures the marginal change in y associated with a very small change in x. It is basically the slope of a function.

6. Marginal analysis relates to a single unit of output, while incremental analysis relates to a specified managerial decision that can involve a choice between two discrete quantities of output (e.g., 10,000 units vs. 15,000 units). Incremental analysis is frequently used as the practical equivalent of marginal analysis.

PRACTICAL APPLICATION

1. Total profit (π) = total revenue(TR) – total cost(TC)

$$= \$20Q - (40 + 4Q + 0.02Q^2) = -40 + 16Q - 0.02Q^2$$

Taking the derivative with respect to Q and setting it equal to zero, we obtain

$$\frac{d\pi}{dQ} = 16 - 0.04Q = 0, \text{ Solving for } Q \text{ yields } Q^* = 40.$$

The maximum profit at $Q^* = 40$ is

$$\pi^* = -40 + 16Q - 0.02Q^2 = -40 + 16(40) - 0.02(40)^2 = 568.$$

2. Set $dy/dx = 0$:

$$\frac{dy}{dx} = 75 - 0.5x = 0, \ \ x = 150.$$

Since $d^2y/dx^2 = -0.5 < 0$, $x = 150$ a maxima has been located.

3. Set $dy/dx = 0$ to locate all maxima and minima.

$$\frac{dy}{dx} = -600 - 30x + 3x^2 = 0$$

or

$$(3x + 30)(x - 20) = 0$$

(the dual solutions are $x = -10$; $x = 20$).

Taking the second derivative yields $d^2y/dx^2 = -30 + 6x$:

At $x = -10$, $\dfrac{d^2y}{dx^2} = -30 + 6x = -30 + 6(-10) = -90 < 0$ (maxima),

At $x = 20$, $\dfrac{d^2y}{dx^2} = -30 + 6x = -30 + 6(20) = 90 > 0$ (minima).

4a. Given: $TR(Q) = 3{,}200Q - 6Q^2$ and $TC(Q) = 90 + 2Q^2$, the marginal revenue (*MR*) and marginal cost (*MC*) are as follows:

$$MR = \frac{dTR}{dQ} = 3{,}200 - 12Q \ \text{and} \ MC = \frac{dTC}{dQ} = 4Q.$$

At the profit-maximizing output level, $MR = MC$; thus

$$MR = 3{,}200 - \$12Q = 4Q = MC.$$

Solving for Q gives

$Q^* = 200$ units, which is the profit-maximizing quantity of output.

4b. $MR = 3{,}200 - 12Q = 3{,}200 - 12(200) = 800$

4c. $MC = 4Q = 4(200) = 800$

4e. Profits $= TR - TC = 3{,}200Q - 6Q^2 - (90 + 2Q^2) = -90 + 2{,}300Q - 8Q^2$.

When $Q^* = 200$, profits are $-90 + 2{,}300(200) - 8(200)^2 = \$139{,}910$.

5a. Set $dTR/dQ = \$200 - Q = 0$; $Q = 200$.

5b. Set $dTC/dQ = -\$40 + Q = 0$; $Q = 40$.

5c. Total profit (π)

$$= TR - TC = \$200Q - \$0.5Q^2 - (\$1{,}000 - \$40Q + \$0.5Q^2)$$
$$= -\$1{,}000 + \$240Q - Q^2.$$

Set $d\pi/dQ = \$240 - 2Q = 0$; $Q = 120$.

5d. At $Q^* = 20$, we note

$$MR = \frac{dTR}{dQ} = \$200 - Q = \$200 - 120 = \$80,$$

$$MC = \frac{dTC}{dQ} = -\$40 + Q = -\$40 + 120 = \$80.$$

So, $MR = MC = \$80$.

6. Given $TIC = C(Q/2) + S(D/Q)$, taking the derivative of TIC with respect to Q and setting it equal to zero yields:

$$\frac{dTIC}{dQ} = \frac{C}{2} - \frac{SD}{Q^2} = 0 \rightarrow Q^2 = \frac{2SD}{C} \rightarrow Q^* = EOQ = \sqrt{\frac{2SD}{C}}.$$

7. The Lagrangean function is

$$L(x, y, \lambda) = xy + \lambda(6 - x - y).$$

Taking the partial derivative with respect to x, y, and λ, we get

$$\frac{\partial L}{\partial x} = y - \lambda = 0,$$

$$\frac{\partial L}{\partial y} = x - \lambda = 0,$$

$$\frac{\partial L}{\partial \lambda} = 6 - x - y = 0.$$

Solving them simultaneously, we obtain: $x = 3$, $y = 3$, and $\lambda = 3$.

8a. The formulation is as follows:

Maximize $\qquad\qquad Q = M^2 + 5MK + 4K^2,$

subject to $\qquad\qquad \$5M + \$10K = \$1{,}000.$

8b. Solve for M in terms of K and substitute in Q yields:

$$M = 200 - 2K,$$
$$Q = (200 - 2K)^2 + 5(200 - 2K)K + 4K^2$$
$$= 40,000 - 800K + 4K^2 + 1,000K - 10K^2 + 4K^2$$
$$= 40,000 + 200K - 2K^2.$$

Using the first-order condition for an extreme, we find dQ/dK and set it equal to zero we get

$$\frac{dQ}{dK} = 200 - 4K = 0,$$

which means $K = 50$ and hence, $M = 100$.

8c. The Lagrangean function is:

$$L(M, K, \lambda) = M^2 + 5MK + 4K^2 + \lambda(1000 - 5M - 10K).$$

Using the partial derivatives, we obtain

$$\frac{\partial L}{\partial M} = 2M + 5K - 5\lambda = 0,$$

$$\frac{\partial L}{\partial K} = 5M + 8K - 10\lambda = 0,$$

$$\frac{\partial L}{\partial \lambda} = 1,000 - 5M - 10K = 0.$$

Solving these three equations simultaneously, we find $K = 50$, $M = 100$, and $\lambda = 90$.

8d. $\lambda = 90$ means that the output can be increased by 90 units if the cost limitation is increased by \$1; that is, an increase from \$1,000 to \$1,001.

9a. The formulation is as follows:

Maximize $\qquad Z = -60 + 140x + 100y - 10x^2 - 8y^2 - 6xy,$

subject to $\qquad 20x + 40y = 200.$

9b. Solve for x in terms of y and substitute in Z yields:

$20x + 40y = 200$, which leads to $x = \dfrac{200}{20} - \dfrac{40y}{20} = 10 - 2y,$

$$Z = -60 + 140x + 100y - 10x^2 - 8y^2 - 6xy$$
$$= -60 + 140(10 - 2y) + 100y - 10(10 - 2y)^2 - 8y^2 - 6(10 - 2y)y$$
$$= 340 + 160y - 36y^2.$$

Using the first-order condition for an extreme, we find dQ/dK and set it equal to zero we get

$$\frac{dQ}{dK} = 160 - 72y = 0,$$

which means $y = 2.22$ units and $x = 10 - 2y = 10 - 2(2.22) = 5.56$ units.

9c. The Lagrangean function is:

$$L(x, y, \lambda) = -60 + 140x + 100y - 10x^2 - 8y^2 - 6xy + \lambda(200 - 20x - 40y).$$

Using the partial derivatives, we obtain

$$\frac{\partial L}{\partial x} = 140 - 20x - 6y + 20\lambda = 0,$$

$$\frac{\partial L}{\partial y} = 100 - 16x - 6y + 40\lambda = 0,$$

$$\frac{\partial L}{\partial \lambda} = 200 - 20x - 40y = 0.$$

Solving these three equations simultaneously, we find $x = 5.56$, $y = 2.22$, and $\lambda = 0.774$

9d. $\lambda = 0.774$ means that profits can be increased by $0.774 if one additional unit of raw material were available; that is, an increase from 200 units to 201 units.

10. The Lagrangean function requires two Lagrangean multipliers since there are two constraint equations. We will denote them with λ_1 and λ_2.

$$L(x, z, w, \lambda_1, \lambda_2) = 10xzw - 3w^2 + \lambda_1(12 - x - z - w) + \lambda_2(2 - x + w).$$

The partial derivative equations are as follows:

$$\frac{\partial L}{\partial x} = 10zw - \lambda_1 - \lambda_2 = 0,$$

$$\frac{\partial L}{\partial z} = 10xw - \lambda_1 = 0,$$

$$\frac{\partial L}{\partial w} = 10xz - 6w - \lambda_1 + \lambda_2 = 0,$$

$$\frac{\partial L}{\partial \lambda_1} = 12 - x - z - w = 0,$$

$$\frac{\partial L}{\partial \lambda_2} = 2 - x + w = 0.$$

3
DEMAND AND SUPPLY: THEORY AND ANALYSIS

KEY TERMS

demand function mathematical relationship showing how the quantity demanded of a good or service responds to changes in a number of economic factors, such as its own price, the prices of substitutes and complementary goods, income, and advertising.

demand schedule table or tabular representation of the quantity demanded at various possible prices during a given time period, all other things remaining equal. The data from a demand schedule can be used to construct a *demand curve.*

demand curve graph of a demand schedule in which price is on the vertical axis and quantity demanded is on the horizontal axis.

average revenue total revenue per unit of output, that is total revenue divided by output.

marginal revenue change of total revenue with respect to quantity demanded.

point price elasticity ratio of a percentage change in quantity demanded to a percentage change in price.

cross elasticity responsiveness for one product to changes in the price of some other product, holding all other factors constant.

optimal price typically a profit maximizing price.

supply function mathematical relationship showing how the quantity supplied of a good or service responds to changes in these factors.

equilibrium price price of a commodity (good and service) toward which a competitive market will move and, once there, at which it will remain.

Demand analysis is useful in forecasting sales, setting prices, and long-range profit planning. Demand analysis includes:

1. Quantitative expression demand—specification of demand functions

2. Calculation of various elasticities of demand

3. Estimation of demand functions

4. Forecasting sales

5. Pricing decisions

The first two topics are covered in this chapter. The other topics are discussed in later chapters.

DEMAND FUNCTION

Economic theory tells us that demand for a particular product depends on its price, i.e.,

$$Q_d = f(P).$$

Economic theory goes one step further, stating that

$$Q_d = f(P, P_c, Y, A,...),$$

where P = its own price, P_C = the prices of substitutes and complementary goods, Y = income, and A = advertising. *Demand function* is a mathematical relationship showing how the quantity demanded of a good or service responds to changes in these factors. Explanatory factors other than its own price are called *demand shifters*. The effect of each explanatory factor on the quantity demanded may be estimated statistically with time-series or cross-sectional data.

DEMAND SCHEDULE

Demand schedule is a table or tabular representation of the quantity demanded at various possible prices during a given time period, all other things remaining equal. The data from a demand schedule can be used to construct a *demand curve*.

DEMAND CURVE

Demand curve is a graph of a demand schedule, showing the negative relationship between price and quantity demanded during a period of time, all other

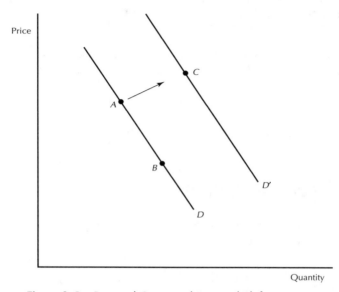

Figure 3–1. Demand Curve and Demand Shifters

things remaining the same. Price is on the vertical axis and quantity demanded is on the horizontal axis.

Notice that the change in demand from point A to B is due to a change in price. The change in demand from point A to C is not due to price, but a shift in demand.

SHIFT IN DEMAND

Market shifters create increase or decrease in demand for a good brought about by a change in any factor *other than* the price of the product. These factors include (1) consumers' incomes, (2) the prices of substitute or complementary goods, and (3) consumers' tastes. Graphically, a shift in demand may be represented by a parallel movement of the demand curve.

MARKET DEMAND CURVE

The *market demand curve* for a product represents the various amounts that consumers as a group are willing and able to purchase at various alternative prices at a specific moment in time when other factors influencing consumer behavior are held constant. Thus, the market demand curve isolates the relationship between price and the quantity demanded by all consumers. It is found by summing the quantities of a good that each consumer is willing and able to purchase at each and every alternative price.

DEMAND AND REVENUE

The total revenue of a firm is directly related to the demand for the firm's product or service. Total revenue (*TR*) is a function of price and quantity demanded, i.e.,

$$TR = f(P, Q) = P \times Q.$$

For example, if $P = 500 - 0.02Q$, then $TR = PQ = (500 - 0.2Q)Q = 500Q - 0.02Q^2$

AVERAGE REVENUE

Average revenue (*AR*) is total revenue per unit of output, that is total revenue received divided by output, i.e.,

$$AR = \frac{TR}{Q} = \frac{500Q - 0.02Q^2}{Q} = 500 - 0.02Q.$$

MARGINAL REVENUE

Marginal revenue is the rate of change of total revenue with respect to quantity demanded, i.e.,

$$MR = \frac{dTR}{dQ} = \frac{d(500Q - 0.02Q^2)}{dQ} = 500 - 0.04Q.$$

ELASTICITY OF DEMAND

Whether price cutting or an increase in advertising dollars is desirable or not depends largely on the elasticity of demand for the product. One of the most important concepts in demand is elasticity, which tells you how sensitive quantity demanded is to the change in a factor in the demand function. The principal factors involved with demand elasticity are

1. the price of the good (in the case of price elasticity),
2. the price of a substitute product (in the case of cross elasticity),
3. income (in the case of income elasticity),
4. advertising (in the case of advertising elasticity).

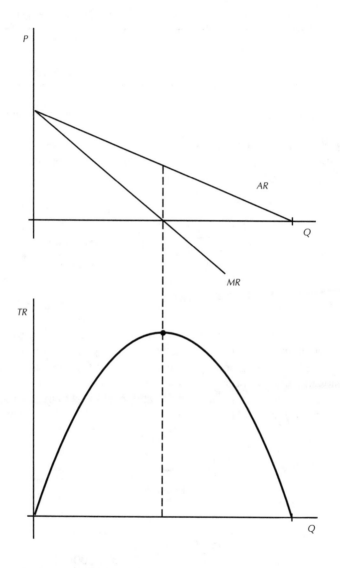

Figure 3–2. Average Revenue, Marginal Revenue, and Total Revenue

PRICE ELASTICITY

Price elasticity, denoted with e_p, is the ratio of a percentage change in quantity demanded (Q) to a percentage change in price (P), as stated as a *positive* term. We classify the price elasticity of demand into three categories:

Price elasticity of demand	Degree of elasticity
$e_p > 1$	Elastic
$e_p = 1$	Unitary
$e_p < 1$	Inelastic

There are two types of price elasticity: (1) arc elasticity and (2) point elasticity.

• *ARC ELASTICITY*

Arc elasticity of demand is the average responsiveness of quantity demanded to a change in price between two different values:

$$e_p = \frac{\dfrac{(Q_2 - Q_1)}{\left[\dfrac{(Q_2 + Q_1)}{2}\right]}}{\dfrac{(P_2 - P_1)}{\left[\dfrac{(P_2 + P_1)}{2}\right]}} = \frac{(Q_2 - Q_1)}{(P_2 - P_1)} \times \frac{(P_2 + P_1)}{(Q_2 + Q_1)},$$

where P_1, and Q_1 are the original price and quantity, and P_2 and Q_2 are the new price and quantity. In other words, changes in Q and P are calculated as percentages of the average of their respective original and final values. This approach eliminates the problem of the elasticity measure being dependent on which end of the range is viewed as the initial point and results in a more accurate measure of the average relative relationship between the two variables over the range indicated by the data.

Example 1

Given the following:

P	Q
P_1 = $0.60	Q_1 = 400,000
P_2 = 0.50	Q_2 = 800,000

$$e_p = \frac{(800,000 - 400,000)}{(0.5 - 0.6)} \times \frac{(0.5 + 0.6)}{(800,000 + 400,000)} = \frac{400,000}{-0.1} \times \frac{1.10}{1,200,000}$$

$$= -3.667.$$

YOU SHOULD REMEMBER

A negative sign is expected, so the absolute value expression $|e_p|$ is widely adopted in texts.

• *POINT ELASTICITY*

Point elasticity is the elasticity measured at a given point.

$$e_p = \frac{\% \text{ change in } Q}{\% \text{ change in } P} = \frac{\dfrac{dQ}{Q}}{\dfrac{dP}{P}} = \frac{dQ}{dP} \times \frac{P}{Q},$$

where dQ/dP is the slope of the demand function $Q = (P)$.

Example 2

The demand function is given as $Q = 200 - 6P$. The price elasticity at $P = 4$ is computed as follows:

First, $Q = 200 - 6(4) = 176$.

Since $dQ/dP = -6$, the e_p at $P = 4$ is:

$$e_p = -6 \times (4/176) = -0.136,$$

which means that a 1% change in price will bring about a 0.14% change in demand. The product under study is considered price inelastic, since the e_p is less than 1 in absolute value.

TWO EXTREME CASES OF PRICE ELASTICITY

There are two extreme cases: (1) $e_p = 0$ and (2) $e_p = \infty$. If $e_p = 0$, the price elasticity of demand is completely inelastic and the quantity demanded will not change in response to a change in price. The demand curve in this case is a vertical line, as in Figure 3–3, panel (a). If $e_p = \infty$, the price elasticity of demand is

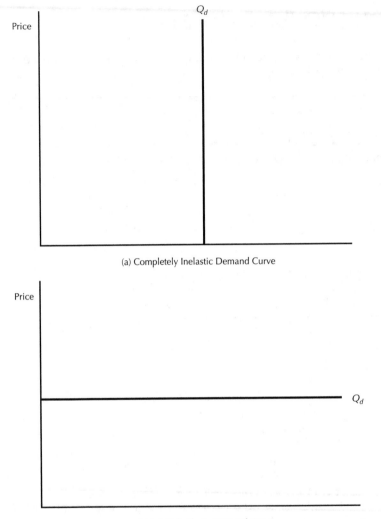

(a) Completely Inelastic Demand Curve

(b) Infinitely Elastic Demand Curve

Figure 3-3. Two Extreme Cases of Price Elasticity of Demand

infinitely elastic and a firm can sell as many units of its product as it wants to at the going market price, but it will lose all of its sales at a higher price. In this case, the demand curve is a horizontal line as seen in Figure 3–3, panel (b). These cases, however, are very rare in reality. The demand for some products, such as table salt, over at least some price ranges may be highly inelastic. Further, we may relate the horizontal demand curve with the purely competitive firm.

LINEAR DEMAND CURVE AND NONCONSTANT PRICE ELASTICITY

The information on price elasticity is useful to see the effect of a change in price on sales. However, you should be careful to know the price elasticity in each price range, since elasticity is not constant along the demand curve.

Example 3

We are given the following demand function: $P = 10 - 2Q$ or $Q = 5 - 0.5P$

In the case of a *linear* demand function (See Figure 3–4), while the slope of a straight-line demand curve is the same at all points, the elasticity for such a curve varies from one point to the next. The reason for this is that in the e_p formula

1. dQ/dP would be constant, but

2. P/Q would fall in the case of a move down and to the right.

TOTAL REVENUE AND PRICE ELASTICITY

Economists have established the following relationships between price elasticity (e_p) and total revenue (TR), which can aid a firm in setting its price.

Price	$e_p > 1$	$e_p = 1$	$e_p < 1$
Price rises	TR falls	No change	TR rises
Price falls	TR rises	No change	TR falls

Example 4

In Example 3, we note that $TR = PQ = (10 - 2Q)Q = 10Q - 2Q^2$ and hence $MR = 10 - 4Q$. Figure 3–5 shows the relationship between TR, price elasticity, and marginal revenue.

---

1. Price elasticities can be used to answer the following types of questions:

    a. What will be the impact on sales of a 5% price increase?

    b. How great a price reduction is necessary to increase sales by 20%?

2. Firms need to be aware of the elasticity of their own demand curves when they set product prices. For example, a profit-maximizing firm would never

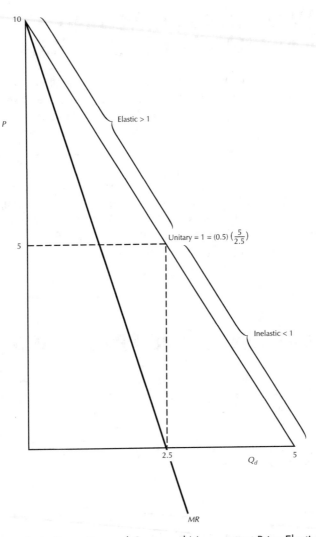

Figure 3–4. Linear Demand Curve and Nonconstant Price Elasticity

choose to lower its price in the inelastic range of its demand curve—such a price decrease would only decrease total sales and at the same time increase costs, since output would be rising. The result would be a drastic decrease in profits. In fact, when costs are rising and the product is inelastic, the firm would have no difficulty passing on the increases by raising the price to the customer.

3. When there are many substitutes and demand is quite elastic, increasing prices may lead to a reduction in total revenue rather than an increase. The result may be lower profits rather than higher profits.

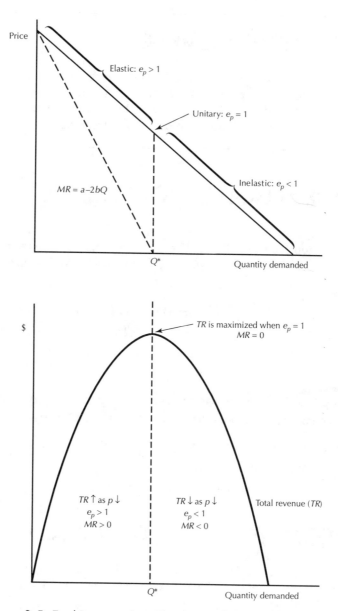

Figure 3–5. Total Revenue, Price Elasticity, and Marginal Revenue

4. Similarly, managers are sometimes surprised by a lack of success of price reductions, this merely being a reflection of the fact that demand is relatively inelastic. In such a case, they may have to rely on other marketing efforts, such as advertising and sales promotion, in an attempt to increase market share.

YOU SHOULD REMEMBER

Various elasticity measures will allow marketing managers to see how effective each of the demand determinants (i.e., advertising, price change, and external factors) is going to be. In this way, marketing resources may be utilized more profitably and efficiently.

CROSS ELASTICITY OF DEMAND

Cross elasticity of demand is the responsiveness for one product to changes in the price of some other product, holding all other factors constant. It measures the closeness of substitutes or the degree of complementality of demand. It is computed as

$$e_{P_X} = \frac{\% \text{ change in } Q}{\% \text{ change in } P_X} = \frac{\dfrac{dQ}{Q}}{\dfrac{dP_X}{P_X}} = \frac{dQ}{dP_X} \frac{P_X}{Q}.$$

1. If $e_{P_X} > 0$, goods are substitutes. A high-cross elasticity means that the commodities are close substitutes (e.g., coffee and tea).

2. If $e_{P_X} < 0$, goods are complements (e.g., high-fidelity components and CDs).

3. If $e_{P_X} = 0$, goods are independent of each other.

INCOME ELASTICITY OF DEMAND

Income elasticity of demand is the responsiveness of quantity demanded to changes in income, holding all other factors constant. It is computed as

$$e_Y = \frac{\% \text{ change in } Q}{\% \text{ change in } P_Y} = \frac{\dfrac{dQ}{Q}}{\dfrac{dY}{Y}} = \frac{dQ}{dY} \frac{Y}{Q}.$$

If $e_Y > 0$, products are normal or superior goods whose demand varies directly with income, holding prices constant. A majority of consumer goods are superior goods. If $e_Y < 0$, products are *inferior* goods. Demand will drop with rising personal income, because, for example, people turn to more expensive foods with higher income. Examples of inferior goods include dried beans, recapped automobile tires, and budget-priced durable goods.

ADVERTISING ELASTICITY OF DEMAND

Advertising elasticity of demand is the percentage change in the quantity sold (or market share) that is associated with a percentage change in the advertising expenditures of that product:

$$e_A = \frac{\% \text{ change in } Q}{\% \text{ change in } A} = \frac{\dfrac{dQ}{Q}}{\dfrac{dA}{A}} = \frac{dQ}{dA}\frac{A}{Q}.$$

It is used as a measure of short-run advertising effectiveness. This elasticity may be affected by a number of factors, such as the stage of the product's market development, the extent to which competitors react to the firm's advertising, either by further advertising or by increased promotional efforts, the importance of other marketing factors (e.g., prices, incomes, tastes, etc.), and the quality and quantity of the firm's past and present advertising.

MARKET SHARE ELASTICITY

Market share elasticity is the percentage change in a firm's market share resulting from a percentage change in the price.

CONSTANT ELASTICITY

The second most commonly specified demand relationship is the *multiplicative* form, which gives constant elasticity. The form is found in power functions. An example is:

$$Q = aP^b A^c Y^d \tag{1}$$

where P = price, A = advertising, and Y = income.
 By definition,

$$e_p = \frac{\% \text{ change in } Q}{\% \text{ change in } P} = \frac{\partial Q}{\partial P} = \frac{\partial Q}{\partial P} \cdot \frac{P}{Q}. \tag{2}$$

Differentiating Equation (1) with respect to price (P), we obtain

$$\frac{\partial Q}{\partial P} = abP^{b-1}A^cY^d.$$

Therefore,

$$e_p = abP^{b-1}A^cY^d \cdot \left(\frac{P}{Q}\right). \tag{3}$$

Substituting (1) for Q in (3) gives

$$e_p = abP^{b-1}A^cY^d \cdot \left(\frac{P}{aP^bA^cY^d}\right). \tag{4}$$

Combining terms and canceling where possible in Equation (4), we obtain

$$e_p = \frac{abP^bA^cY^d}{P} \cdot \frac{P}{aP^bA^cY^d} = b.$$

Thus, the price elasticity of demand is equal to b (whose usual sign is *negative*), the exponent of the price variable in the multiplicative demand function given as in equation (1). Therefore, the elasticity is not a function of the price/quantity (P/Q) ratio and hence is constant. In a similar fashion, we can prove that (1) the income elasticity is c, and (2) the advertising elasticity is d.

YOU SHOULD REMEMBER

The power function form can be transformed into a *log-linear* form using logarithm and then estimated by the least-squares method. Equation (1) is equivalent to

$$\log Q = \log a + b \log P + c \log Y + d \log A$$

The property of constant elasticity is useful because it means that changes in one of the independent variables, such as income, will result in proportionate changes in quantity demanded. Note that the elasticity of a linear function changes over the entire range of the demand curve.

Example 5
Given the demand function in multiplicative form:

$$Q = 2077P^{-0.144}P_X^{0.097}A^{0.314}$$

The price elasticity is always -0.144, which means that a 1% reduction (increase) in price leads to 0.14% increase (decrease) in demand.

OPTIMAL PRICING POLICY AND PRICE ELASTICITY

We note, without a mathematical derivation, the relationship between the point price elasticity of demand, marginal revenue, and price:

$$MR = P\left(1 + \frac{1}{e_p}\right).$$

(Note that e_p is a negative number.)

This follows directly from the mathematical definition of marginal revenue (MR). This formula is useful in setting a firm's pricing policy. From the profit-maximizing condition $MR = MC$, we can derive the formula for determining the profit-maximizing price level, which is shown below.

$$MC = MR$$

$$MC = P\left(1 + \frac{1}{e_p}\right).$$

Solving for the optimal or profit-maximizing P^*, yields

$$P^* = \frac{MC}{\left(1 + \frac{1}{e_p}\right)}.$$

Example 6
Suppose the manager of a toy store notes a 2.5% increase in weekly sales following a 1% price discount on the Bamboo doll. The store's wholesale cost per doll plus display and marketing expenses total $30 per unit. The price elasticity of demand is

$$e_p = \frac{\% \text{ change in } Q}{\% \text{ change in } p} = \frac{-2.5}{1} = -2.5.$$

The profit-maximizing price is then

$$P = \frac{\$30}{1 + \dfrac{1}{-2.5}} = \$50.$$

Suppose the manager can reduce, through quantity buying, marginal costs per unit by \$3 to \$27. Then the new optimal price is:

$$P = \frac{\$27}{\left(1 + \dfrac{1}{-2.5}\right)} = \$45.$$

Thus, the profit-maximizing price would fall by \$5 following a \$3 reduction in the store's marginal costs.

SUPPLY FUNCTION

Up to this point we focused on the demand side of the market, which represents half of the forces that determine the price in a market. The other determinant is market supply. Economic theory tells us that supply for a particular product depends on its price, i.e.,

$$Q_s = f(P).$$

Economic theory goes one step further, stating that

$$Q_s = f(P, P_X, W, ...),$$

where P = its own price, P_X = the prices of technologically related goods, W = the value of some other variables that affect supply, such as the existing technology or weather. *Supply function* is a mathematical relationship showing how the quantity supplied of a good or service responds to changes in these factors (see Figure 3–6). Explanatory factors other than its own price are called *supply shifters*. The effect of each explanatory factor on the quantity supplied may be estimated statistically with time-series or cross-sectional data.

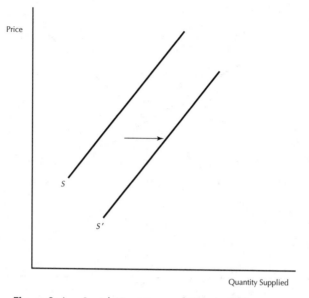

Figure 3-6. Supply Function and Supply Shifters

SHIFT IN SUPPLY

A shift in the supply of a product is brought about by a change in any factor other than the price of the product. Graphically, a shift in supply is illustrated as a parallel movement of the supply curve. A rightward (leftward) shift or an increase (decrease) in supply implies that more (less) product is supplied than before the increase (decrease) at every price. Supply shifters include (1) input prices, (2) technology, (3) number of firms, (4) substitutes in production, and (5) excise taxes.

MARKET EQUILIBRIUM

Equilibrium in a competitive market is determined by the intersection of the market demand and supply curves. Equilibrium price is the price of a commodity (good and service) toward which a competitive market will move and, once there, at which it will remain. It is the price at which the market "clears"—that is, the price determined by the intersection of the market forces of demand and supply (see Figure 3–7). Equilibrium quantity is the quantity that corresponds to the *equilibrium price.* It is the output level at which the market "clears."

$$Q_d = Q_s$$

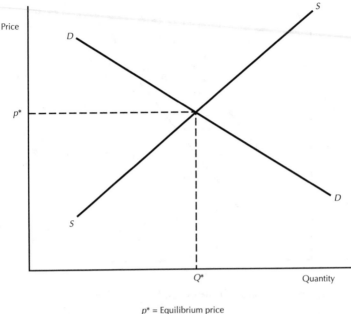

p^* = Equilibrium price
Q^* = Equilibrium quantity

Figure 3–7.   Market Equilibrium

Example 7

The following relations describe monthly demand and supply functions for dry cleaning services in the local area:

$$Q_d = 50 - 2P \text{ (demand)},$$

$$Q_s = -20 + 5P \text{ (supply)}.$$

The equilibrium price-output combination is determined as follows:
At equilibrium,

$$Q_d = Q_s,$$

$$50 - 2P = -20 + 5P,$$

$$-7P = -70; P = \$10.$$

To find the equilibrium quantity, we simply plug this price into either the demand or the supply function. For example, using the supply function, we find that $Q_s = -20 + 5P = -20 + 5(10) = 30$ units.

KNOW THE CONCEPTS

TERMS FOR STUDY

advertising elasticity
arc elasticity
average revenue
complementary goods
constant elasticity
demand curve
demand function
demand schedule
demand shifters
equilibrium

income elasticity
inferior goods
linear demand function
marginal revenue
normal goods
optimal price
point price elasticity
substitute goods
supply
supply shifters

DO YOU KNOW THE BASICS?

1. What does demand theory and analysis involve? List what is used in determining a firm's revenue.

2. What are demand shifters? Give examples.

3. Define total revenue, average revenue, and marginal revenue. Explain the relationships among these.

4. What are the factors associated with demand elasticity?

5. Distinguish between arc elasticity and point elasticity.

6. What is the special feature of a linear demand curve in terms of price elasticity?

7. Describe the relationship between price elasticity of demand and total revenue.

8. Give two good examples of how price elasticity can be used for marketing decisions.

9. How do you know whether a product is a normal good or an inferior good?

10. What type of function form would give *constant* elasticity of demand?

11. Write down the relationship between the point price elasticity of demand, marginal revenue, and price.

PRACTICAL APPLICATION

1. A valve manufacturer is considering raising the price of its valves from the current average price of $2,000 per unit. It is currently selling 600 units per month, but trying to bring its sales down to its maximum output of 500 units per month. If the firm's price elasticity of demand is −2 over the range of $2,000 to $2,500 per valve, what will the new price have to be in order to bring demand in line with capacity?

2. Lilex Watch, Inc. is considering lowering the price of its watches from the current $80 per unit to $70 per unit. It sells 2,000 units per month. If the watch's price elasticity of demand is −2, what will be the new quantity sold?

3. The Sunhee Bags, Inc. has estimated the following demand function for its deluxe sleeping bag in the San Francisco Bay area:

$$P = 600 - 0.3Q$$

   a. Determine the MR and TR functions.

   b. At what price would Sunhee Bags fail to sell any sleeping bags?

   c. What is the maximum quantity Sunhee Bags could sell?

   d. What is the maximum revenue that the firm could receive?

   e. For a given percentage change in price, what would be the percentage change in quantity demanded at the output level $Q = 700$?

   f. What is the arc price elasticity of demand for the quantity range of 700–800 units?

4. Given the following demand curve:

$$Q = 250 - 0.5P$$

   Determine the corresponding total revenue (TR) function, marginal revenue (MR) function, and the average revenue (AR) function.

5. Given the following demand curve:

$$P = 400 - 3Q$$

   Determine the corresponding total revenue (TR) function, marginal revenue (MR) function, and the average revenue (AR) function.

6. The marketing department of a compact automaker has determined the following demand functions for their cars:

$$Q = 150{,}000 - 52P + 80P_C + 0.3A + 0.5Y$$

where Q = the number of the firm's cars sold weekly

P = the price of the firm's car

P_C = the price of a close competitor's car

A = weekly advertising dollars spent

Y = average family disposable income

a. If $P = \$12{,}000$, $P_C = \$10{,}000$, $A = \$310{,}000$, and $Y = \$25{,}000$, derive the demand function and determine the price elasticity of demand.

b. Comment on the price elasticity obtained in part a. If the firm raises price, what will happen to total revenue?

c. Assuming the values given in part a, calculate the income elasticity of demand. Interpret your answer.

d. Determine the cross elasticity of demand between two competing cars. Interpret your answer.

7. The demand for your product has been estimated to be

$Q_A = 8{,}500 - 4P_A - 2P_B + P_C - 0.1Y$, where P = price and Y = income. The relevant price and income data are as follows: $P_A = 10$, $P_B = 50$, $P_C = 50$, and $Y = 40{,}000$.

a. Which goods are substitutes for product A? Which are complements?

b. Is A an inferior or a normal good?

c. How much of product A will be purchased?

8. a. Derive the following formula:

$$MR = P\!\left(1 + \frac{1}{e_p}\right)$$

b. Explain the relationship between marginal revenue (MR) and the price elasticity of demand (e_p).

9. Suppose the manager of a toy store notes a 2% increase in weekly sales following a 1% price discount on the Bamboo doll. The store's wholesale cost per doll plus display and marketing expenses total \$15 per unit.

a. What is the store's point price elasticity of demand?

b. Calculate the optimal price.

c. Suppose the manager can reduce, through quantity buying, marginal costs per unit by $1 to $14. What is the new optimal price?

10. Your company's food product has its own price elasticity of demand of -0.8. If the price of food increased by 5 percent, what would happen to the quantity of food demanded and the total revenue for your company's food product?

11. The following relations describe monthly demand and supply functions for dry cleaning services in the local area:

$$Q_d = 40,000 - 4,000P \qquad \text{(demand)}$$
$$Q_s = -10,000 + 10,000P \qquad \text{(supply)}$$

a. At what average price level would demand equal zero?

b. At what average price level would supply equal zero?

c. Find the equilibrium price-output combination?

ANSWERS

DO YOU KNOW THE BASICS?

1. Demand analysis includes (a) quantitative expression of demand (specification of demand functions), (b) calculation of various elasticities of demand, (c) estimation of demand functions, (d) forecasting sales, and (e) pricing decisions.

2. Demand shifters are factors that create increase or decrease in demand for a good brought about by a change in any factor *other than* the price of the product. They include (1) consumers' incomes, (2) the prices of substitute or complementary goods, and (3) consumers' tastes. Graphically, a shift in demand may be represented by a parallel movement of the *demand curve*.

3. *Total revenue (TR)* of a firm is directly related to the demand for the firm's product or service. *Average revenue (AR)* is total revenue per unit of output, that is total revenue received divided by output., i.e., $AR = TR/Q$. *Marginal revenue (MR)* is the rate of change of total revenue with respect to quantity demanded, i.e., $MR = dTR/dQ$. The total revenue is maximized when MR is equal to zero.

4. The principal factors involved with demand elasticity are (1) the price of the good (in the case of price elasticity), (2) the price of a substitute product (in the case of cross elasticity), (3) income (in the case of income elasticity), and (4) advertising (in the case of advertising elasticity).

5. Arc elasticity of demand is the average responsiveness of quantity demanded to a change in price between two different values, while point elasticity is the elasticity measured at a given point.

6. In the case of a *linear* demand function, while the slope of a straight line demand curve is the same at all points, the elasticity for such a curve varies from one point to the next.

7. Economists have established the following relationships between price elasticity (e_p) and total revenue (*TR*), which can aid a firm in setting its price.

Price	$e_p > 1$	$e_p = 1$	$e_p < 1$
Price rises	TR falls	No change	TR rises
Price falls	TR rises	No change	TR falls

8. Price elasticities can be used to answer the following types of questions: (a) what will be the impact on sales of a 5% price increase? (b) how great a price reduction is necessary to increase sales by 20%?

9. If income elasticity (e_Y) is greater than zero, products are normal or superior goods whose demand varies directly with income, holding prices constant. If $e_Y < 0$, products are *inferior* goods.

10. The *multiplicative* form (or power function) gives constant elasticity. The form is found in power functions. An example is $Q = aP^b A^c Y^d$.

11. The relationship between the point price elasticity of demand, marginal revenue, and price is:

$$MR = P\left(1 + \frac{1}{e_p}\right)$$

PRACTICAL APPLICATION

1.

$$e_p = \frac{(Q_2 - Q_1)}{\left[\dfrac{(Q_2 + Q_1)}{2}\right]} = \frac{(Q_2 - Q_1)}{(P_2 - P_1)} \times \frac{(P_2 + P_1)}{(Q_2 + Q_1)},$$

$$-2 = \frac{500 - 600}{P_2 - 2{,}000} \times \frac{P_2 + 2{,}000}{500 + 600}$$

$$= \frac{-100(P_2 + 2{,}000)}{1{,}100(P_2 - 2{,}000)}$$

$$-2(11P_2 - 22,000) = -P_2 - 2,000$$
$$-22P_2 + 44,000 = -P_2 - 2,000$$
$$-21P_2 = -46,000$$
$$P_2 = \$2,190.48$$

2.
$$-2 = \frac{Q_2 - 2,000}{70 - 80} \times \frac{70 + 80}{Q_2 + 2,000}$$

$$-2 = \frac{150(Q_2 - 2,000)}{-10(Q_2 + 2,000)}$$

$$-2(-10Q_2 - 20,000) = 150Q_2 - 300,000$$
$$20Q_2 + 40,000 = 150Q_2 - 300,000$$
$$-130Q_2 = -340,000$$
$$Q_2 = 2,615.38$$

3a. Given $P = 600 - 0.3Q$:
$$TR = PQ = (600 - 0.3Q)\,Q = 600Q - 0.3Q^2$$

$$MR = \frac{dTR}{dQ} = 600 - 0.6Q$$

3b. At $P = \$600$, $Q = 0$ since $P = 600 - 0.3(0) = \$600$.

3c. $P = 600 - 0.3Q$, so $Q = 2,000 - 10/3P$

At a price of 0, $Q = 2,000 - 10/3(0) = 2,000$ units.

3d. *TR* will be maximized when $MR = 0$.

$$MR = \frac{dTR}{dQ} = 600 - 0.6Q = 0; \; Q = 1,000 \text{ units.}$$

At $Q = 1,000$ *units*, $TR = 600Q - 0.3Q^2 = 600(1,000) - 0.3(1,000)^2 = \$300,000$

3e.

$$e_p = \frac{\% \text{ change in } Q}{\% \text{ change in } P} = \frac{dQ/Q}{dP/P} = \frac{dQ}{dP}\frac{P}{Q}$$

First,

$$\frac{dQ}{dP} = -10/3$$

Then, at $Q = 700$, $P = 390$,

$e_p = -(10/3) \times (390/700) = -1.86$. The point elasticity of demand is -1.86, so the percentage change in quantity demanded would be -1.86 times the percentage change in price.

3f. Since $P = 600 - 0.3Q$,

$$\text{At } Q = 700, P = 600 - 0.3(700) = \$390$$

$$\text{At } Q = 800, P = 600 - 0.3(800) = \$360$$

Therefore,

Arc elasticity of demand

$$\frac{(Q_2 - Q_1)}{(P_2 - P_1)} \times \frac{(P_2 + P_1)}{(Q_2 + Q_1)} = \frac{(800 - 700)}{(360 - 390)} \frac{(360 + 390)}{(800 + 700)} = -1.67$$

4.

$$Q = 250 - 0.5P \rightarrow 0.5P = 250 - Q \rightarrow P = 500 - 2Q$$

$$TR = PQ = (500 - 2Q)Q = 500Q - 2Q^2$$

$$MR = \frac{dTR}{dQ} = 500 - 4Q$$

$$AR = \frac{TR}{Q} = 500 - 2Q$$

5.

$$TR = PQ = (400 - 3Q)Q = 400Q - 3Q^2$$

$$MR = \frac{dTR}{dQ} = 400 - 6Q$$

$$AR = \frac{TR}{Q} = 400 - 3Q$$

6a. The demand function is: $Q = 150,000 - 52P + 80P_C + 0.3A + 0.5Y = 150,000 - 52P + 80(10,000) + 0.3(310,000) + 0.5(25,000) = 563,000 - 52P$

Hence, $Q = 1,055,500 - 52P = 1,055,500 - 52(12,000) = 431,500$

6b. The price elasticity of demand is

$$e_p = \frac{\% \text{ change in } Q}{\% \text{ change in } P} = \frac{\partial Q}{\partial P} \cdot \frac{P}{Q} = -52 \frac{12,000}{431,500} = -1.45 = 1.45 > 1.$$

Demand for the car is elastic and thus if the price is raised, total revenue will drop sharply.

6c. The income elasticity is

$$e_Y = \frac{\% \text{ change in } Q}{\% \text{ change in } Y} = \frac{\partial Q}{\partial Y} \cdot \frac{Y}{Q} = 0.5\frac{25,000}{431,500} = 0.029 < 1.$$

Since the income elasticity is greater than 0 but less than 1, the car is normal but not superior. If income goes up, demand will rise but not at the same rate of increase as income.

6d. The cross elasticity is

$$e_{P_c} = \frac{\% \text{ change in } Q}{\% \text{ change in } P_c} = \frac{\partial Q}{\partial P_c} \cdot \frac{P_C}{Q} = 80\frac{10,000}{431,500} = 1.85 > 1.$$

Since the cross elasticity is greater than 0, these two cars are substitutes.

7a. C is a substitute for A, while B is a complement for A.

7b. A is an inferior good, as indicated by a *negative* sign associated with the income variable.

7c. $Q_A = 8,500 - 4P_A - 2P_B + P_C - 0.1Y = 8,500 - 4(10) - 2(15) + (50) - 0.1(40,000) = 4,480$.

8a. By definition,

$$MR = \frac{dTR}{dQ} = \frac{d(P \times Q)}{dQ} = \frac{d[f(Q) \times Q)]}{dQ} = f(Q) + f'(Q)\,Q = P + Q\frac{dP}{dQ}$$

$$= P\left(1 + \frac{Q}{P}\frac{dP}{dQ}\right) = P\left(1 + \frac{1}{e_p}\right)$$

8b. We observe that

$MR > 0$ when $e_p > 1$

$MR = 0$ when $e_p = 1$

$MR < 0$ when $e_p < 1$

9a.

$$e_p = \frac{\% \text{ change in } Q}{\% \text{ change in } P} = \frac{-2}{1} = -2$$

9b. The profit-maximizing price is then:

$$P = \frac{\$15}{1 + 1/-2} = \$30$$

9c. The new optimal price is:

$$P = \frac{\$14}{1 + 1/-2} = \$28$$

Thus, the profit-maximizing price would fall by $2 following a $1 reduction in the store's marginal costs.

10.

$$e_p = \frac{\% \text{ change in } Q}{\% \text{ change in } P} \rightarrow -0.8 = \frac{\% \text{ change in } Q}{5\%}$$

Percentage change in $Q = -0.8(5) = -4\%$. The demand for food will fall by 4% if the price increases by 5%. Since the price elasticity is less than 1, demand is inelastic. Thus, the price increase will lead to an increase in your total revenue.

11a. Set $Q_d = 0$ and solve for P.

$$Q_d = 40{,}000 - 4{,}000P = 0; \; P = \$10.$$

11b. Set $Q_s = 0$ and solve for P.

$$Q_s = -10{,}000 + 10{,}000P = 0; \; P = \$1$$

11c. At the market equilibrium, $Q_d = Q_s$.

$$40{,}000 - 4{,}000P = -10{,}000 + 10{,}000P$$

$50{,}000 = 14{,}000P$; $P = \$3.57$, Substituting $P = \$3.57$ into either the demand and the supply function yields:

$$Q_d = 40{,}000 - 4{,}000P = 40{,}000 - 4{,}000(\$3.57) = 25{,}720 \text{ units.}$$

4

DEMAND ESTIMATION

KEY TERMS

consumer surveys method that involves interviewing potential customers to estimate demand relations.

market experiments studies of consumer behavior in actual or simulated market settings.

identification problem statistical problem encountered in the estimation of the parameters of one function, such as demand function when simultaneous relations exist.

linear regression regression that deals with a straight-line relationship between variables.

regression analysis statistical procedure for estimating mathematically the average relationship between the dependent variable (sales, for example) and one or more independent variables (price and advertising, for example).

simple regression regression analysis that involves one independent variable. For example, the demand for automobiles is a function of its price only.

multiple regression statistical procedure that attempts to assess the relationship between the dependent variable and two or more independent variables.

least-squares method statistical method in regression analysis aimed at finding a regression line of *best fit*.

coefficient of determination proportion of the total variation in the dependent variable that is explained by the regression equation.

standard error of the estimate standard deviation of the regression.

t-test test for statistical significance of the regression coefficients.

---

f-test test used to determine the overall significance of the regression model.

homoscedasticity constant variance. One of the assumptions required in a regression in order to make valid statistical inferences about population relationships.

multicollinearity condition that exists when the independent variables are highly correlated with each other.

Durbin-Watson statistic summary measure of the amount of autocorrelation in the error terms of the regression.

In the previous chapter, the theory of demand was developed; the concepts of demand elasticity were introduced and analyzed. In this chapter we explore the procedures that may be used in making empirical estimates of demand functions. With demand estimation, we will be able to quantitatively calculate the various elasticities and determine the impact of a change in various factors, such as price, income, or advertising on quantity demanded. Essentially there are two major approaches to demand estimation: direct and statistical. Direct approaches to demand estimation include consumer surveys and market experiments. Statistical estimation of the demand function primarily rests on econometrics and regression analysis.

CONSUMER SURVEYS

Consumers are questioned about their likely response to such things as sensitivity to price change, willingness to buy, or awareness of advertising campaigns. By aggregating the data obtained, the firm can develop a better understanding of key factors in its demand function. An advantage is that in short-term sales forecasting, subjective information about consumer attitudes and expectations, obtainable only through interview methods, often makes the difference between an accurate estimate and one that misses by a wide margin. It is fraught with potential pitfalls. One is that consumers are frequently unable, and at times unwilling, to provide accurate answers to hypothetical questions about how they would respond to changes in major demand variables.

MARKET EXPERIMENTS

Market experiments involve examining the way consumers behave in real-market situations. A firm varies prices, advertising, and other controllable variables in the demand function, with the variations occurring either over time or between markets and observes the impact on quantity demanded. An advantage is that because important variables in the demand function, such as price and advertising, are controlled by the experimenter, the firm can gain some insight regarding the short-run effects. Wide swings in important demand-related factors can be gained. Or a feel can be developed for the price elasticity or cross elasticity of demand for a product. Major drawbacks are

a. These experiments are extremely expensive to undertake on a large scale.

b. Because of the high cost and the risk involved, the duration of the test is likely to be short. The experimenter is thus forced to examine short-run data and must attempt to extend it to a longer period.

c. Possible changes in external economic conditions or competitor behavior during the market test can undermine the validity of the results.

YOU SHOULD REMEMBER

Each technique of demand estimation has important pros and cons. Firms must make their choice of demand estimation method, or an appropriate combination of methods, on the basis of individual estimation problem characteristics.

IDENTIFICATION PROBLEM

We often encounter a statistical problem in the estimation of the parameters of one function, such as the demand function when simultaneous relations exist. When the same two endogenous variables appear in at least two different equations in a simultaneous model, a problem exists of identifying which relationship can be estimated on the basis of data, because all the variables change simultaneously. For instance, both supply curves and demand curves may be specified with quantity as the dependent variable, and price as the explanatory variable. Any observations available are actually all the same, namely at the intersection point of demand and supply. It is impossible to distinguish the demand curve from the true supply curve or any other line which passes through the intersection point. (See Figure 4–1.) The scatter of dots arises because both the supply curves and demand curves are shifting (possibly in unobservable ways).

In order to distinguish between equations, their specifications require knowledge of actual shifts in demand or supply due to changes in some factor which affects only one of the curves. When the problem is serious, consumer surveys and market experiments can be used to gain important demand information.

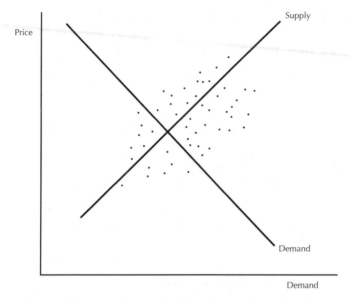

Figure 4–1. Identification Problem: Demand and Supply

ECONOMETRICS AND REGRESSION ANALYSIS

A major empirical work is done within the framework of *econometrics*. Econometrics is concerned with empirical testing of economic theory using various estimation methods, including *regression analysis*. The technique of regression analysis is perhaps the best-known and most-frequently-used technique in developing estimates of demand function.

REGRESSION ANALYSIS

Regression analysis is a statistical procedure for estimating mathematically the average relationship between the dependent variable and the independent variable(s). *Simple regression* involves one independent variable, price or advertising in a demand function, whereas *multiple regression* involves two or more variables, that is price and advertising together.

LEAST-SQUARES METHOD

The least-squares method is widely used in regression analysis for estimating the parameter values in a regression equation. The regression method includes all the observed data and attempts to find a line of best fit. To find this line, a technique called the *least-squares method* is used.

We first assume a linear relation: $Y = \alpha + \beta X + e$, where α and β are the true (but unknown) population parameters of the regression line and $e =$ an error term. In the real world, our task is to find an estimate of α and β from a sample data. Thus, we wish to find $Y' = a + bX$, where a and b are estimates of α and β, respectively, and Y' is the calculated value of Y given a particular value of X and our estimated relationship. Then

$$Y = a + bX + u,$$

where u is the error term for our estimated relationship and is an estimate of e, the population error term.

Thus,

$$u = Y - Y'.$$

The least-squares criterion requires that the line of best fit be such that the sum of the squares of the errors (or the vertical distance in Figure 4–2 from the observed data points to the line) is a minimum, i.e.,

$$\text{Minimum: } \Sigma u^2 = \Sigma(Y - a - bX)^2.$$

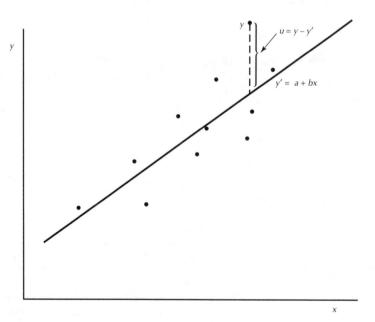

Figure 4–2. Scattergraph: y and y'

Using differential calculus we obtain the following equations, called *normal equations*:

$$\Sigma Y = na + b\Sigma X$$

$$\Sigma XY = a\Sigma X + b\Sigma X^2$$

Solving the equations for b and a yields

$$b = \frac{n\Sigma XY - (\Sigma X)(\Sigma Y)}{n\Sigma X^2 - (\Sigma X)^2}$$

$$a = \overline{Y} - b\overline{X}$$

$$\text{where } \overline{Y} = \frac{\Sigma Y}{n} \text{ and } \overline{X} = \frac{\Sigma X}{n}$$

EXAMPLE 1

DHG Oil Company has observed the following price-quantity relationships over the last six periods:

Period	Price (X)	Quantity demanded (Y)
1	1.20	250
2	1.21	245
3	1.25	200
4	1.17	310
5	1.15	375
6	1.19	280
	7.17	1,660

To illustrate the computations of b and a, we will refer to the data in Table 4–1. All the sums required are computed and shown below.

Table 4–1.   Computed Sums

Period	Price (X)	Quantity demanded(Y)	XY	X-squared	Y-squared
1	1.20	250	300.00	1.4400	62,500
2	1.21	245	296.45	1.4641	60,025
3	1.25	200	250.00	1.5625	40,000
4	1.17	310	362.70	1.3689	96,100
5	1.15	375	431.25	1.3225	140,625
6	1.19	280	333.20	1.4161	78,400
	7.17	1,660	1,973.60	8.5741	477,650

From the table above:

$\Sigma X = 7.17; \Sigma Y = 1,660;$ $\Sigma XY = 1,973.60;$ $\Sigma X^2 = 8.5741$

$X = \dfrac{\Sigma X}{n} = \dfrac{7.17}{6} = 1.20;$ $Y = \dfrac{\Sigma Y}{n} = \dfrac{1,660}{6} = 276.67$

Substituting these values into the formula for b first:

$$b = \frac{n\Sigma XY - (\Sigma X)(\Sigma Y)}{n\Sigma X^2 - (\Sigma X)^2} = \frac{(6)(1,973.60) - (7.17)(1,660)}{(6)(8.5741) - (7.17)^2} = \frac{-60.60}{0.0357} = -1,697.48,$$

$$a = \overline{Y} - b\overline{X} = 276.67 - (-1,697.48)(1.20) = 2,305.15$$

Thus, $Y' = 2,305.15 - 1,697.48\ X.$

Note that ΣY^2 is not used here but rather is computed for r-squared (r^2).

EXAMPLE 2

Assume advertising of $1.10 is to be expended for next year; the projected sales for the next year would be computed as follows:

$$Y' = 2,305.15 - 1,697.48X = 2,305.15 - 1,697.48(1.10) = \$437.92$$

ASSUMPTIONS UNDERLYING REGRESSION ANALYSIS

To make valid inferences from sample data about population relationships, four assumptions must be satisfied: (1) *linearity,* (2) *constant variance (homoscedasticity),* (3) *independence, and* (4) *normality.* A violation of any one of these assumptions reduces the validity of the least-squares technique for estimating demand relationships.

• *LINEARITY*

In the population, X and Y are linearly related. The hypothesized population relation is $Y = \alpha + \beta X + u,$ where α and β are the true (but unknown) parameters of the regression line. We assume that errors, u, have an average or expected value of zero, i.e., $E(u) = 0$, which leads to $E(Y) = \alpha + \beta X$. The deviation of the actual value of Y from the true regression line is called the error term (or the disturbance term), which is defined as $Y - Y'$.

YOU SHOULD REMEMBER

Before attempting a least-squares regression approach, it is extremely important to plot the observed data on a diagram, called the scatter-graph (See Figure 4–3). The reason is that you might want to make sure that a linear (straight-line) relationship existed between *Y* and *X* in the past sample. If for any reason there was a nonlinear relationship detected in the sample, the linear relationship we assumed, $Y' = a + bX$, would not give us a good fit. In order to obtain a good fit and achieve a high degree of accuracy, you should be familiar with statistics relating to regression, such as *r*-squared (r^2) and *t*-value, which are discussed later.

• *CONSTANT VARIANCE (HOMOSCEDASTICITY)*

Also called *homoscedasticity,* the assumption is that the variance of the *X*'s is constant for all *X*'s, i.e., as *X* changes, the dispersion does not change. This indicates that there is uniform scatter or dispersion of points about the regression line. The scatter diagram is the easiest way to check for constant variance. Note in Figure 4–4 that this assumption is valid for the first chart, but not the second. Violation of this assumption is called *heteroscedasticity.*

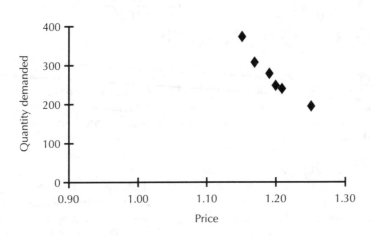

Figure 4–3.   Scatter Diagram

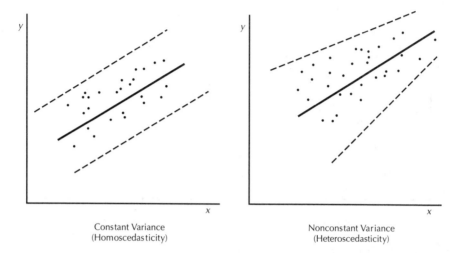

Figure 4–4.   Homoscedasticity vs. Heteroscedasticity

If the constant-variance assumption does not hold, the accuracy of the b coefficient is open to question. It will ruin the validity of important statistical tests associated with regression analysis.

• *INDEPENDENCE*

It is further assumed that the u's are independent of each other, i.e., the occurrence of an error of one magnitude does not cause an error of another size. If the u's are not independent, the problem of *serial correlation* (also called *autocorrelation) is* present. (See Figure 4–5.) To illustrate, when observations are taken in successive time periods, the disturbances that arose in a period t may not be independent from those that arose in previous periods $t-1$, and so on. When autocorrelation exists, the standard errors of the regression coefficients are seriously underestimated. As a result, the use of a t-statistic may yield incorrect conclusions concerning the significance of the individual predictor (i.e., independent) variables. (The t-statistic and standard error are explained in the next section.) Furthermore, the predictions of the Y variable made from the regression equations will be more variable than is ordinarily anticipated from least-squares estimation. The computation of standard errors is based on independent observations. If observations are not independent, there simply are not enough observations in the sample. Fortunately, computer programs usually have tests for serial correlation.

• *NORMALITY*

The fourth assumption is that the points around the regression line are normally distributed. That is, the u values are normally distributed—or at least t-distributed. This assumption is necessary concerning inferences about Y', a, and b. For example,

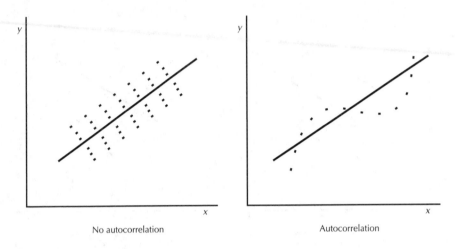

No autocorrelation   Autocorrelation

Figure 4–5.   Autocorrelation

the normality assumption is necessary to make probability statements using the standard error of the estimate.

REGRESSION STATISTICS

Regression analysis is a statistical method. Hence, it uses a variety of statistics to tell about the accuracy and reliability of the regression results. They include:

1. Correlation coefficient (r) and coefficient of determination (r^2)

2. Standard error of the estimate (S_e) and prediction confidence interval

3. Standard error of the regression coefficient (S_b) and confidence interval

4. t-statistic

Each of these statistics is explained below.

CORRELATION COEFFICIENT (r) AND COEFFICIENT OF DETERMINATION (r^2)

The correlation coefficient r measures the degree of correlation between Y and X. The range of values it takes on is between -1 and $+1$. More widely used, however, is the coefficient of determination, designated r^2 (read as r-squared).

Simply put, r^2 tells us how good the estimated regression equation is. In other words, it is a measure of "goodness of fit" in the regression. Therefore, the higher the r^2, the more confidence we have in our estimated equation.

YOU SHOULD REMEMBER

A low r^2 is an indication that the model is inadequate for explaining the Y variable. The general causes for this problem are

1. the use of a wrong functional form,

2. the poor choice of an X variable as the predictor,

3. the omission of some important variable or variables from the model.

EXAMPLE 3

The statement "Sales is a function of price with $r^2 = 70$ percent," can be interpreted as "70 percent of the total variation of sales is explained by the regression equation and the change in price and the remaining 30 percent is accounted for by something other than price, such as advertising and income."

As shown in Figure 4–6, the total deviation of the dependent variable Y for its mean $\overline{Y}$ can be divided into two parts.

$$(Y - \overline{Y}) \quad = \quad (Y - Y') \quad + \quad (Y' - \overline{Y})$$

(Total Deviation) (Unexplained Deviation) (Explained Deviation)

The measure of the goodness of fit of a regression line, expressed by the coefficient of determination (r^2), is made by comparing $\Sigma(Y' - \overline{Y})^2$, the explained sum of squares with the total sum of the squares $\Sigma(Y - \overline{Y})^2$.

That is,

$$r^2 = \frac{\Sigma(Y' - \overline{Y})^2}{\Sigma(Y - \overline{Y})^2} = \frac{\text{Explained variance}}{\text{Total variance}}.$$

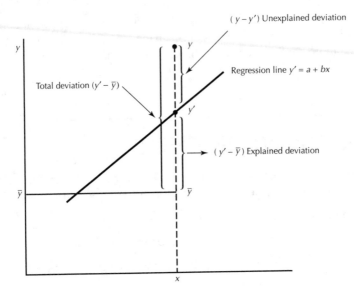

Figure 4–6. Fundamental Measures of Variance (Deviation)

Thus, the coefficient of determination represents the proportion of the total variation in Y that is explained by the regression equation. It has the range of values between 0 and 1.

YOU SHOULD REMEMBER

The sum of squares of the explained deviation *plus* the sum of squares of the unexplained deviation *equals* the total sum of squares.

In a simple regression situation, however, there is a shortcut method available:

$$r^2 = \frac{[n\Sigma XY - (\Sigma X)(\Sigma Y)]^2}{[n\Sigma X^2 - (\Sigma X)^2][n\Sigma Y^2 - (\Sigma Y)^2]}.$$

Comparing this formula with the one for b, we see that the only additional information we need to compute r^2 is ΣY^2.

EXAMPLE 4

To illustrate the computations of various regression statistics, we will refer to the data in Table 4–1. Using the shortcut method for r^2,

$$r^2 = \frac{[(6)(1,973.60) - (7.17)(1,660)]^2}{[(6)(8.5741) - (7.17)^2][(6)(477,650) - (1,660)^2]} = \frac{(-60.60)^2}{(0.0357)(110,300)}$$

$$= \frac{3,672.36}{3,937.71} = 0.9326 = 93.26\%.$$

This means that about 93.26 percent of the total variation in sales is explained by price and the remaining 6.74 percent is still unexplained. A relatively high r^2 indicates that the estimated demand function is quite reliable and price is an excellent determinant of demand.

STANDARD ERROR OF THE ESTIMATE (S_e) AND PREDICTION CONFIDENCE INTERVAL

The standard error of the estimate, designated S_e, is defined as the standard deviation of the regression. It is computed as

$$S_e = \sqrt{\frac{\Sigma(Y - Y')^2}{n - 2}} = \sqrt{\frac{\Sigma Y^2 - a\Sigma Y - b\Sigma XY}{n - 2}}.$$

This statistic can be used to gain some idea of the accuracy of our predictions.

EXAMPLE 5

Going back to our example data, S_e is calculated as

$$S_e = \sqrt{\frac{(477,650) - (2,305.15)(1,660) - (-1,697.48)(1,973.60)}{6 - 2}}$$

$$= \sqrt{\frac{1,247.5}{4}} = 17.66.$$

Suppose you wish to make a prediction regarding an individual Y value, such as a prediction about the sales when price is $1.10. Usually, we would like to have some objective measure of the confidence we can place in our prediction, and one such measure is a *confidence* (or *prediction*) *interval* constructed for Y.

A confidence interval for a predicted Y, *given a value for X*, can be constructed in the following manner.

$$Y' \pm t\, S_e \sqrt{1 + \frac{1}{n} + \frac{(X_p - \bar{X})^2}{\Sigma X^2 - \dfrac{(\Sigma X)^2}{n}}},$$

where Y' = the predicted value of Y given a value for X;

X_p = the value of an independent variable used as the basis for prediction.

Note: t is the critical value for the level of significance employed. For example, for a significance level of 0.025 (which is equivalent to a 95% confidence level in a two-tailed test), the critical value of t for 4 degrees of freedom is 2.776 (See Table 5 in Appendix II).

YOU SHOULD REMEMBER

Degrees of freedom (*df*) is the number of observations beyond the absolute minimum needed to calculate a given regression line or statistic. For example, to compute a constant term, *a*, at least one observation is needed; to compute *a* and *b*, at least two observations are required; and so on.

EXAMPLE 6

If you want to have a 95 percent confidence interval of your prediction, the range for the prediction, given a price of $1.10, would be between $356.93 and $518.91, as determined as follows: Note that from Example 2, $Y' = 2{,}305.15 - 1{,}697.X = 2{,}305.15 - 1{,}697.48(\$1.10) = \$437.92$

The confidence interval is therefore established as follows:

$$\$437.92 \pm (2.776)(17.66) \sqrt{1 + \frac{1}{6} + \frac{(1.10 - 1.195)^2}{8.5741 - \dfrac{(7.17)^2}{6}}}$$

$$= \$437.92 \pm (2.776)(17.66)(1.638)$$

$$= \$437.92 \pm 80.30$$

which means the range for the prediction, given an advertising expense of $1.10 would be between $357.62 and $518.22. Note that $357.62 = $437.92 − 80.30 and $518.22 = $437.92 + 80.30.

YOU SHOULD REMEMBER

Many managerial economics texts use $Y' \pm t\,S_e$ for the prediction interval, ignoring the adjustment factor. In Example 6, the interval is $\$437.92 \pm (2.776)(17.66)$.

STANDARD ERROR OF THE REGRESSION COEFFICIENT (S_b)

The standard error of the regression coefficient, designated S_b, and the t-statistic are closely related. S_b is calculated as

$$S_b = \frac{S_e}{\sqrt{\Sigma(X - \overline{X})^2}}$$

or in shortcut form

$$S_b = \frac{S_e}{\sqrt{\Sigma X^2 - \overline{X}\Sigma X}}.$$

S_b gives an estimate of the range where the true coefficient will "actually" fall. Just as S_e was used to determine confidence intervals for your prediction, S_b can be used to estimate confidence intervals of the true value of the regression coefficient with varying degrees of confidence. The intervals are

$$b \pm t\,S_b.$$

t-STATISTIC

t-statistics (or t-value) is a measure of the statistical significance of an independent variable X in explaining the dependent variable Y. It is determined by

$$t = \frac{b - \beta}{S_b}.$$

Since we wish to test the hypothesis that $\beta = 0$, we substitute $\beta = 0$ into this formula, which means that we essentially divide the estimated regression coefficient b by its standard error S_b. It is then compared with the table t-value to determine if the null hypothesis is true.

Note: The t-statistic basically measures how many standard errors the coefficient is away from zero. The higher the t-value, the greater the confidence we have in the coefficient as a predictor. Low t-values are indications of low reliability of the predictive power of that coefficient.

EXAMPLE 7

The *Sb* for our example is

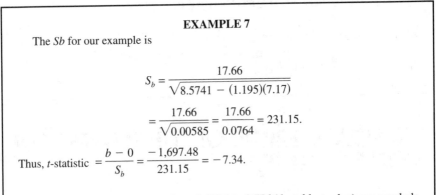

$$S_b = \frac{17.66}{\sqrt{8.5741 - (1.195)(7.17)}}$$

$$= \frac{17.66}{\sqrt{0.00585}} = \frac{17.66}{0.0764} = 231.15.$$

Thus, t-statistic $= \frac{b - 0}{S_b} = \frac{-1,697.48}{231.15} = -7.34.$

Since $t = 7.34$ (the absolute value of -7.34) > 2.776 (the table t-value), we conclude that the null hypothesis is false and therefore the b coefficient is statistically significant.

YOU SHOULD REMEMBER

1. t-statistic is more relevant to multiple regressions that have more than one b's.

2. r^2 tells you how good the forest (overall fit) is while t-statistic tells you how good an individual tree (an independent variable) is.

   In summary, the table t-value, based on a degree of freedom and a level of significance, is used:

1. to set the prediction range—upper and lower limits—for the predicted value of the dependent variable,

2. to estimate confidence intervals within which the true value of the regression coefficient falls,

3. as a cutoff value for the t-test.

USE OF EXCEL FOR REGRESSION

Spreadsheet programs such as *Excel* have a regression routine which you can use without any difficulty. You can access the regression tool by completing the following steps:

1. Click the Tools menu

2. Click Data Analysis

3. Click Regression

After you choose the Regression command, the Regression dialog box appears, which asks you to select the Y-Range, the X-Range, and the Output Range. After selecting these ranges, you can click the OK button and Excel will calculate the least-squares values for the parameters a and b (along with other summary statistics), as shown below.

Summary Output

Regression Statistics

Multiple R	0.96572
R Square	0.93261
Adjusted R Square	0.91577
Standard Error	17.5983
Observations	6

ANOVA

	df	SS	MS	F	Significance F
Regression	1	17,144.54	17,144.54	55.35873	0.001742641
Residual	4	1,238.796	309.6989		
Total	5	18,383.33			

	Coefficients	Standard Error	t-Stat	P-value	Lower 95%	Upper 95%
Intercept	2,305.15	272.7282	8.452204	0.001073	1,547.937731	3,062.37
X Variable 1	−1,697.48	228.1452	−7.44035	0.001743	−2,330.912925	−1,064.05

YOU SHOULD REMEMBER

Note from the Excel regression output that

1. $b = -1,697.48$ and $a = 2,305.15$; therefore, the estimated demand function is

$$Y' = 2,305.15 - 1,697.48X$$

2. $r^2 = 0.93261$

3. $S_e = 17.5983$

4. $S_b = 228.1452$

5. t for the regression coefficient = -7.44035

The computer output numbers are *different* from manually obtained numbers due to rounding errors. Computer numbers are more accurate because the computer carries computations to more decimal digits.

MULTIPLE REGRESSION

Multiple regression analysis is a powerful statistical technique that is perhaps the most widely used one by forecasters. Multiple regression attempts to estimate statistically the average relationship between the dependent variable (e.g., sales) and two or more independent variables (e.g., price, advertising, income, etc.).

In reality, forecasters will face more multiple regression situations than simple regression. In order to obtain a good fit and achieve a high degree of accuracy, they should be familiar with statistics relating to regression, such as r-squared (r^2) and t-value.

Note: Look beyond the statistics we discussed here. Furthermore, forecasters will have to perform additional tests unique to multiple regression.

APPLICATIONS

Applications of multiple regression are numerous. Multiple regression analysis is used to do the following:

1. To find the overall association between the dependent variable and a host of explanatory variables. For example, total costs are explained by volume, productivity, and technology.

2. To attempt to identify the factors that influence the dependent variable. For example,

   a. factors critical in affecting sales include price levels, advertising expenditures, consumer take-home income, taste, and competition;

   b. financial analysts might seek causes of a change in stock prices or price-earnings (*P-E*) ratios by analyzing growth in earnings, variability of earnings, stock splits, inflation rates, beta, and dividend yields;

    c. advertising directors wish to study the impact on consumer buying of advertising budgets, advertising frequency, media selection, and the like;

    d. personnel managers attempt to determine the relationship between employee salary levels and a host of factors, such as industry type, union leadership, competitive salaries, unemployment, skill levels, and geographical location.

3. To use it as a basis for providing sound forecasts of the dependent variable. For example, sometimes cash collections from customers are forecasted from credit sales of prior months because cash collections lag behind sales.

THE MODEL

It takes the following form:

$$Y = b_0 + b_1 X_1 + b_2 X_{2...} + b_k X_k + u$$

where Y = dependent variable, X's = independent (explanatory) variables, b's = regression coefficients, u = error term.

STATISTICS TO LOOK FOR IN MULTIPLE REGRESSIONS

In multiple regressions that involve more than one independent (explanatory) variable, managers must look for the following statistics:

- t-statistics
- $\bar{r}^2$ (r-bar squared) and F-statistic
- Multicollinearity
- Autocorrelation (or serial correlation)

• *t-STATISTICS*

The t-statistic was discussed earlier, but is taken up again because it is more valid in multiple regressions than in simple regressions. The t-statistic shows the significance of each explanatory variable in predicting the dependent variable. It is desirable to have as large (either positive or negative) a t-statistic as possible for each independent variable. Generally, a t-statistic greater than $+2.0$ or less than -2.0 is acceptable. Explanatory variables with low t-values can usually be eliminated from the regression without substantially decreasing r^2 or increasing the standard error of the regression. In a multiple regression situation, the t-statistic is defined as

$$t\text{-statistic} = \frac{b_i}{S_{b_i}},$$

where $i = i$th independent variable

$\bar{r}^2$ (r-BAR SQUARED) AND F-STATISTIC

r^2 tends to increase if the number of coefficients (k) to be estimated increases (i.e., degrees of freedom diminishes). $\bar{r}^2$, read as r-bar squared, is used as a more appropriate test for goodness of fit for multiple regressions. $\bar{r}^2$ is a corrected or adjusted r^2 to account for the degrees of freedom. It is a downward adjustment to r^2 in light of the number of observations and estimated coefficients.

$$\bar{r}^2 = r^2 - (1 - r^2)\frac{(k-1)}{(n-k)},$$

where n = number of observations
k = number of coefficients to be estimated

An alternative test of the overall explanatory power of a regression equation is the F-test. It is a formal test of the null hypothesis: $b_1 = b_2 = \cdots = b_k = 0$.

The F-statistic is defined as

$$F = \frac{\dfrac{r^2}{(k-1)}}{\dfrac{(1-r^2)}{(n-k)}} = \frac{\dfrac{\text{Explained variation}}{(k-1)}}{\dfrac{\text{Unexplained variation}}{(n-k)}}$$

Virtually all computer programs for regression analysis show an F-statistic. If the F-statistic is greater than the F-value in the table (Table 6 in Appendix II), it is concluded that the regression equation is statistically significant in overall terms. Table 6 shows critical values of the F-distribution (a) for various levels of statistical significance or confidence levels and (b) for two degrees-of-freedom characteristics of the F-statistic, one $(k-1)$ related to the numerator and the other $(n-k)$ associated with the denominator.

MULTICOLLINEARITY

When using more than one independent variable in a regression equation, there is sometimes a high correlation between the independent variables themselves. Multicollinearity occurs when these variables interfere with each other. Homeownership and family income provide an example of multicollinearity. If two variables move up and down together, the least-squares method can assign one variable an arbitrarily high coefficient and the other an arbitrarily low coefficient, the two largely offsetting each other. As it damages the reliability of obtained regression coefficients, it also damages the ability to draw well-supported conclusions about the significance of individual variables from t-tests.

There are two ways to get around the problem of multicollinearity.

1. One of the highly correlated variables may be dropped from the regression.

2. The structure of the equation may be changed using one of the following methods.

   a. Divide both the left- and right-hand side variables by some series that will leave the basic economic logic but remove multicollinearity.

   b. Estimate the equation on a first-difference basis.

AUTOCORRELATION (SERIAL CORRELATION)

Autocorrelation is another major pitfall often encountered in regression analysis. It occurs where there is a correlation between successive errors. The Durbin-Watson statistic provides the standard test for autocorrelation. The table below provides a rough guide for the values of the Durbin-Watson statistic.

Durbin-Watson Statistic	Autocorrelation
Between 1.5 and 2.5	No Autocorrelation
Below 1.5	Positive Autocorrelation
Above 2.5	Negative Autocorrelation

Autocorrelation usually indicates that an important part of the variation of the dependent variable has not been explained. If there is autocorrelation, the least-squares method may seriously underestimate the standard error. Calculations drawn from r^2 and t-tests are likely to be unreliable and less meaningful. The best solution to this problem is to search for other explanatory variables to include in the regression equation.

USE OF REGRESSION SOFTWARE

Excel does not calculate statistics, such as the Durbin-Watson statistic. You have to go to regression packages, such as *Statistical Analysis System (SAS), Minitab,* and *Statistical Packages for Social Scientists (SPSS)*, to name a few.

The following example illustrates the use of computer software for multiple regression.

EXAMPLE 8

Stanton Consumer Products Corporation wishes to develop a forecasting model for its dryer sale by using multiple regression analysis. The marketing department has prepared the following sample data.

Month	Sales of Washers (X_1)	Disposable Income (X_2)	Savings (X_3)	Sales of Dryers (Y)
January	$45,000	$16,000	$71,000	$29,000
February	42,000	14,000	70,000	24,000
March	44,000	15,000	72,000	27,000
April	45,000	13,000	71,000	25,000
May	43,000	13,000	75,000	26,000
June	46,000	14,000	74,000	28,000
July	44,000	16,000	76,000	30,000
August	45,000	16,000	69,000	28,000
September	44,000	15,000	74,000	28,000
October	43,000	15,000	73,000	27,000

Figure 4–7 contains the output that results from using a popular software, SPSS.

1. *The regression equation.* We see that

$$Y' = -45.796 + 0.597X_1 + 1.177X_2 + 0.405X_3.$$

2. *The coefficient of determination.* Note that $r^2 = 0.983$.

   In the case of multiple regression, $\bar{r}^2$ is more appropriate and equals 0.975. It is a modest downward adjustment to r^2 based on the size of the sample analyzed relative to the number of estimated coefficients. This tells us that 97.5 percent of total variation in sales of dryers is explained by the three explanatory variables. The remaining 2.5 percent was unexplained by the estimated equation.

3. *The standard error of the estimate (S_e).* This is a measure of dispersion of actual sales around the estimated equation. The output shows $S_e = 0.28612$.

4. *Computed t.* We read from the output

Equation Number 1   Dependent Variable.   SALESDRY (Sales of dryers)

Block Number 1.   Method: Enter   SALESWAS (Sales of washers) INCOME   SAVINGS

Variable(s) Entered on Step Number
  1.   SAVINGS
  2.   SALESWAS
  3.   INCOME

Multiple R	0.99167
R Square	0.98340
Adjusted R Square	0.97511
Standard Error	0.28613

-- Variables in the Equation --

Variable	B	SE B	Beta	Tolerance	VIF	T
SALESWAS	0.596972	0.081124	0.394097	0.964339	1.037	7.359
INCOME	1.176838	0.084074	0.752425	0.957217	1.045	13.998
SAVINGS	0.405109	0.042234	0.507753	0.987080	1.013	9.592
(Constant)	–45.796348	4.877651				–9.389

Analysis of Variance

	DF	Sum of Squares	Mean Square
Regression	3	29.10878	9.70293
Residual	6	0.49122	0.08187

F = 118.51727   Signif F = 0.0000

Collinearity Diagnostics

Number	Eigenval	Cond Index	Variance Constant	Proportions SALESWAS	INCOME	SAVINGS
1	3.99470	1.000	0.00002	0.00004	0.00033	0.00005
2	0.00429	30.505	0.00538	0.00705	0.91815	0.02968
3	0.00078	71.687	0.00509	0.39949	0.07280	0.55230
4	0.00023	130.826	0.98950	0.59341	0.00872	0.41796

Durbin-Watson Test = 2.09377

Figure 4–7. SPSS Regression Output

t-Statistic	
X_1	7.359
X_2	13.998
X_3	9.592

All *t* values are greater than a rule of thumb table *t*-value of 2.0. (Strictly speaking, with $n - k = 10 - 4 = 6$ degrees of freedom and a level of significance of, say, 0.01, we see from Table 5 in Appendix II that the table *t*-value is 3.707.) For a two-sided test, the level of significance to look up was 0.005. In any case, we conclude that all three explanatory variables we have selected were statistically significant.

5. *Multicollinearity diagnostics.* Collinearity diagnostics indicate very little correlations among the independent variables. No visible sign of multicollinearity exists.

6. *F-test.* From the output, we see that $F = 118.51727$. At a significance level of 0.01, our *F*-value is far above the value of 9.78 (which is from Table 6 in Appendix V), so we conclude that the regression as a whole is highly significant.

7. *Serial correlation test.* The SPSS regression output shows a Durbin-Watson value of 2.09377. Since it is between 1.5 and 2.5, no autocorrelation exists.

8. *Conclusion.* Based on statistical considerations, we see that:
   - the estimated equation had a good fit,
   - all three variables are significant explanatory variables,
   - the regression as a whole is highly significant,
   - no autocorrelation exists,
   - the model developed can be used as a forecasting equation with a great degree of confidence.

KNOW THE CONCEPTS

TERMS FOR STUDY

coefficient of determination
consumer surveys
Durbin-Watson statistic
F-test
homoscedasticity
identification problem
least-squares method
linear regression
market experiments

multicollinearity
multiple regression
$\bar{r}^2$ (*r*-bar squared)
regression analysis
simple regression
standard error of the estimate
standard error of the regression
   coefficient
t-test

DO YOU KNOW THE BASICS?

1. Why is the identification problem often serious for demand estimation?

2. What criteria must be met if regression-based analysis is to provide an accurate estimate of demand relationships?

3. What are "consumer surveys"? What are some of the problems associated with the use of consumer surveys to estimate the demand for a firm's product?

4. Explain market experiments: what they are, how they may be used, and any limitations that they might have.

5. Distinguish between simple regression and multiple regression. Give an example of each.

6. List five basic assumptions underlying regression analysis. What happens if these assumptions are violated?

7. What does a low r^2 mean? What are some causes for this? What is r-bar squared ($\bar{r}^2$)?

8. Describe a circumstance in which multicollinearity is likely to be a problem, and describe a possible remedy.

9. What are the uses of the t-table value obtained based on a given degree of freedom and a given level of significance?

10. What is the primary use of standard errors?

PRACTICAL APPLICATION

1. The following are the advertising and sales data of Jupiter Corporation over an eight-month period.

Advertising (000 omitted)	Sales (000 omitted)
320	$2,600
200	1,500
230	2,150
240	2,250
720	4,700
560	3,700
470	3,300
750	4,750

   a. Develop the demand equation by using the method of least squares.

   b. Compute the coefficient of determination.

   c. Comment on the choice of advertising in predicting sales. Is advertising a good predictor?

2. A government economist wishes to establish the relationship between annual family income X and savings Y. A sample of 100 families has been made and the following calculations have been obtained (X and Y are measured in thousands of dollars):

$$\Sigma X = \$1{,}239 \qquad \Sigma Y = \$79 \qquad \Sigma XY = \$1{,}613$$

$$\Sigma X^2 = \$17{,}322 \qquad \Sigma Y^2 = \$293$$

   a. Determine the equation for the estimated regression line.

   b. State the meaning of the slope b and the intercept value a.

   c. Compute the coefficient of determination r^2.

   d. Calculate the standard error of the estimate S_e.

   e. Write down the expression for the predicted range of Y (use the table t-value $= 1.98$ with 98 degrees of freedom and a 5 percent significance level).

3. You want to estimate the demand function for gasoline. Given the following data and the regression output from Excel:

Period	Price (P)	Quantity demanded(Q)
1	1.20	300
2	1.30	295
3	1.25	298
4	1.33	275
5	1.27	266
6	0.99	360
7	1.15	325
8	1.36	266
9	1.19	311
10	1.22	325
	12.26	3,021

SUMMARY OUTPUT

Regression Statistics	
Multiple R	0.9128
R Square	0.8333
Adjusted R Square	0.8124
Standard Error	12.826
Observations	10

ANOVA

	df	SS	MS	F	Significance F
Regression	1	6,576.785	6,576.785	39.97698	0.000227161
Residual	8	1,316.115	164.5143		
Total	9	7,892.9			

	Coefficients	Standard Error	t-Stat	P-value	Lower 95%	Upper 95%
Intercept	616.13	49.83278	12.36403	1.71E−06	501.2194022	731.0488
X Variable 1	−256.15	40.51178	−6.32274	0.000227	−349.5656425	−162.725

a. Write the estimated demand function.

b. What is r^2? What does that number indicate?

c. Compute the point elasticity of demand when the price is $1. Is this product price elastic?

d. Determine the confidence interval for the price coefficient (the table t-value with a 5% significance level and 8 (10 − 2) degrees of freedom is 2.306).

e. What is t-value for the regression coefficient? What does that indicate?

f. Can this estimated relationship be improved? What would you suggest?

4. Using linear regression analysis, Dokdo Home Improvement Company estimated its demand function for roofing and achieved the following realities:

$$Q = 244 - 0.1057P + 1.35P_c + 0.0251 \text{ with } r^2 = 0.65,$$

where P_C = price of a competing firm's average bid and I = average annual household income.

a. What would an $\bar{r}^2$ of 0.65 indicate?

b. Can you think of a potentially important variable that Dokdo has ignored in its demand analysis?

5. A study of the demand for imported motorcycles based on two years of monthly data (24 observations) showed the following demand function

$$Q = 3.25P^{-2.5} \, P_X^{3.5} \, A^{2.5} \quad I^4$$
$$(1) \quad (1.5) \, (0.8) \, (1.5)^*$$
$$r^{-2} = 0.92$$

The asterisk indicates the standard errors of the exponents in the multiplicative demand function where Q = the quantity of motorcycles imported, P = average motorcycle price, P_X = the average price of imported compact cars, A = motorcycle industry advertising, and I = average disposable family income.

a. What share of overall variation in demand is explained by the regression equation? What share is left unexplained?

b. Are the factors in this demand function statistically significant? If so, on what basis do you come to that conclusion?

c. Is the demand for imported motorcycles elastic with respect to price?

d. Are imported motorcycles a normal good?

e. Are motorcycles and compact cars substitutes?

6. Complete Fitness, Inc., a health club chain, estimated its demand function based on monthly sales by four outlets during the past year (a total of 36 observations):

$$Q = 410 - 4P + 2P_C + 8A + 50T - 5W$$
$$(1.5) \quad (0.8) \quad (3.5) \quad (15) \quad (2.4)^*,$$
$$r^{-2} = 0.98,$$
$$S_e = 15,$$

where Q = membership sales (in units), P = average membership price (in dollars), P_C = average membership price charged by competitors (in dollars), A = advertising expenditures (in thousands of dollars), T = time (in months of continuous operation), W = weather (in average monthly temperature).

a. What share of overall variation in membership sales is explained by the regression equation? What share is left unexplained?

b. Using a 95 percent confidence level (or a 5 percent significance level), which independent factors have an influence on membership sales?

c. During a recent month, for the Seal Beach outlet $P = \$750$, $P_C = \$600$, $A = \$67,500$, $T = 3$ years, and $W = 70°$. Derive the relevant demand curve for Complete Fitness memberships.

ANSWERS

DO YOU KNOW THE BASICS?

1. The identification problem occurs when many factors that influence product demand also affect product supply. When two economic relations, such as demand and supply functions, are so interrelated so as to make empirical estimation of the relations impossible, we say that we are unable to identify the individual functions.

2. The regression model must be properly specified. In other words, the range of factors influencing demand must be properly identified and the correct functional form must be employed. Many statistics, such as r^2 and t-tests, are used to ascertain whether these conditions are satisfied.

3. Potential and actual customers are questioned about various factors affecting their demand for a firm's product. Two problems are: (a) consumers may not be able to respond accurately to specific questions, such as proposed price changes, and (b) such surveys may be prohibitorily expensive.

4. A market experiment is conducted by varying those factors that supposedly affect the demand and which are under control, such as pricing or advertising. The experiment can be expensive and risky. It may not generate a sufficiently large number of observations to make reliable estimates of the demand function.

5. *Simple regression* involves one independent variable, price or advertising in a demand function, whereas *multiple regression* involves two or more variables, that is, price and advertising together.

6. The five assumptions that must be satisfied are as follows: (1) *linearity,* (2) *constant variance (homoscedasticity),* (3) *independence,* (4) *normality,* (5) *no multicollinearity.* When these assumptions are not satisfied, the sample values a and b are *not* the reliable estimates of the population values α and β.

7. A low r^2 is an indication that the model is inadequate for explaining the Y variable. The general causes for this problem are: (a) the use of a wrong functional form, (b) a poor choice of an X variable as the predictor, and/or (c) the omission of some important variable or variables from the model. $\bar{r}^2$ is a corrected or adjusted r^2 to account for the degrees of freedom. It is a downward adjustment to r^2 in light of the number of observations and estimated coefficients.

8. Multicollinearity occurs when two (or more) independent variables are closely related with each other. Homeownership and family income provide an example of multicollinearity. If two variables move up and down together, the least-squares method can assign one variable an arbitrarily high coefficient and the other an arbitrarily low coefficient, the two largely offsetting each other. One remedy is to drop one of the highly correlated variables from the regression.

9. The t-table value is used (a) to set the prediction range—upper and lower limits set with a specified level of confidence (e.g., 95 percent)—for the predicted value of the dependent variable, (b) to set the confidence interval for regression coefficients, and (c) as a cutoff value for the t-test.

10. The standard error of the estimate, S_e, is used to set a prediction range for the value of the dependent variable with varying degrees of confidence, while the standard error of the regression coefficient, S_b, gives an estimate of the range where the true coefficient will "actually" fall.

PRACTICAL APPLICATION

1a. Based on the method of least squares, we obtain:

Advertising X	Sales Y	XY	X^2	Y^2
$320	$2,600	$832,000	$102,400	$6,760,000
200	1,500	300,000	40,000	2,250,000
230	2,150	494,500	52,900	4,622,500
240	2,250	540,000	57,600	5,062,500
720	4,700	3,384,000	518,400	22,090,000
560	3,700	2,072,000	313,600	13,690,000
470	3,300	1,551,000	220,900	10,890,000
750	4,750	3,562,500	562,500	22,562,500
$3,490	$24,950	$12,736,000	$1,868,300	$87,927,500

From the table:

$n = 8$, $\Sigma X = \$3,490$, $\Sigma Y = \$24,950$, $\Sigma XY = \$12,736,000$, $\Sigma X^2 = \$1,868,300$.

Substituting these values into the formula for b first:

$$b = \frac{n\Sigma XY - (\Sigma X)(\Sigma Y)}{n\Sigma X^2 - (\Sigma X)^2} = \frac{(8)(12,736,000) - (3,490)(24,950)}{(8)(1,868,300) - (3,490)^2} = \$5.35,$$

$$a = \frac{\Sigma Y}{n} - b\frac{\Sigma X}{n} = \frac{24,950}{8} - (5.35)\left(\frac{3,490}{8}\right) = 3,119 - 2,334 = \$785.$$

Thus, the regression model is $785 + $5.35 X.

1b.

$$r^2 = \frac{[(8)(12,736,000) - (3,490)(24,950)]^2}{[(8)(1,868,300) - (3,490)^2][(8)(87,927,500) - (24,950)^2]}$$

$$= 0.9801 = 98.01\%.$$

1c. Advertising was an excellent choice in explaining the behavior of sales as the high r-squared indicated: 98.01 percent of the total change in sales was explained by advertising alone. Only 1.99 percent was due to chance.

2a.

$$b = \frac{(100)(1,613) - (1,239)(79)}{(100)(17,322) - (1,239)^2} = \frac{63,419}{197,079} = 0.3218$$

$$a = \frac{79}{100} - (0.3218)\frac{1,239}{100} = -3.1971$$

Therefore, the estimated relationship between annual income and savings is:

$$-\$3.1971 + \$0.3218 \text{ per dollar of annual income.}$$

2b. The b value, $0.3218, means that an average family saves about $0.32 for every dollar they earn annually. The intercept value a (-3.1971) means that an average family has an annual debt of $3,197.10.

2c.

$$r^2 = \frac{(63,419)^2}{(197,079)[(100)(293) - (79)^2]}$$

$$= \frac{(63,419)^2}{(197,079)(23,059)} = 0.885$$

2d.

$$S_e = \sqrt{\frac{293 - (-3.1971)(79) - (0.3218)(1,613)}{100 - 2}}$$

$$= 0.52$$

2e.

$$Y' \pm (1.98)(0.52) \sqrt{1 + \frac{1}{n} + \frac{(X_p - \bar{X})^2}{\Sigma X^2 - \frac{(\Sigma X)^2}{n}}}$$

3a. $Q = 616.13 - 256.15P$

3b. $r^2 = 83.33\%$, which means the total variation in quantity demand is explained by price alone. The remaining 16.67% is still unexplained.

3c. At $P = \$1$, $Q = 616.13 - 256.15P = 616.13 - 256.15(\$1) = 359.98$

$$e_{Pc} = \frac{\% \text{ change in } Q}{\% \text{ change in } P} = \frac{dQ}{dP} \cdot \frac{P}{Q} = (-256.15)\left(\frac{1}{359.98}\right) = 0.71 < 1.$$

The product is not sensitive to price change.

3d. The intervals are $b \pm t\, S_b = -256.15 \pm (2.306)(40.512) = -256.15 \pm 93.42$. The range then is -349.57 to -162.73

3e. The t-value $= -6.32$, which is greater than 2 (in absolute value). The regression coefficient is statistically significant.

3f. The addition of advertising or income may improve the estimated demand relationship.

4a. An r^2 of 0.65 indicates that the regression model has explained 65 percent of the variation in Q. It also means it has not explained 35 percent of the variation.

4b. Explanatory factors, such as annual advertising expenditures, annual average rainfall, and the number of degree days, might have been overlooked.

5a. $\bar{r}^2 = 0.92$ means that 92 percent of the total variation in demand is explained by the regression model. This implies that 8 percent of demand variation remains unexplained.

5b. All four factors are statistically significant since their t-values are greater than 2.

5c. The exponents of multiplicative demand functions are elasticity estimates. Since the price elasticity of demand is -4, motorcycle demand is elastic with respect to price provided.

5d. Motorcycles are a normal good because the exponent associated with family income is positive.

5e. Motorcycles and compact cars are substitutes since the exponent for compact car price is positive (i.e., $3 > 0$).

6a. $\overline{r}^2 = 0.98$ means that 98 percent of the total variation in demand is explained by the regression model. This implies that only 2 percent of demand variation remains unexplained.

6b. With a sample size $n = 36$ and a model featuring $k = 6$ coefficients, the relevant number of degrees of freedom $(n - k)$ is 30. As a rule of thumb, we use a t-value of 2 (or more precisely 2.042 with 30 degrees of freedom and a significance level of 5%) to test whether or not a given independent variable influences Q. All the variables are statistically significant, as shown below.

Variable	Computed t-value = b/S_b	Influence
Price (P)	$4/1.5 = 2.67 > 2.042$	Yes
Competitor price (P_c)	$2/0.8 = 2.5 > 2.042$	Yes
Advertising (A)	$8/3.5 = 2.29 > 2.042$	Yes
Time (T)	$50/15 = 3.33 > 2.042$	Yes
Weather (W)	$5/2.4 = 2.083 > 2.042$	Yes

6c. The demand curve for Complete Fitness memberships is given by the expression:

$$Q = 410 - 4P + 2P_c + 8A + 50T - 5W$$
$$= 410 - 4P + 2(600) + 8(67.5) + 50(36) - 5(70)$$
$$= 3{,}600 - 4P$$

5

BUSINESS AND ECONOMIC FORECASTING

KEY TERMS

moving average in a time series an average that is updated as new information is received.

exponential smoothing forecasting technique that uses a weighted moving average of past data as the basis for a forecast.

mean squared error (MSE) average sum of the variations between the historical sales data and the forecast values for the corresponding periods.

trend analysis statistical procedure for estimating mathematically the average relationship between the dependent variable (sales, for example) and time. Trends are the general upward or downward movements of the average over time.

barometric forecasting use of economic indicators, such as leading indicators, to predict turning points in economic activity.

econometric models statistically based models where relationships among economic variables are expressed in mathematical equations, single or simultaneous in nature, and then estimated using such techniques as regression methods.

input-output analysis models that are concerned with the flows of goods among industries in an economy or among branches of a large organization.

Management typically operates under conditions of uncertainty or risk. Probably the most important function of business is forecasting. A forecast is a starting point for planning. The objective of forecasting is to reduce risk in decision making. In business, forecasts are the basis for capacity planning, production and inventory planning, manpower planning, planning for sales and market share, financial planning and budgeting, planning for research and development, and top management's strategic planning. Sales forecasts are especially crucial aspects of many financial management activities, including budgets, profit planning, capital expenditure analysis, and acquisition and merger analysis.

Figure 5–1 illustrates how sales forecasts relate to various managerial functions of business.

WHO USES FORECASTS?

Forecasts are needed for marketing, production, purchasing, manpower, and financial planning. Further, top management needs forecasts for planning and implementing long-term strategic objectives and planning for capital expenditures. More specifically, marketing managers use sales forecasts to (1) determine opti-

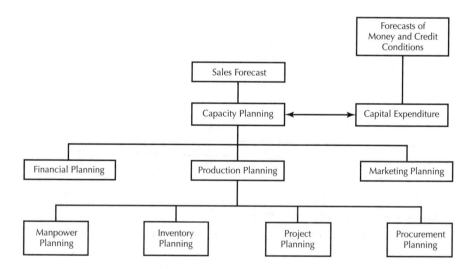

Figure 5–1. Sales Forecasts and Managerial Functions

mal sales-force allocations, (2) set sales goals, and (3) plan promotions and advertising. Other things, such as market share, prices, and trends in new product development, are required.

Production planners need forecasts in order to (a) schedule production activities, (b) order materials, (c) establish inventory levels, and (d) plan shipments. Some other areas that need forecasts include material requirements (purchasing and procurement), labor scheduling, equipment purchases, maintenance requirements, and plant capacity planning.

As shown in Figure 5–1, as soon as the company makes sure that it has enough capacity, the production plan is developed. If the company does not have enough capacity, it will require planning and budgeting decisions for capital spending for capacity expansion.

On this basis, the financial manager must estimate the future cash inflow and outflow. He must plan cash and borrowing needs for the company's future operations. Forecasts of cash flows and the rates of expenses and revenues are needed to maintain corporate liquidity and operating efficiency. In planning for capital investments, predictions about future economic activity are required so that returns or cash inflows accruing from the investment may be estimated.

Forecasts must also be made of money and credit conditions and interest rates so the cash needs of the firm may be met at the lowest possible cost. The finance and accounting functions must also forecast interest rates to support the acquisition of new capital, the collection of accounts receivable to help in planning working capital needs, and capital equipment expenditure rates to help balance the flow of funds in the organization. Sound predictions of foreign exchange rates are increasingly important to financial managers of multinational companies (MNCs).

Long-term forecasts are needed for the planning of changes in the company's capital structure. Decisions as to whether to issue stock or debt in order to maintain the desired financial structure of the firm require forecasts of money and credit conditions.

The personnel department requires a number of forecasts in planning for human resources in the business. Workers must be hired and trained, and for these personnel there must be benefits provided that are competitive with those available in the firm's labor market. Also, trends that affect such variables as labor turnover, retirement age, absenteeism, and tardiness need to be forecast as input for planning and decision making in this function.

Service businesses, such as banks, insurance companies, restaurants, and cruise ships, need various projections for their operational and long-term strategic planning. Take a bank, for example. The bank has to forecast:

- demands of various loans and deposits

- money and credit conditions so that it can determine the cost of money it lends

TYPES OF FORECASTS

The types of forecasts used by businesses and other organizations may be classified in several categories, depending on the objective and the situation for which a forecast is to be used. Three types are discussed below.

• *SALES FORECASTS*

The sales forecast gives the expected level of sales for the company's goods or services throughout some future period and is instrumental in the company's planning and budgeting functions. It is the key to other forecasts and plans.

• *FINANCIAL FORECASTS*

Although the sales forecast is the primary input to many financial decisions, some financial forecasts need to be made independently of sales forecasts.

• *ECONOMIC FORECASTS*

Economic forecasts, or statements of expected future business conditions, are published by governmental agencies and private economic forecasting firms. Businesses can use these forecasts and develop their own forecasts about external business conditions that will affect their product demand. Economic forecasts cover a variety of topics, including GDP, levels of employment, interest rates, and foreign exchange rates.

FORECASTING METHODOLOGY

There is a wide range of forecasting techniques that the company may choose from. There are basically three approaches to forecasting: qualitative, quantitative, and methods used for economic forecasting. They are as follows:

1. Qualitative approach—forecasts based on judgment and opinion

> executive opinions
>
> delphi technique
>
> sales-force polling
>
> consumer surveys

2. Quantitative approach

> naive methods
>
> moving averages
>
> exponential smoothing

trend analysis

decomposition of time series

simple regression

multiple regression

3. Economic forecasting methodology

barometric forecasting

econometric models

input-output analysis

opinion polling

Quantitative models work superbly as long as little or no systematic change in the environment takes place. When patterns or relationships do change, by themselves, the objective models are of little use. It is here where the qualitative approach based on human judgment is indispensable. Because judgmental forecasting also bases forecasts on observation of existing trends, they too are subject to a number of shortcomings. The advantage, however, is that they can identify systematic change more quickly and interpret better the effect of such change on the future.

SELECTION OF FORECASTING METHOD

The choice of a forecasting technique is significantly influenced by the stage of the product life cycle, and sometimes by the firm or industry for which a decision is being made.

In the beginning of the product life cycle, relatively small expenditures are made for research and market investigation. During the first phase of product introduction, these expenditures start to increase. In the rapid growth stage, considerable amounts of money are involved in the decisions; therefore a high level of accuracy is desirable. After the product has entered the maturity stage, the decisions are more routine, involving marketing and manufacturing. These are important considerations when determining the appropriate sales forecast technique.

After evaluating the particular stages of the product, and firm and industry life cycles, a further probe is necessary. Instead of selecting a forecasting technique by using whatever seems applicable, decision makers should determine what is appropriate. Some of the techniques are quite simple and rather inexpensive to develop and use, whereas others are extremely complex, require significant amounts of time to develop, and may be quite expensive. Some are best suited for short-term projections, whereas others are better prepared for intermediate- or long-term forecasts.

What technique or techniques to select depends on the following criteria.

1. What is the cost associated with developing the forecasting model compared with potential gains resulting from its use? The choice is one of a benefit-cost trade-off.

2. How complicated are the relationships that are being forecasted?

3. Is it for short-run or long-run purposes?

4. How much accuracy is desired?

5. Is there a minimum tolerance level of errors?

6. How much data are available? Techniques vary in the amount of data they require.

THE QUALITATIVE APPROACH

The qualitative (or judgmental) approach can be useful in formulating short-term forecasts and also can supplement the projections based on the use of any of the qualitative methods. Four of the better-known qualitative forecasting methods are executive opinions, the delphi method, sales-force polling, and consumer surveys.

EXECUTIVE OPINIONS

The subjective views of executives or experts from sales, production, finance, purchasing and administration are averaged to generate a forecast about future sales. Usually this method is used in conjunction with some quantitative method, such as trend extrapolation. The management team modifies the resulting forecast based on their expectations.

The advantage of this approach is that the forecasting is done quickly and easily, without the need of elaborate statistics. Also, the jury of executive opinions may be the only feasible means of forecasting in the absence of adequate data. The disadvantage, however, is that of "group think." This is a set of problems inherent to those who meet as a group. Foremost among these problems are high cohesiveness, strong leadership, and insulation of the group. With high cohesiveness, the group becomes increasingly conforming through group pressure that helps stifle dissension and critical thought. Strong leadership fosters group pressure for unanimous opinion. Insulation of the group tends to separate the group from outside opinions, if given.

THE DELPHI METHOD

The delphi method is a group technique in which a panel of experts are individually questioned about their perceptions of future events. The experts do not meet as a group in order to reduce the possibility that consensus is reached because of dominant personality factors. Instead, the forecasts and accompanying arguments are summarized by an outside party and returned to the experts along with further questions. This continues until a consensus is reached by the group, especially after only a few rounds. This type of method is useful and quite effective for long-range forecasting. The technique is done by "questionnaire" format, and thus, it eliminates the disadvantages of group think. There is no committee or debate. The experts are not influenced by peer pressure to forecast a certain way, as the answer is not intended to be reached by consensus or unanimity. Low reliability is cited as the main disadvantage of the delphi method, as well as lack of consensus from the returns.

SALES-FORCE POLLING

Some companies use as a forecast source sales people who have continual contacts with customers. They believe that the sales force who are closest to the ultimate customers may have significant insights regarding the state of the future market. Forecasts based on sales-force polling may be averaged to develop a future forecast, or they may be used to modify other quantitative and/or qualitative forecasts that have been generated internally in the company. The advantages to this way of forecast are that (1) it is simple to use and understand, (2) it uses the specialized knowledge of those closest to the action, (3) it can place responsibility for attaining the forecast in the hands of those who most affect the actual results, and (4) the information can be easily broken down by territory, product, customer or salesperson.

The disadvantages include salespeople being overly optimistic or pessimistic regarding their predictions and inaccuracies due to broader economic events that are largely beyond their control.

CONSUMER SURVEYS

Some companies conduct their own market surveys regarding specific consumer purchases. Surveys may consist of telephone contacts, personal interviews, or questionnaires as a means of obtaining data. Extensive statistical analysis is usually applied to survey results in order to test hypotheses regarding consumer behavior.

COMMON FEATURES AND ASSUMPTIONS INHERENT IN FORECASTING

Forecasting techniques are quite different from each other. But there are certain features and assumptions that underlie the business of forecasting. They are

1. Forecasting techniques generally assume that the same underlying causal relationship that existed in the past will continue to prevail in the future. In other words, most of the techniques are based on historical data.

2. Forecasts are very rarely perfect. Therefore, for planning purposes, allowances should be made for inaccuracies. For example, the company should always maintain a safety stock in anticipation of stock-outs.

3. Forecast accuracy decreases as the time period covered by the forecast (that is, the time horizon) increases. Generally speaking, a long-term forecast tends to be more inaccurate than a short-term forecast because of the greater uncertainty.

4. Forecasts for groups of items tend to be more accurate than forecasts for individual items because forecasting errors among items in a group tend to cancel each other out. For example, industry forecasting is more accurate than individual firm forecasting.

STEPS IN THE FORECASTING PROCESS

There are six basic steps in the forecasting process.

1. Determine the what and why of the forecast and what will be needed. This will indicate the level of detail required in the forecast (for example, forecast by region, forecast by product), the amount of resources (for example, computer hardware and software, manpower) that can be justified, and the level of accuracy desired.

2. Establish a short-term or long-term time horizon. More specifically, project for the next year or for several years.

3. Select a forecasting technique. Refer to the criteria discussed before.

4. Gather the data and develop a forecast.

5. Identify any assumptions that had to be made in preparing the forecast and using it.

6. Monitor the forecast to see if it is performing in a manner desired. Develop an evaluation system for this purpose. If it is not performing as desired, go to step 1.

NAIVE MODELS, MOVING AVERAGES, AND SMOOTHING METHODS

This section discusses several forecasting methods that fall in the quantitative approach category. The discussion includes naive models, moving averages, exponential smoothing, and time series. Regressions were covered in the previous chapter.

NAIVE MODELS

Naive forecasting models are based exclusively on historical observation of sales or other variables, such as earnings and cash flows being forecast. They do not attempt to explain the underlying causal relationships that produce the variable being forecast.

Naive models may be classified into two groups. One group consists of simple projection models. These models require inputs of data from recent observations, but no statistical analysis is performed. The second group is made up of models that, while naive, are complex enough to require a computer. Traditional methods, such as classical decomposition, moving average, and exponential smoothing models, are some examples.

- Advantages: It is inexpensive to develop, store data, and operate.

- Disadvantages: It does not consider any possible causal relationships that underly the forecasted variable.

1. A simple example of a naive model type would be to use the actual sales of the current period as the forecast for the next period. Let us use the symbol Y'_{t+1} as the forecast value and the symbol Y_t as the actual value. Then,

$$Y'_{t+1 = Y_t}$$

2. If you consider trends, then $Y'_{t+1 =} Y_t + (Y_t - Y_{t-1})$.

This model adds the latest observed absolute period-to-period change to the most recent observed level of the variable.

3. If you want to incorporate the rate of change rather than the absolute amount, then

$$Y'_{t+1} = Y_t \frac{Y_t}{Y_{t-1}}.$$

Example 1

Consider the following sales data:

Month	20X1 Monthly Sales of Product
1	$3,050
2	2,980
3	3,670
4	2,910
5	3,340
6	4,060
7	4,750
8	5,510
9	5,280
10	5,504
11	5,810
12	6,100

The forecasts for January 20X2 based on the aforementioned three models are as follows:

1. $Y'_{t+1} = Y_t = \$6,100$

2. $Y'_{t+1} = Y_t + (Y_t - Y_{t-1}) = \$6,100 + (\$5,810 - \$5,504) = \$6,100 + \$306 = \$6,406$

3. $Y'_{t+1} = Y_t \frac{Y_t}{Y_{t-1}}.$

   $= \$6,100 \frac{\$6,100}{\$5,810} = \$6,100 \,(1.05)$

   $= \$6,405.$

YOU SHOULD REMEMBER

The naive models can be applied, with very little need of a computer, to develop forecasts for sales, earnings, and cash flows. They must be compared with more sophisticated models, such as the regression method, for forecasting efficiency.

MOVING AVERAGES

Moving averages are averages that are updated as new information is received. With the moving average, a manager simply employs the most recent observations to calculate an average, which is used as the forecast for the next period.

Example 2

Assume that the marketing manager has the following sales data.

Date	Actual Sales (Y_t)
Jan. 1	46
2	54
3	53
4	46
5	58
6	49
7	54

In order to predict the sales for the seventh and eighth days of January, the manager has to pick the number of observations for averaging purposes. Let us consider two cases: one is a six-day moving average and the other is a three-day average (See Figure 5–2).

Case 1

$$Y'_7 = \frac{46 + 54 + 53 + 46 + 58 + 49}{6} = 51$$

$$Y'_8 = \frac{54 + 53 + 46 + 58 + 49 + 54}{6} = 52.3$$

where Y' = predicted

Case 2

$$Y'_7 = \frac{46 + 58 + 49}{3} = 51,$$

$$Y'_8 = \frac{58 + 49 + 54}{3} = 53.6.$$

In terms of weights given to observations, in case 1, the old data received a weight of 5/6, and the current observation got a weight of 1/6. In case 2, the old data received a weight of only 2/3 while the current observation received a weight of 1/3.

Thus, the marketing manager's choice of the number of periods to use in a moving average is a measure of the relative importance attached to old versus current data.

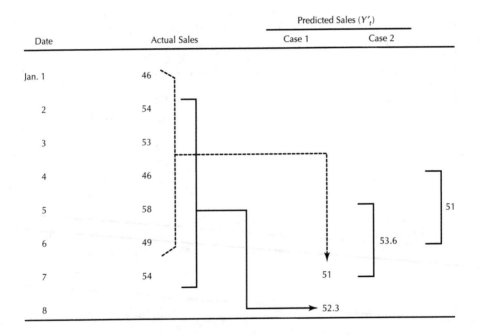

Date	Actual Sales	Predicted Sales (Y'_t)	
		Case 1	Case 2
Jan. 1	46		
2	54		
3	53		
4	46		
5	58		
6	49		53.6
7	54	51	51
8		52.3	

Figure 5–2. Moving Average Calculations

ADVANTAGES AND DISADVANTAGES

The moving average is simple to use and easy to understand. However, there are two shortcomings.

- It requires you to retain a great deal of data and carry it along with you from forecast period to forecast period.

- All data in the sample are weighted equally. If more recent data are more valid than older data, why not give it greater weight?

The forecasting method known as exponential smoothing gets around these disadvantages.

EXPONENTIAL SMOOTHING

Exponential smoothing is a popular technique for short-run forecasting by financial managers. It uses a weighted average of past data as the basis for a forecast. The procedure gives heaviest weight to more recent information and smaller weights to observations in the more distant past. The reason for this is that the future is more dependent upon the recent past than on the distant past. The method is known to be effective when there is randomness and no seasonal fluctuations in the data. One disadvantage of the method, however, is that it does not include industrial or economic factors, such as market conditions, prices, or the effects of competitors' actions.

YOU SHOULD REMEMBER

Exponential smoothing is known to be effective when there is randomness and no seasonal fluctuations in the data.

• THE MODEL:

The formula for exponential smoothing is:

$$Y'_{t+1} = \alpha Y_t + (1 - \alpha)Y'_t$$

or in words,

$$Y'_{new} = \alpha Y_{old} + (1 - \alpha)Y'_{old}$$

where Y'_{new} = Exponentially smoothed average to be used as the forecast, Y_{old} = most recent actual data, Y'_{old} = most recent smoothed forecast, and α = smoothing constant.

The higher the α, the higher the weight given to the more recent information.

Example 3

The following data on sales are given below.

Time period (t)	Actual sales (1000)(Y_t)
1	$60.0
2	64.0
3	58.0
4	66.0
5	70.0
6	60.0
7	70.0
8	74.0
9	62.0
10	74.0
11	68.0
12	66.0
13	60.0
14	66.0
15	62.0

To initialize the exponential smoothing process, we must have the initial forecast. The first smoothed forecast to be used can be

1. First actual observations.

2. an average of the actual data for a few periods.

For illustrative purposes, let us use a six-period average as the initial forecast Y'_7 with a smoothing constant of $\alpha = 0.40$. Then

$$Y'_7 = (Y_1 + Y_2 + Y_3 + Y_4 + Y_5 + Y_6)/6$$

$$= (60 + 64 + 58 + 66 + 70 + 60)/6 = 63.$$

Note that $Y_7 = 70$. Then Y'_8 is computed as follows:

$$Y'_8 = \alpha Y_7 + (1 - \alpha)\, Y'_7$$

$$= (0.40)(70) + (0.6)(63)$$

$$= 28.0 + 37.80 = 65.80.$$

Similarly,

$$Y'_9 = \alpha Y_8 + (1 - \alpha)\, Y'_8$$

$$= (0.40)(74) + (0.60)(65.80)$$

$$= 29.60 + 39.48 = 69.08$$

and

$$Y'_{10} = \alpha Y'_9 + (1 - \alpha) Y'_9$$

$$= (0.40)(62) + (0.60)(69.08)$$

$$= 24.80 + 41.45 = 66.25.$$

By using the same procedure, the values of Y'_{11}, Y'_{12}, Y'_{13}, Y'_{14}, and Y'_{15} can be calculated. The following table shows a comparison between the actual sales and predicted sales by the exponential smoothing method.

Due to the negative and positive differences between actual sales and predicted sales, the forecaster can use a higher or lower smoothing constant (α), in order to adjust his prediction as quickly as possible to large fluctuations in the data series. For example, if the forecast is slow in reacting to increased sales (that is to say, if the difference is negative), he might want to try a higher value. For practical purposes, the optimal may be picked by minimizing what is known as the *mean squared error (MSE)*, which is the average sum of the variations between the historical sales data and the forecast values for the corresponding periods.

$$MSE = (Y_t - Y'_t)^2 / (n - i),$$

where i = the number of observations used to determine the initial forecast (in our example, $i=6$).

Table 5-1.   Comparison of Actual Sales and Predicted Sales

Time period (t)	Actual sales (Y_t)	Predicted sales (Y'_t)	Difference ($Y_t - Y'_t$)	Difference^2 ($Y_t - Y'_t)^2$
1	$60.0			
2	64.0			
3	58.0			
4	66.0			
5	70.0			
6	60.0			
7	70.0	63.00	7.00	49.00
8	74.0	65.80	8.20	67.24
9	62.0	69.08	−7.08	50.13
10	74.0	66.25	7.75	60.06
11	68.0	69.35	−1.35	1.82
12	66.0	68.81	−2.81	7.90
13	60.0	67.69	−7.69	59.14
14	66.0	64.61	1.39	1.93
15	62.0	65.17	−3.17	10.05
				307.27

In our example,

$$MSE = \frac{307.27}{15 - 6} = \frac{307.27}{9} = 34.$$

The idea is to select the α that minimizes MSE.

TREND ANALYSIS

Trends are the general upward or downward movements of the average over time. These movements may require many years of data to determine or describe them. They can be described by a straight line or a curve. The basic forces underlying the trend include technological advances, productivity changes, inflation, and population change.

Trend analysis is a special type of simple regression. This method involves a regression whereby a trend line is fitted to a time series of data. In practice, however, one typically finds linear curves used for business forecasting.

LINEAR TREND

The *linear* trend line equation can be shown as

$$Y = a + b\,t,$$

where t = time.

The formula for the coefficients a and b are essentially the same as the cases for simple regression. However, for regression purposes, a time period can be given a number so that $\Sigma t = 0$. When there is an odd number of periods, the period in the middle is assigned a zero value. If there is an even number, then -1 and $+1$ are assigned the two periods in the middle, so that again $\Sigma t = 0$.

With $\Sigma t = 0$, the formula for b and a reduces to the following:

$$b = \frac{n\Sigma tY}{n\Sigma t^2}$$

$$a = \frac{\Sigma Y}{n}$$

Example 4

Case 1 (odd number)

	19X1	19X2	19X3	19X4	19X5	
$t =$	-2	-1	0	$+1$	$+2$	

Case 2 (even number)

	19X1	19X2	19X3	19X4	19X5	19X6
$t =$	-3	-2	-1	$+1$	$+2$	$+3$

In each case $\Sigma t = 0$.

Example 5

Consider ABC Company, whose historical sales follows.

Year	Sales (in millions)
19X1	$ 10
19X2	12
19X3	13
19X4	16
19X5	17

Because the company has five years' data, which is an odd number, the year in the middle is assigned a zero value.

Year	t	Sales (in millions) (Y)	tY	t^2	Y^2
19X1	−2	$10	−20	4	100
19X2	−1	12	−12	1	144
19X3	0	13	0	0	169
19X4	+1	16	16	1	256
19X5	+2	17	34	4	289
	0	68	18	10	958

$$b = \frac{(5)(18)}{(5)(10)} = \frac{90}{50} = 1.8,$$

$$a = \frac{68}{5} = 13.6.$$

Therefore, the estimated trend equation is

$$Y' = \$13.6 + \$1.8\ t.$$

To project 19X6 sales, we assign +3 to the t value for the year 19X6.

$$Y' = \$13.6 + \$1.8\ (3)$$

$$= 19.$$

ECONOMIC FORECASTING

Economic forecasting is typically concerned with predicting future values of key economic variables, such as gross domestic product, inflation, interest rates, and unemployment.

BAROMETRIC FORECASTING

Barometric methods involve the use of economic indicators, such as leading indicators to predict turning points in economic activity. It is used primarily to identify potential future changes in general business conditions or conditions of a specific industry rather than conditions for a specific firm. The series chosen serve as barometers of economic change. Types of indicators frequently used are

1. *Coincident indicators*: These are the types of economic indicator series that tend to move up and down in line with the aggregate economy and, therefore, are measures of current economic activity. Examples are Gross Domestic Product (GDP), retail sales, and industrial production.

2. *Lagging indicators*: These are the economic series of indicators that follow or trail behind aggregate economic activity. There are currently six lagging indicators published by the government comprising of unemployment rate, business expenditures, labor cost per unit, loans outstanding, bank interest rates, and book value of manufacturing and trade inventories.

3. *Leading indicators*: More exactly known as *Index of Leading Economic Indicators (LEI)*, it is the economic series of indicators that tend to predict future changes in economic activity; officially called Composite Index of 11 Leading Indicators. This index was designed to reveal the direction of the economy in the next six to nine months. This series is the government's main barometer for forecasting business trends. Each of the series has shown a tendency to change before the economy makes a major turn—hence, the term "leading indicators." The index is designed to forecast economic activity six to nine months ahead (1987=100).

   The Index consists of 11 indicators, and are subject to revision. For example, petroleum and natural gas prices were found to distort the data from crude material prices and were subsequently dropped from that category.

   This series consists of:

   • *Average workweek of production workers in manufacturing.* Employers find it a lot easier to increase the number of hours worked in a week than to hire more employees.

- *Initial claims for unemployment insurance.*
  The number of people who sign up for unemployment benefits signals changes in present and future economic activity.

- *Change in consumer confidence.*
  It is based on the University of Michigan's survey of consumer expectations. The index measures consumers' optimism regarding the present and future state of the economy and is based on an index of 100 in 1966. Note that consumer spending buys two-thirds of the gross domestic product (GDP: all goods and services produced in the economy), so any sharp change could be an important factor in an overall turnaround.

- *Percent change in prices of sensitive crude materials.*
  Rises in prices of such critical materials as steel and iron usually mean factory demands are going up, which means factories plan to step up production.

- *Contracts and orders for plant and equipment.*
  Heavier contracting and ordering usually lead economic upswings.

- *Vendor performance.*
  Vendor performance represents the percentage of companies reporting slower deliveries. As the economy grows, firms have more trouble filling orders.

- *Stock prices.*
  A rise in the common stock index indicates expected profits and lower interest rates. Stock market advances usually precede business upturns by three to eight months.

- *Money supply.*
  A rising money supply means easy money that sparks brisk economic activity. This usually leads recoveries by as much as fourteen months.

- *New orders for manufacturers of consumer goods and materials.*
  New orders mean more workers hired, more materials and supplies purchased, and increased output. Gains in this series usually lead recoveries by as much as four months.

- *Residential building permits for private housing.*
  Gains in building permits signal business upturns.

- *Factory backlogs of unfilled durable goods orders.*
  Backlogs signify business upswings.

The LEI is found in *Business Conditions Digest* published by the Bureau of Economic Analysis of the U.S. Department of Commerce. If the index is consistently rising, even only slightly, the economy is chugging along and a setback is unlikely. If the indicator drops for three or more consecutive months, look for an economic slowdown and possibly a recession in the next year or so. A rising (consecutive percentage increases in) indicator is bullish for the economy and the stock market, and vice versa.

These 11 components of the index are adjusted for inflation. Rarely do these components of the index all go in the same direction at once. Each factor is weighted. The composite figure is designed to tell only in which direction business will go. It is not intended to forecast the magnitude of future ups and downs.

As a further tool and aid to understanding business conditions, a series known as *diffusion indexes* are used. Unlike a composite index, such as the LEI, a diffusion index indicates the percentage of economic series that experience increases over the time interval being measured. Often, the 50 percent mark is used as a guide. For example, if more than 50 percent of the leading indicators are rising, it might be plausible to predict an upturn in aggregate economic activity. In a more general sense, however, diffusion indexes can be employed to help measure and interpret the breadth and intensity of recessions and recoveries, the state of economic conditions, and the degree of optimism or pessimism on the part of businessmen.

Barometric models have the following limitations:

1. No series accurately signals changes in other economic variables on a consistent basis.

2. It may still indicate only the direction of future change, little or nothing about the magnitude of the change.

ECONOMETRIC MODELS

The approach employs statistically based models where relationships among economic variables are expressed in mathematical equations, single or simultaneous in nature and then estimated using such techniques as regression methods. The simplest kind of econometric models is a single equation, expressing some dependent variable as a function of some other set of variables. For example, GDP might be expressed as a function of past GDP (GDP-t), construction activity (C), changes in the unemployment rate(ΔU), and the level of interest rates (I). A linear model expressing this relation is

$$GDP = a + bGDP_{-t} + cC + d\Delta U + eI.$$

Some models attempt to capture the complexity of the entire economy; they may contain hundreds of equations that must all be estimated simultaneously. The *Wharton model* is a good example. Multiple equation systems, however, are difficult and expensive to construct.

Example 6

Suppose that a major U.S. automaker wishes to project GDP as a step toward forecasting the demand for autos. The company has developed the following econometric model:

$$GDP = C + I + G,$$

$$C = 60 + 0.7Y,$$

$$I = 200 + 0.3\pi_{t-1},$$

$$G = 800$$

$$Y = GDP - T$$

$$T = 0.3GDP,$$

$$\pi_{t-1} = 900,$$

where C = consumption, I = investment, G = government expenditure, Y = disposable income, T = tax receipts, and π_{t-1} = prior year's corporate profit. (Figures are in billions of dollars.)

We will calculate GDP, step by step, as follows:

1. $I = 200 + 0.3\pi_{t-1} = 200 + 0.3(900) = 470.$

2. $GDP = C + I + G = 60 + 0.7Y + 470 + 800 = 60 + 0.7(GDP - T) + 470 + 800$

   $= 60 + 0.7(GDP - 0.3GDP) + 470 + 800 = 60 + 0.49GDP + 470 + 800,$

   0.51 GDP $= 1,330,$

   GDP $= 2,608$ (*in billions of dollars*).

INPUT-OUTPUT ANALYSIS

Input-output analysis, also called *interindustry analysis,* is the input-output approach to forecasting. It employs historical tabular data on intersectional output and material flows to predict demand and supply changes for individual industries. An input-output matrix table, as shown in Figure 5–3, is the source of this method. The table is very useful in evaluating the effects of a change in demand in one industry on other industries (i.e., a change in oil prices and its resulting effect on demand for cars, then steel sales, then iron ore and limestone sales). The *total requirements* table prepared as a part of the input-output table shows the *direct*, as well as *indirect*, requirements of each industry listed in the left-hand column (supplying industry) in order to produce one dollar's worth of output for the industry identified at the top of each column (producing industry). This table makes it pos-

		Producers			Final Product Markets			Row totals
		X	Y	Z	Personal Consumption	Government	Exports	
Producers	X	12	4	52	42	30		140
	Y	7		17	32	22	4	82
	Z		31		67			98
Value Added	Wages	102	27	22				151 ⎫ GDP =
	Profit plus Depreciation	19	20	7				46 ⎭ $197
Column totals		140	82	98	141	52	4	

GDP= $197

Figure 5–3. Input-Output Table

sible to compute the impacts on various industries in the economy that result from changes in the final demand for products of one or more industries.

Input-output analysis for forecasting, however, suffers from two major limitations:

1. The development of accurate and updated supplements to the original *Commerce Department* input-output table is prohibitively expensive.

2. The method is a *linear* approach to forecasting and thereby fails to capture some possible *nonlinear* relations.

Example 7

You are presented the following total requirements table (per dollar of output for final consumption) for a simple economy:

Supplying Industry	Producing Industry X	Y	Z
X	1.07	0.28	0.67
Y	0.04	1.05	0.18
Z	0.01	0.35	1.06

If Industry Y is expected to sell $1 million worth of goods to final demand, Industries X, Y, and Z must produce in total:

X: $1 million x 0.28 = $0.28 million worth of goods

Y: $1 million x 1.05 = $1.05 million worth of goods

Z: $1 million x 0.35 = $0.35 million worth of goods

OPINION POLLING

This is a qualitative and subjective method of predicting economic activity or some particular phase of it. The surveys include:

1. Surveys of business executives' intentions on what to spend on plant and equipment, made independently by McGraw-Hill, Department of Commerce, Securities and Exchange Commission, and the Conference Board

2. Surveys of consumers' finances, buying plans, and confidence, made independently by the University of Michigan and the Conference Board

3. Surveys of business plans regarding inventory changes, made by the National Association of Purchasing Agents

The surveys seem to do well in forecasting turning points of business, but are not that useful for predicting the magnitude of change.

MEASURING ACCURACY OF FORECASTS

The performance of a forecast should be checked against its own record or against that of other forecasts. There are various statistical measures that can be used to measure performance of the model. Of course, the performance is measured in terms of forecasting error, where error is defined as the difference between a predicted value and the actual result.

$$\text{Error } (e) = \text{Actual } (A) - \text{Forecast } (F).$$

MEAN-SQUARED ERROR (MSE),

One commonly used measure for summarizing historical errors is mean-squared errors discussed earlier.

THE *U* STATISTIC

There is still a number of statistical measures for measuring accuracy of the forecast. Two standards may be identified. First, one could compare the forecast being evaluated with a naive forecast to see if there are vast differences. The naive forecast can be anything like the same as last year, moving average, or the output of an exponential smoothing technique. In the second case, the forecast may be compared against the outcome when there is enough to do so. The comparison may be against the actual level of the variable forecasted, or the change observed may be compared with the change forecast.

The Theil U Statistic is based upon a comparison of the predicted change with the observed change. It is calculated as:

$$U = 1/n\Sigma(F - A)^2/[(1/n)\Sigma F^2 + (1/n)\Sigma A^2].$$

As can be seen, $U = 0$ is a perfect forecast, since the forecast would equal actual and $F - A = 0$ for all observations. At the other extreme, $U = 1$ would be a case of all incorrect forecasts. The smaller the value of U, the more accurate are the forecasts. If U is greater than or equal to 1, the predictive ability of the model is lower than a naive no-change extrapolation.

KNOW THE CONCEPTS

TERMS FOR STUDY

naive models
delphi method
moving average
exponential smoothing
trend analysis

mean squared error (MSE)
barometric forecasting
econometric models
input-output analysis

DO YOU KNOW THE BASICS?

1. Discuss the difference between quantitative and qualitative (judgmental) forecasting methods. What circumstances would warrant one over the other?

2. Discuss the role of forecasting in production/operations management.

3. Illustrate, by examples of typical applications, the various types of qualitative forecasting techniques often used.

4. Define a time series.

5. How are moving averages calculated?

6. What is exponential smoothing, and when is it most effective?

7. Explain the two popular measures of forecast accuracy.

8. What are the basic steps in forecasting? Discuss each.

9. How are quantitative and judgmental forecasts used together in practice?

PRACTICAL APPLICATION

1. Develop a forecast for the next period, given the data below, using a 3-period moving average.

Period	Demand (Y_t)
1	19
2	20
3	18
4	19
5	17

2. Consider the data below:

Period	Demand (Y_t)
11	81
12	75
13	82

   a. Determine a naive forecast for period 14.

   b. Using exponential smoothing with $\alpha = 0.2$ and exponentially smoothed forecast for period 12 = 80, what would the forecast for period 14 be?

3. Given the data below, make an appropriate forecast for the following year, using a linear trend line.

Period	Demand (Y_t)
1	110
2	110
3	120
4	140
5	150

4. The AZ Ice Cream Shoppe has recorded the demand for a particular flavor during the first seven days of August.

Date	Actual Sales (Y_t)
Aug. 1	56
2	64
3	63
4	56
5	68
6	59
7	64

Predict the sales for the eighth day of August, using (a) a five-day moving average and (b) a three-day average.

5. Develop a forecast for period 6 using an alpha of 0.4 and period 1 value as the initial forecast.

Period	Number of customer complaints
1	45
2	34
3	35
4	42
5	48

6. The following time series shows the sales of a particular product over the past 12 months:

Month	Sales
1	105
2	135
3	120
4	105
5	90
6	120
7	145
8	140
9	100
10	80
11	100
12	110

Compute the exponential-smoothing values for the time series and MSE (Assume $\alpha = 0.5$).

7. Data for total cash collections and credit sales are given below.

Cash collections (000 omitted)	Credit sales (000 omitted)
4	6
8	7
8	9
6	5
7	8
5	6

a. Fit a linear regression line using the method of least squares. Estimate the cash collections when credit sales is $8.

b. Compute the coefficient of determination.

c. Does the regression equation need to be improved?

8. The Viacam Manufacturing Company makes a product called Zone. Some of the manufacturing expenses are easily identified as fixed or directly variable with production. Management is confronted with the problem of preparing a budget for the indirect manufacturing costs. The following details are provided for the first 5 months of the past year:

Month	Number of Units Produced X	Indirect Manufacturing Costs Y
1	100	$1,000
2	200	1,250
3	300	2,250
4	400	2,500
5	500	3,750

Determine the cost function using the method of least squares.

9. A consumer product maker's marketing manager has developed a linear trend equation that can be used to forecast annual sales of its popular SH shampoo:

$$Y = 17,500 + 23,000t$$

(fitted using the data covering the period 1995–2001)

a. Are annual sales increasing or decreasing? By how much?

b. Predict sales for 2002 (Assume the t value assigned for 1998 is zero).

10. The Hume Company, Inc. has recorded the following sales (000 omitted) since its inception in 1982:

1994	$10	2000	$125
1995	20	2001	150
1996	30	2002	180
1997	45	2003	220
1998	70	2004	270
1999	90		

a. Calculate 2005 sales, using the method of least squares.

b. Compute the coefficient of determination.

c. Comment on the reliability of the estimated sales equation, together with the necessary assumptions if the estimated equation is to be used to predict sales.

11. Suppose that a major U.S. automaker wishes to project GDP as a step toward forecasting the demand for autos. The company has developed the following econometric model:

$$GDP = C + I + G$$

$$C = 200 + 0.8Y$$

$$I = 300 + 0.3\pi_{t-1}$$

$$G = 1,000$$

$$Y = GDP - T$$

$$T = 0.4GDP$$

$$\pi_{t-1} = 1,000$$

where C = consumption, I = investment, G = government expenditure, Y = disposable income, T = tax receipts, and π_{t-1} = prior year's corporate profit. (Figures are n billions of dollars). Given the information above, forecast GDP using the multiple equation system.

12. You are presented the following input-output table that represents the total requirements—direct and indirect—for a simple economy:

	Producing Industry		
Supplying Industry	A	B	C
A	1.07	0.28	0.67
B	0.04	1.05	0.18
C	0.01	0.35	1.06

a. If Industry *A* is expected to sell $3 million worth of goods to final demand, how much must industry *A* produce in total?

b. If industry *A* is expected to sell $3 million worth of goods to final demand, how much must industries *B* and *C* produce?

ANSWERS

DO YOU KNOW THE BASICS?

1. Quantitative methods are based on the analysis of historical data while qualitative (judgmental) methods depend on expert opinion. Obviously, if historical data is unavailable, quantitative methods cannot be used. Such would be the case with technology forecasts. For such data as sales and costs, quantitative approaches are useful. Quite frequently a combination of the two is used.

2. Forecasts are needed in order to (1) plan resource requirements, such as production facilities, (2) workforce levels and planning purchases of materials, and (3) for financial planning and capacity planning.

3. Expert opinion—new technologies or new products unlike any currently on the market.

   Delphi method—space travel, long range economic conditions.

   Sales-force polling or consumer surveys—new products, restaurants, fast food, consumer appliances.

4. A time series is a set of observations measured at successive points in time or over successive periods of time.

5. A moving average is an average of the most recent *n* data values for any point in time.

6. Exponential smoothing is a weighting of the current actual value and the previous forecast. As such, it is essentially a weighted average of the previous time series values with more emphasis placed on the most recent observations. It is known to be effective when there is randomness and no seasonal fluctuations in the data.

7. Forecast errors are measured by mean absolute deviation (MAD) and mean squared error (MSE). These enable one to quantitatively measure forecast errors.

8. (a) Preliminary data analysis of scatter diagram. (b) determination of forecasts choice of method: quantitative and/or judgmental. (c) evaluation and determination of a final forecast—consideration of accuracy and implications

of errors, data collection and processing. (d) control and feedback—comparison of actual observations with forecasts.

9. Since quantitative methods are slow to adapt to unexpected changes in the environment, qualitative (judgmental) forecasts are often also used. Quantitative forecasts are frequently modified by judgmental forecasts.

PRACTICAL APPLICATION

1. $(18 + 19 + 17)/3 = 18$

2a. Naive: 82

2b. $Y'_{13} = \alpha Y_{12} + (1 - \alpha) Y'_{12} = (0.2)(75) + (0.8)(80) = 79$

$Y'_{14} = \alpha Y_{13} + (1 - \alpha)Y'_{13}(0.20)(82) + (0.80)(79) = 16.4 + 63.2 = 79.6$

3.

Time	t	Demand Y	tY	t^2
1	-2	110	-220	4
2	-1	110	-110	1
3	0	120	0	0
4	1	140	140	1
5	2	150	300	4
	0	630	110	10

$$b = 5(110/5(10) = 11$$

$$a = 630/5 = 126$$

$$Y = 126 + 11t = 126 + 11(3) = 159 \text{ (for period 6, } t = 3)$$

4a. using a five-day moving average

$$Y'_8 = \frac{63 + 56 + 68 + 59 + 64}{5} = 62$$

where Y' = predicted

4b. Using a three-day average.

$$Y'_8 = \frac{68 + 59 + 64}{3} = 63.6$$

5.

Period	Number of customer complaints	Forecast $= Y'_{t+1} = \alpha Y_t + (1-\alpha) Y'_t$
1	45	
2	34	45
3	35	$0.4(34) + 0.6(45) = 40.6$
4	42	$0.4(35) + 0.6(40.6) = 38.4$
5	48	$0.4(42) + 0.6(38.4) = 39.8$

For period 6: $.4(48) + .6(39.8) = 43.1$

6.

Month	Sales	Forecast	Error	Error Squared
1	105			
2	135	105	30	900
3	120	$0.5(135) + 0.5(105) = 120$	0	0
4	105	$0.5(120) + 0.5(120) = 120$	-15	225
5	90	$0.5(105) + 0.5(120) = 112.50$	-22.5	506.25
6	120	$0.5(90) + 0.5(112.5) = 101.25$	18.75	351.56
7	145	$0.5(120) + 0.5(101.25) = 110.63$	34.37	1,181.30
8	140	$0.5(145) + 0.5(110.63) = 127.81$	12.19	148.60
9	100	$0.5(140) + 0.5(127.81) = 133.91$	-33.91	1,149.89
10	80	$0.5(100) + 0.5(133.91) = 116.95$	-36.95	1,365.30
11	100	$0.5(80) + 0.5(116.95) = 98.48$	1.52	2.31
12	110	$0.5(100) + 0.5(98.48) = 99.24$	10.76	115.78
				5,945.99

$$MSE = \frac{\Sigma (Y_t - Y'_t)^2}{n-1} = \frac{5,945.99}{12-1} = 540.54$$

7a.

Y	X	XY	X^2	Y^2
4	6	24	36	16
8	7	56	49	64
8	9	72	81	64
6	5	30	25	36
7	8	56	64	49
5	6	30	36	25
$38	41	268	291	254

$$b = \frac{(6)(268) - (41)(38)}{(6)(291) - (41)(41)} = \frac{50}{65} = 0.77,$$

$$a = 38 / 6 - (0.77)(41 / 6) = 1.07.$$

The estimated regression equation is

$$Y' = \$1.07 + \$0.77X,$$

where Y' = estimated cash collections and X = credit sales

The estimated cash collection for credit sales of $8 will be

$$Y' = \$1.07 + \$0.77(8) = \$7.23.$$

7b. $r^2 = \dfrac{(50)^2}{(65)[(6)(254) - (38)^2]} = \dfrac{2,500}{5,200} = 0.48$

$$= 48\%,$$

which means that the credit sales account for only 48 percent of the change in cash collections.

7c. The answer is yes. A low r^2 (48 percent) indicates that credit sales was not good enough to fully explain the behavior of cash collections. 52 percent is still unexplained by the estimated equation. Often factors like interest rates may be responsible for part of the variation in cash collections.

8.

X	Y	XY	X²
100	$1,000	$ 100,000	10,000
200	1,250	250,000	40,000
300	2,250	675,000	90,000
400	2,500	1,000,000	160,000
500	3,750	1,875,000	250,000
1,500	10,750	3,900,000	550,000

From the table:

$$n = 5 \ \Sigma X = 1,500 \ \Sigma Y = 10,750 \ \Sigma XY = 3,900,000 \ \Sigma X^2 = 550,000$$

Substituting these values into the formula for b first:

$$b = \frac{n\Sigma XY - (\Sigma X)(\Sigma Y)}{n\Sigma X^2 - (\Sigma X)^2} = \frac{(5)(3,900,000) - (1,500)(10,750)}{(5)(550,000) - (1,500)^2} = \frac{3,375,000}{500,000}$$

$$= 6.75,$$

$$a = (\Sigma Y/n) - b\ (\Sigma X/n) = 10,750/5 - (6.75)(1,500/5) = \$125.$$

Thus, the regression equation is $125 + $6.75 X.

9a. Annual sales are increasing by $2,300 per year.

9b. Note that the *t*-value for the year 2002 is 4. Hence, $Y = 17,500 + 23,000\ (4)$ = $109,500.

10a. For regression purposes, a year can be given a number so that the $\Sigma X = 0$. Since the company has 11 years of data, which is an odd number, the year in the middle is assigned a zero value.

Year	X	Sales Y (000 omitted)	XY	X^2	Y^2
1994	−5	$10	−50	25	100
1995	−4	$ 20	−80	16	400
1996	−3	$ 30	−90	9	900
1997	−2	$ 45	−90	4	2,025
1998	−1	$ 70	−70	1	4,900
1999	0	$ 90	0	0	8,100
2000	+1	$ 125	125	1	15,625
2001	+2	$ 150	300	4	22,500
2002	+3	$ 180	540	9	32,400
2003	+4	$ 220	880	16	48,400
2004	+5	$ 270	1,350	25	72,900
	0	$1,210	2,815	110	208,250

$$b = \frac{(11)(2,815)}{(11)(110)} = \frac{30,965}{1,210} = \$25,59$$

$$a = \frac{1,210}{11} = \$110$$

Therefore, the estimated equation is:

$$Y' = \$110 + \$25.59X,$$

where Y' = estimated sales and X = year index value.

To calculate 2005 sales, we assign $+6$ to the X value for the year 2005.

Thus, $Y' = \$110 + \$25.59(+6) = \$263.54$.

10b. $r^2 = \dfrac{(30,965)^2}{(1,210)[(11)(208,250) - (1,210)^2]} = 0.958$

10c. The high r^2 (0.958) ensures that annual sales shows an increasing trend.

11. We will calculate GDP, step by step, as follows:

1. $I = 300 + 0.3\pi_{t-1} = 300 + 0.3\,(1,000) = 600$

2. $GDP = C + I + G = 200 + 0.8Y + 600 + 1,000$

   $\qquad = 200 + 0.8(GDP - T) + 600 + 1,000$

   $\qquad = 200 + 0.8(GDP - 0.4GDP) + 600 + 1,000$

   $\qquad = 220 + 0.48GDP + 600 + 1,000$

$0.52\ GDP = 1,800$

$GDP = 3,462$ (in billions of dollars)

12a. Industry A must produce \$3 million $\times$ 1.07 $=$ \$3.21 million worth of goods.

12b. Industry B must produce \$3 million $\times$ 0.04 $=$ \$0.12 million worth of goods.

Industry C must produce \$3 million $\times$ 0.01 $=$ \$0.03 million worth of goods.

6
PRODUCTION THEORY AND ANALYSIS

KEY TERMS

production function engineering relation that defines the maximum amount of output that can be produced with a given set of inputs.

linear production function production function that assumes a perfect linear relationship between all inputs and total output.

Leontief production function production function in which inputs are used in fixed proportions.

Cobb-Douglas production function production function that assumes some degree of substitutability among inputs.

marginal revenue product net addition to total revenue attributable to the addition of one unit of the variable productive service.

average product total amount of output divided by the amount of the input used to produce the output.

marginal product change in the quantity of output resulting from a one-unit change in the quantity of input used.

marginal rate of technical substitution rate that measures reduction in one input per unit increase in the other that is just sufficient to maintain a constant level of output.

expansion path graphical device used to illustrate the amount of capital and labor that a firm will use as it expands its operations.

returns to scale increase in output arising from a proportionate increase in all inputs.

isocost curve curve or line showing the combinations of any inputs that can be bought with a fixed sum of money.

> **optimal employment rule** profit-maximizing rule that says that the marginal revenue product of an input is exactly equal to the input price.

Management's production decision problems may be considered to fall into the following four types:

1. How much, in total, shall be spent on the purchase of inputs?

2. How shall this amount be divided among the various types of inputs?

3. How much of each type of input will be allocated to each type of output?

4. How much of each final product shall the firm produce?

PRODUCTION FUNCTION

The production function is an engineering relation that defines the maximum amount of output that can be produced with a given set of inputs. Mathematically, the production function is denoted as:

$$Q = F(L, K)$$

where Q = the maximum amount of output, K = capital , and L = labor. The function can take many different forms.

LINEAR PRODUCTION FUNCTION

The *linear* production function assumes a perfect linear relationship between all inputs and total output:

$$Q = ak + bL$$

Example 1

Given $Q = 3K + 4L$, if 9 units of capital and 4 units of labor are employed, the total output will be 43 units: $Q = 3(9) + 4(4) = 43$.

LEONTIEF PRODUCTION FUNCTION

Also called the fixed-proportions production function, the *Leontief production function* assumes that inputs are used in fixed proportions. It is given by

$$Q = \text{mim } \{aK, bL\}$$

Example 2

Given $Q = \min \{3K, 4L\}$, if 5 units of capital and 4 units of labor are employed, the total output will be 15 units: $Q = \min \{3(5), 4(4)\} = \min \{15, 16\} = 15$. Note the minimum of the numbers "15" and "16" is 15.

COBB-DOUGLAS PRODUCTION FUNCTION

The *Cobb-Douglas production function* is between the extremes of the linear production function and the Leontief production function. Unlike the linear function, the relationship between output and the inputs is not linear. Unlike the Leontief function, inputs need not be used in fixed proportions. The form is

$$Q = K^a L^b.$$

Example 3

Given $Q = K^{1/2}L^{1/2}$, if 4 units of labor and 9 units of capital are employed, the total output will be 6 units: $Q = (9)^{1/2}(4)^{1/2} = (3)(2) = 6$.

YOU SHOULD REMEMBER

There are many other forms for production function, including constant elasticity of substitution (*CES*) function, which is not covered here.

MEASURES OF PRODUCTIVITY

A useful consideration that needs to be taken into account in business decision making is the determination of the productivity of inputs in the production process. Productivity measures are useful for evaluating the efficiency of a production process and in making input decisions that yield maximum profits. The three important measures of productivity are total product, average product, and marginal product.

• *TOTAL PRODUCT*

Total product (*TP*) is the maximum level of output that can be obtained with given inputs.

Example 4

A garage door maker has the following production function:

$$Q = 0.2K^2 + 0.3KL + 0.4L^2$$

Assume a weekly rate of use where $L = 100$ labor hours and $K = 30$ machine hours. The total product per week is $Q = 0.2(30)^2 + 0.3(30)(100) + 0.4(100)^2 = 180 + 900 + 4,000 = 5,080$ units.

• *AVERAGE PRODUCT*

The average product (*AP*) is the total amount of output divided by the amount of the input used to produce a given amount of output. The average product of labor (AP_L) is equal to total product (*TP*) divided by the amount of labor (*L*) used in the production of output (*Q*):

$$AP_L = Q/L.$$

Similarly, the average product of capital (AP_K) is:

$$AP_K = Q/K$$

Example 5

From Example 4: $Q = 0.2K^2 + 0.3KL + 0.4L^2$ and $L = 100$ labor hours and $K = 30$ machine hours.

$$AP_L = \frac{Q}{L} = \frac{0.2K^2}{L} + 0.3K + 0.4L =$$

$$\frac{0.2(30)^2}{100} + 0.3(30) + 0.4(100) = 180 + 9 + 40 = 229 \text{ units.}$$

$$AP_K = \frac{Q}{K} = 0.2K + 0.3L + \frac{0.4L^2}{K} = 0.2(30) + 0.3(100) + \frac{0.4(100)^2}{(30)}$$

$$6 + 30 + 133.33 = 169.33 \text{ units.}$$

• *MARGINAL PRODUCT*

The marginal product (*MP*) of an input is the change in the quantity of output resulting from a one unit change in the quantity of input used. Thus, the marginal product of labor (MP_L) is

$$\frac{\Delta Q}{\Delta L} = \frac{dQ}{dL}$$

and the marginal product of capital (MP_K) is

$$\frac{\Delta Q}{\Delta K} = \frac{dQ}{dK}$$

Example 6

From Example 4: $Q = 0.2K^2 + 0.3KL + 0.4L^2$

$$MP_L = \frac{\partial Q}{\partial L} = 0.3K + 0.8L = 0.3(30) + 0.8(100) = 89,$$

$$MP_K = \frac{\partial Q}{\partial K} = 0.4K + 0.3L = 0.4(30) + 0.3(100) = 42.$$

RELATIONSHIP AMONG TOTAL PRODUCT, MARGINAL PRODUCT, AND AVERAGE PRODUCT

The profit-oriented firm is deeply interested in how its output will vary with respect to the quantity used of an input. The reason is that such information is essential for determining the profit-maximizing level of output. Figure 6–1 shows graphically the relationship among total product, marginal product, and average product. We observe that

a. as the usage of an input increases, MP initially increases (increasing marginal returns), then begins to decline (decreasing marginal returns), and eventually becomes negative (negative marginal returns);

b. AP increases when MP > AP; otherwise, MP < AP.

From 0 to 3 units of variable input, the quantity of output increases at an increasing rate and the MP function is rising. Such behavior of output denotes increasing returns to input. Diminishing marginal returns begin at point A. Between 3 and 7 units of variable input, output increases at a decreasing rate. Because MP is a positive yet diminishing value, this portion of the production function reflects decreasing returns to input. Output is maximum at 7 units of input and MP, being equal to the slope of the production function, is zero. Beyond 7 units of input, input is present in uneconomic proportions relative to the available fixed input; the marginal products of additional units of input are negative and negative returns to input are encountered. The AP of input reaches its maximum value at that point where a ray drawn from the origin is just tangent to the production function (point B). The MP function passes through the apex of the AP product function.

MARGINAL REVENUE PRODUCT

Marginal revenue product (MRP) is the net addition to total revenue attributable to the addition of one unit of the variable productive service or the dollar value of the marginal product (MP) of an input. The marginal revenue product (MRP) of an input is equal to MP multiplied by the MR of the commodity.

OPTIMAL EMPLOYMENT RULE

A profit-maximizing firm will employ units of a variable productive service until the point is reached at which the MRP of an input is exactly equal to the input price.

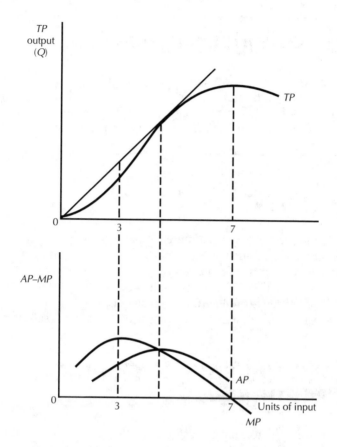

Figure 6–1. Graphical Relationship Among Total Product, Marginal Product, and Average Product

Marginal revenue product of the input (MRP_i) = Price of an input (P_i)
For example, an optimal employment rule is

Marginal revenue product of labor (MRP_L) = price of labor (w),

assuming that the firm is a wage taker.

YOU SHOULD REMEMBER

We defined profit maximization as requiring that $MR = MC$. This was looking at the matter from the output side. From the input side, we note $MRP = P$. The two rules are logically identical. They are simply different ways of stating the maximum-profit condition.

ISOQUANT

Also known as producers' indifference curve or isoproduct curve, an isoquant curve traces out the combinations of any two or more inputs that give rise to the same level of output (see Figure 6–2). These combinations must be the most efficient ones (i.e., any point on an isoproduct curve shows the minimum quantities of the inputs needed to produce the given output). Isoproduct curves are typically drawn as being convex to the origin because of the assumed substitutability of inputs.

MARGINAL RATE OF TECHNICAL SUBSTITUTION

Marginal rate of technical substitution (*MRTS*) is the rate that measures the reduction in one input per unit increase in the other that is just sufficient to maintain a constant level of output. The marginal rate of technical substitution of labor and capital ($MRTS_{LK}$) at a point on an *isoquant* is equal to the absolute value of the slope of the isoquant at that point. It is also equal to the ratio of the marginal products:

$$MRTS_{LK} = \frac{MP_K}{MP_L}.$$

SUBSTITUTABILITY OF INPUTS

There are three general types of shapes of an isoquant, as shown in Figure 6–3. In panel (a), the isoquants are right angles indicating that inputs *a* and *b* are *not substitutable* (or *perfect complements*). In this case, one particular combination of inputs are required to produce a specified level of output. Output cannot rise without increased quantities of both inputs. An example of this would be tires and a battery for an automobile. In this case, the *MRTS* will be zero, since when an

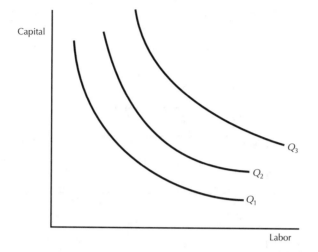

Capital

Q_3

Q_2

Q_1

Labor

Figure 6–2. Isoquants

additional unit of input a is used, there is no amount of input b that can be given up if a given level of output is to be maintained.

The other extreme case is where inputs a and b are perfect substitutes, as shown in panel (b). In this case inputs can be substituted for each other at a fixed rate while the firm maintains the same level of output. The isoquant will be a straight line and have a constant slope and *MRTS*. Natural gas and fuel oil are considered close substitutes in energy production.

Panel (c) depicts, however, the most common case where inputs are imperfect substitutes. They can be substituted for each other at changing rates. In other words, the rate at which one input can be given up in return for one more unit of another input while maintaining the same level of output diminishes as the amount of input a being used increases. That is, the *MRTS* diminishes. In general, capital and labor are imperfect substitutes.

YOU SHOULD REMEMBER

The choice of which input combination to use is easy in the first two cases—panel (a) and (b). In the first case, no input combination decision can be made. In the second case, the decision is in favor of cheaper input. We tend to concentrate our discussion on the case of inputs that are imperfect substitutes whose *MRTS* is diminishing.

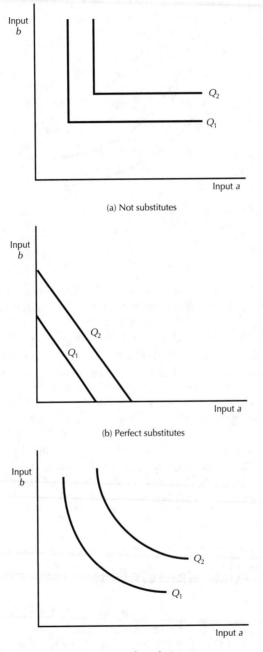

(a) Not substitutes

(b) Perfect substitutes

(c) Imperfect substitutes

Figure 6–3. Substitutability of Inputs

THE STAGES OF PRODUCTION

Typically, there are three stages of production of special significance for analyzing the efficiency with which resource inputs are used (See Figure 6–4). A *production function* that exhibits the qualities of increasing, decreasing, and negative returns can be separated into three stages. Stage I covers the entire range of increasing returns to variable input, and the point of *diminishing marginal returns (DMR)* is reached (Point A) and passed. It ends when the point of *diminishing average return (DAR)* is reached (point B). Stage II covers the portion where the quantity of output rises at a decreasing rate; accordingly, the *marginal product (MP)* of variable input is declining, although it is still positive. Stage III coincides with the range of input where additional usage of variable inputs is associated with the decline in output but *MP* is negative.

ISOCOST CURVE

An isocost curve is a curve or line showing the combinations of any inputs (e.g., labor and capital) that can be bought with a fixed sum of money. It is analogous with the consumer's budget line, but relates to the firm's purchase of inputs. The total cost of inputs are:

$$wL + rK = C,$$

where w = the wage rate (the price of labor) and r = interest rate (the price of capital). This equation can be converted into the formula for an isocost line as follows:

$$K = \frac{C}{r} - \left(\frac{w}{r}\right)L$$

Thus, along an isocost line, K is a linear function of L with a vertical intercept of C/r and a slope of $-w/r$. The varying values of C will create isocost lines that are parallel to each other.

EXPANSION PATH

An expansion path is a graphical device used to illustrate the amount of capital and labor that a firm will use as it expands its operations. The optimum combination is at the point of tangency between the isoquant and the isocost line. The expansion path is then determined by the locus of tangents between isoquants and isocost lines. With reference to the firm, that is the curve traced out by joining up the factor input choices at each output level.

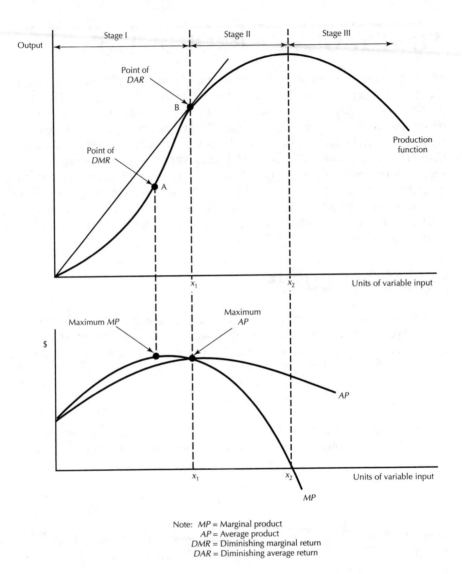

Figure 6–4. Three Stages of Production

Note: MP = Marginal product
       AP = Average product
       DMR = Diminishing marginal return
       DAR = Diminishing average return

For given input prices, the curve indicates what the firm's chosen path of expansion (points A, B, C in Figure 6–5) will be in terms of factor input combinations. With a cost-minimizing firm any point on this curve will satisfy the condition that the ratio of the marginal physical product of any two-factor input will equal the ratio of their prices.

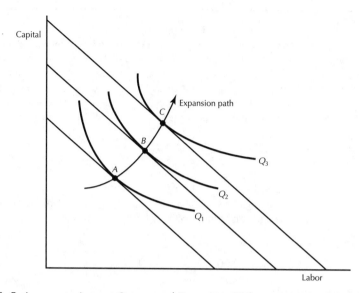

Figure 6–5. Isoquants, Isocost Curves and Expansion Path

COST MINIMIZATION—COST-MINIMIZING INPUT RULE

The tangency of the isocost curve with the isoproduct curve defines the least-cost (optimal) combination of inputs for the production of a given level of output. For a least-cost combination of inputs, the following condition has to hold:

$$\frac{MP_L}{w} = \frac{MP_K}{r},$$

which states that to minimize the cost of producing a given level of output, the marginal product per dollar spent should be equal for all inputs.

Alternatively, a firm should employ inputs such that the marginal rate of substitution is equal to the ratio of input prices.

$$\frac{MP_L}{MP_K} = \frac{w}{r}.$$

Example 7

A grower of strawberries estimates that strawberry output would increase 2,500 per month with an additional 1,000 gallons of water per month provided by an irrigation system. Alternatively, strawberry output could be increased by 1,000 with an additional 2 tons of fertilizer per month. Assuming the cost of water is $.05 per gallon and that fertilizer is $20 per ton, is the farm using an optimal combination of water and fertilizer?

For a least-cost combination of inputs, the following condition has to hold:

$$\frac{MP_L}{w} = \frac{MP_K}{r},$$

MP_L = 2,500 and MP_K = 1,000,
w = 1,000 gallons per month $\times$ $0.05 per gallon = $50 per month,
r = 2 tons per month $\times$ $20 per ton = $40 per month.

Therefore,

$$\frac{2,500}{50} = 50 > \frac{1,000}{40} = 25$$

50 > 25, which is not a least-cost combination of inputs since output per additional dollar spent is greater for water than for fertilizer.

RETURNS TO SCALE

The returns to scale of a production system represents the increase in output arising from a proportionate increase in all inputs. It refers to how output changes when all inputs are increased by the same multiple. There are three possibilities: increasing, constant, and decreasing returns to scale. If output increases by a greater multiple than that by which the inputs are increased, then *increasing returns to scale* are present. If output increases by the same multiple, *constant returns to scale* are present. Finally, if output increases by a smaller multiple, *decreasing returns to scale* are present. Returns to scale play an important role in economic decisions. They affect the optimal scale or plant size of a firm and its production facilities. They also affect the nature of competition in an industry and thus, are important in determining the profitability in a particular sector of the economy.

Returns to scale	Condition
Increasing return to scale	Percentage increase in output > percentage increase in inputs
Constant return to scale	Percentage increase in output = percentage increase in inputs
Decreasing return to scale	Percentage increase in output < percentage increase in inputs

Returns to scale can be evaluated in a number of ways, including the following:

1. Compare the percentage increase in output with any given percentage increase in inputs

2. Use a more general algebraic approach

Example 8

Given the production function $Q = 10L + 15K + 20KL$

a. If $L = K = 100$, then

$$Q_1 = 10(100) + 15(100) + 20(100)(100) = 202,500$$

Increase each unit by one percent yields:

$Q_2 = 10(101) + 15(101) + 20(101)(101) = 206,545$, which implies a 2 percent increase in output ($Q_2/Q_1 = 1.02$), and therefore, the function exhibits *increasing* returns to scale.

b. Alternatively, for a k percent inures in all inputs (where $k > 1$) we observe:

$$Q_1 = 10L + 15K + 20KL,$$

$$Q_2 = 10L + 15K + 20KL = 10(kL) + 15(kK) + 20(kL)(kK) =$$

$$k(10L + 15K + 20kKL).$$

Since $k > 1$, $Q_2 > Q_1$. So the function exhibits *increasing* returns to scale.

OUTPUT ELASTICITY AND RETURNS TO SCALE

The output elasticity measures how sensitive output is to a change in an input used. It is calculated as

$$e_Q = \frac{\% \text{ change in } Q}{\% \text{ change in } X} = \frac{\partial Q}{\partial X} \cdot \frac{X}{Q},$$

where X represents all inputs (capital, labor, etc.). This measure can also be used to estimate returns to scale, based on the following criteria:

Output elasticity	Returns to scale
$e_Q > 1$	Increasing
$e_Q = 1$	Constant
$e_Q < 1$	Decreasing

KNOW THE CONCEPTS

TERMS FOR STUDY

average product
Cobb-Douglas production
Leontief production function
linear production function
marginal product
marginal rate of technical substitution

marginal revenue product
optimal employment rule
output elasticity
production function
returns to scale
total product

DO YOU KNOW THE BASICS?

1. Give several different forms of production function.

2. How does the Cobb-Douglas function differ from other forms?

3. What is marginal revenue product (*MRP*)? What is its significance in profit maximization?

4. Briefly describe three stages of production.

5. What is output elasticity? How is it calculated?

6. Describe the graphical relationship between marginal product and average product.

7. State the condition for the least-cost (optimal) combination of inputs.

8. Give two examples of perfect substitutes.

9. If inputs are not substitutable, there is no decision made on input combination. Comment.

PRACTICAL APPLICATION

1. Anaheim Company, a film processor, has the following production function:

$$Q = 0.5K^2 + 0.3KL + 0.4L^2$$

Assume a weekly rate of use where $L = 100$ labor hours and $K = 30$ film developing hours. Determine the following:

a. The total product per week.

b. The marginal product of labor.

c. The marginal product of capital.

2. John-Jay Opticals, Inc., a maker of optical supplies estimated the following production function:

$$Q = 20L^{0.75}K^{0.30},$$

where Q = plastic cases produced per eight-hour shift, L = units of labor, and K = units of capital employed.

a. Calculate the number of plastic cases completed per eight-hour shift when $L = 10$ and $K = 100$.

b. Calculate the marginal product of labor when $L = 10$ and $K = 100$.

3. Ding-Dong Farms, Inc. is a grower of oranges. The company estimates that orange output would increase 1,500 per month with an additional 1,000 gallons of water per month provided by an irrigation system. Alternatively, orange output could be increased by 900 with an additional 2 tons of fertilizer per month. Assuming the cost of water is $.06 per gallon and that fertilizer is $25 per ton, is the farm using an optimal combination of water and fertilizer? Why or why not?

4. Agasi Farms, Inc. is a grower of pears. The company estimates that pear output would increase 1,200 per month with an additional 1,000 gallons of water per month provided by an irrigation system. Alternatively, pear output could be increased by 1,000 with an additional 2 tons of fertilizer per month. Assuming the cost of water is $.06 per gallon and that fertilizer is $25 per ton, is the farm using an optimal combination of water and fertilizer? Why or why not?

5. Determine whether each of the following production functions exhibits increasing, constant, or decreasing returns to scale.

a. $Q = 3,200 + 10L + 5K$

b. $Q = 120K^{0.75} L^{0.25}$

c. $Q = 20L + 4KL + 2L$

d. $Q = 2K^3 + 6K^2L + 6KL^2 + L^3$

e. $Q = \dfrac{.5K^{1.5}}{L^{0.5}}$

f. $Q = 100 + 5L$

6. *ABC* has the following production function:

$$Q = 12KL + 0.7KL^2 - \frac{1}{30} KL^3$$

Determine the following:

a. The maximum output that can be produced when $K = 5$.

b. The level of use of L where average product of labor (AP_L) is at a maximum.

c. The output level where diminishing returns to L occurs.

7. The Southwestern Mining Company has developed the following production function for its coal output:

$$Q = 250L^{0.5}K^{0.6}$$

a. Determine returns to scale, and comment on it.

b. Determine returns to scale for each factor input.

8. The Nova Coal Mining Company has developed the following production function for is coal output:

$$Q = 300L^{0.5}K^{0.5},$$

where Q = Coal output (in thousands of tons), L = Labor (in hundreds of workers), and K = Capital (in hundreds of millions of dollars).

At peak production, the company is expected to employ 10,000 workers and require $900 million in capital outlays. Coal output is sold at a competitive market price of $40 per ton.

a. Determine the maximum annual wage the company would be willing to pay in order to attract a force of 10,000 workers.

b. How many workers would the company willingly hire in view of union demands for a $20,000 annual wage?

9. The total product of labor (per hour) for a firm is given by:

$$Q = 30L - 0.5L^2$$

a. Determine the marginal product of labor.

b. How many workers should the firm employ if the wage rate is $30 per hour and the marginal revenue product is $24?

ANSWERS

KNOW THE BASICS

1. Examples are linear production function, Leontief production function, and Cobb-Douglas production function.

2. The Cobb-Douglas production function is between the extremes of the linear production function and the Leontief production function. Unlike the linear function, the relationship between output and the inputs is not linear. Unlike the Leontief function, inputs need not be used in fixed proportions.

3. Marginal revenue product (*MRP*) is the net addition to total revenue attributable to the addition of one unit of the variable productive service or the dollar value of the marginal product (*MP*) of an input. The *MRP* of an input is equal to *MP* multiplied by the market price of the commodity. A profit-maximizing firm will employ units of a variable productive service until the point is reached at which the *MRP* of an input is exactly equal to the input price.

4. Three stages of production are of special significance for analyzing the efficiency with which resource inputs are used. Stage I covers the entire range of increasing returns to variable input and the point of *diminishing marginal returns (DMR)* is reached (Point A) and passed. It ends when the point of *diminishing average return (DAR)* is reached (point B). Stage II covers the portion where the quantity of output rises at a decreasing rate; accordingly, the *marginal product (MP)* of variable input is declining, although it is still positive. Stage III coincides with the range of input where additional usage of variable inputs is associated with the decline in output but *MP* is negative.

5. The output elasticity measures how sensitive output is to a change in an input used. It is calculated as:

$$e_Q = \frac{\% \text{ change in } Q}{\% \text{ change in } X} = \frac{\partial Q}{\partial X} \cdot \frac{X}{Q},$$

where X represents all inputs (capital, labor, etc.). This measure can also be used to estimate returns to scale.

6. As the usage of an input increases, *MP* initially increases (increasing marginal returns), then begins to decline (decreasing marginal returns), and eventually becomes negative (negative marginal returns). As long as *MR* increases *MP* > *AP*; otherwise, *MP* < *AP*.

7. The tangency of the isocost curve with the isoproduct curve defines the least-cost (optimal) combination of inputs for the production of a given level of out-

put. For a least-cost combination of inputs, the following condition has to hold: $MP_W/P_W = MP_F/P_F.$

8. In the area of baking, honey and brown sugar are often nearly perfect substitutes.

9. The statement is true. For example, an auto requires one engine, one battery, and four wheels; no other combination will do. Another example would be yeast and flour for a specified bread.

PRACTICAL APPLICATION

1a. $Q = 0.5(30)^2 + 0.3(30)(100) + 0.4(100)^2 = 450 + 900 + 4,000 = 5,350$

1b. $MP_L = \dfrac{\partial Q}{\partial L} = 0.3K + 0.8L = 0.3(30) + 0.8(100) = 89$

1c. $MP_K = \dfrac{\partial Q}{\partial K} = K + 0.3L = (30) + 0.2(100) = 50$

2a. $Q = 20L^{0.75}K^{0.30} = 20(10)^{0.75}(100)^{0.30} = 20(5.623)(3.981) = $ 447.70 plastic cases

2b. $MP_L = \dfrac{\partial Q}{\partial L} = (20)(0.75)L^{-0.25} K^{0.30} = 33.58$

3. For a least-cost combination of inputs, the following condition has to hold:

$$\frac{MP_L}{w} = \frac{MP_K}{r}$$

$MP_L = 1,500$ and $MP_K = 900$

$w = 1,000$ gallons per month $\times$ \$0.06 per gallon $=$ \$60 per month

$r = 2$ tons per month $\times$ \$25 per ton $=$ \$50 per month

Therefore, does

$$\frac{1,500}{60} = \frac{900}{50} ?$$

No, $25 > 18$, which is not a least-cost combination of inputs, since output per additional dollar spent is greater for water than for fertilizer.

4. $MP_L = 1,200$ and $MP_K = 1,000$

$w = 1,000$ gallons per month $\times$ \$0.06 per gallon $=$ \$60 per month

$r = 2$ tons per month $\times$ \$25 per ton $=$ \$50 per month

Therefore, does

$$\frac{1{,}200}{60} = \frac{1{,}000}{50}?$$

Yes, 20 = 20, which is a least-cost combination of inputs, since output per additional dollar spent is equal for both water and for fertilizer.

5a. Let $L = 10$ and $K = 10$;

$$Q_1 = 3{,}200 + 10(10) + 5(10) = 3{,}350$$

Increase each unit by 100% yields:

$$Q_2 = 3{,}200 + 10(20) + 5(20) = 3{,}500,$$
$$Q_2 - Q_1 = 3{,}500 - 3{,}350 = 150.$$

A 100% necroses in inputs produces a 4.47% increase in output, the function exhibits *decreasing* returns to scale.

5b. $Q_1 = 120K^{0.75} L^{0.25}$ Increase each unit by k percent,

$$Q_2 = 120(kK)^{0.75} (kL)^{0.25} = k (120K^{0.75} L^{0.25}) = k Q_1$$

A k percent increase in inputs yields a k percent increase in output, so the function exhibits *constant* returns to scale.

5c. $Q = 20L + 2K + 4KL$

Let $L = K = 100$, then

$$Q_1 = 20(100) + 2(100) + 4(100)(100) = 42{,}200.$$

Increase each unit by one percent yields:

$Q_2 = 20(101) + 2(101) + 4(101)(101) = 43{,}026$, which implies a 2 percent increase in output ($Q_2/Q_1 = 43{,}026/42{,}200 = 1.02$), and therefore, the function exhibits *increasing* returns to scale.

5d. Let $L = 10$ and $K = 10$,

$$Q_1 = 2(10)^3 + 6(10)^2(10) + 6(10)(10)^2 + (10)^3 =$$
$$2{,}000 + 6{,}000 + 6{,}000 + 1{,}000 = 15{,}000$$

Increase each unit by 100% yields

$$Q_2 = 2(20)^3 + 6(20)^2(20) + 6(20)(20)^2 + (20)^3$$
$$= 16{,}000 + 48{,}000 + 48{,}000 + 8{,}000 = 120{,}000,$$
$$120{,}000 - 15{,}000 = 105{,}000;$$

$105{,}000/15{,}000 = 7 = 700\%$, which exhibits *increasing* returns to scale.

5e. Let $L = 10$ and $K = 10$,

$$Q_1 = 0.5K^{1.5}/L^{0.5} = 0.5(10)^{0.5}/(10)^{0.5} = 0.5(10) = 5.$$

Increase each unit by 100% yields

$$Q_2 = 0.5K^{1.5}/L^{0.5} = 0.5(20)^{0.5}/(20)^{0.5} = 0.5(20) = 10$$

A 100% necroses in inputs produces a 100% increase in output, the function exhibits *constant* returns to scale.

5f. Let $L = 10$ and $K = 10$,

$$Q_1 = 100 + 5(10) = 150.$$

Increase each unit by 100% yields

$$Q_2 = 100 + 5(20) = 200,$$
$$200 - 150 = 50, \quad \frac{50}{150} = 0.3333 = 33.33\%.$$

A 100 percent necroses in inputs produces a 33.33% increase in output, the function exhibits *decreasing* returns to scale.

6a. $Q = 12KL + 0.7KL^2 - \dfrac{1}{30}KL^3$

at $K = 5$,

$$TP_L = 12(5)L + 0.7(5)L^2 - \frac{1}{30}(5)L^3$$
$$= 60L + 3.5L^2 - \frac{1}{6}L^3$$

Setting MP_L equal to zero yields

$$MP_L = \frac{\partial Q}{\partial L} = 60 + 7L - 0.5L^2 = 0,$$
$$(-0.5L + 10)(L + 6) = 0.$$

So $L = 20$ (Ignore $L = -6$) is a maximum since

$$\frac{\partial^2 Q}{\partial L^2} = 7 - L = 8 - 20 = -12 < 0.$$

The maximum output then is 1,267 units:

at $L = 20$,

$$TP_L = 60L + 3.5L^2 - \frac{1}{6}L^3$$

$$= 60(20) + 3.5(20)^2 - \frac{1}{6}(20)^3 = 1,267$$

6b. $TP_L = 60L + 3.5L^2 - 1/6L^3$

$$AP_L = \frac{TP_L}{L} = \frac{\left(60L + 3.5L^2 - \frac{1}{6}L^3\right)}{L}$$

$$= 60 + 3.5L - \frac{1}{6}L^2.$$

To find the maximum AP_L, we set this equal to zero and solve for L, as follows:

$$\frac{dAP_L}{dL} = 3.5 - \frac{1}{3}L = 0, L = 10.5,$$

which is a maximum since

$$\frac{d^2 AP_L}{dL^2} = -\frac{1}{3} < 0.$$

The output level where AP_L is maximized is 823 units:

$$TP_L = 60L + 3.5(10.5)^2 - \frac{1}{6}(10.5)^3 = 823.$$

6c. Diminishing marginal returns begin where MP_L is maximized.

$$MP_L = \frac{\partial Q}{\partial L} = 60 + 7L - 0.5L^2,$$

$$\frac{dMP_L}{dL} = 7 - 1 = 0, \ L = 7,$$

which is a maximum since

$$\frac{d^2 MP_L}{dL^2} = -1 < 0.$$

So at $L = 7$,

$$TP_L = 60L + 3.5L^2 - \frac{1}{6}L^3 = 60(7) + 3.5(7)^2 - \frac{1}{6}(7)^3 = 534.$$

Diminishing marginal returns to the labor input begin where output is 534 units.

7a. $Q = 250L^{0.5}K^{0.6} = 250(kL)^{0.5}(kK)^{0.6} = k^{0.5}k^{0.6} \ 250L^{0.5}K^{0.6} = k^{1.1} \ Q,$

i.e., $k^{1.1} > k$, indicates that the above production function exhibits *increasing* returns to scale.

7b. Returns to each factor can be determined by examining how each marginal product changes with increased usage.

Returns to Labor:

$$MP_L = \frac{\partial Q}{\partial L} = 125L^{-0.5}K^{0.6}, \frac{d^2 MP_L}{dL^2} = -62.5 \ L^{-1.5}K^{0.6} < 0.$$

Therefore, returns to labor are decreasing.

Returns to Capital:

$$MP_K = \frac{\partial Q}{\partial K} = 125L^{0.5}K^{-0.4}, \frac{d^2 MP_L}{dL^2} = -50L^{0.5}K^{-1.4} < 0.$$

Therefore, returns to labor are decreasing.

8a. We use the optimal employment rule:

Price of an input (P_i) = Marginal revenue product of the input (MRP_i)

For labor, Price of labor = marginal revenue product of labor, or

$$w = MP_L \times MR_Q$$
$$= (150L^{-0.5}K^{0.5})(\$40 \times 1,000 \text{ tons})$$
$$= [150(100)^{-0.5}(9)^{0.5}](\$40 \times 1,000 \text{ tons}),$$
$$= \$1,800,000 \text{ per hundred workers, or } \$18,000.$$

8b. $w = MP_L \times MR_Q$

$$\$20,000 \times 100 = (150L^{-0.5}K^{0.5})(\$40 \times 1,000 \text{ tons}),$$

$$\$2,000,000 = [150L^{-0.5}(9)^{0.5}](\$40 \times 1,000 \text{ tons}),$$

$$\$2,000,000 = [150L^{-0.5}(9)^{0.5}](\$40 \times 1,000 \text{ tons}),$$

$$\frac{\$2,000,000}{\$18,000,000} = 150L^{-0.5},$$

$$\frac{\$2,000,000}{\$18,000,000} = 1/L^{0.5},$$

$$L^{0.5} = 9,$$

$L = 81$ or 8,100 workers. Thus, at a wage of \$20,000, the company would only be willing to hire 8,100 workers.

9a. $MP_L = \dfrac{\partial Q}{\partial L} = 30 - L$

9b. Using the optimal employment rule,

$$w = MP_L \times MR_Q,$$
$$\$30 = (30-L) \times \$24,$$
$$\$30 = \$720 - \$24L,$$
$$L = 23.$$

The firm should hire 23 workers per hour.

7

LINEAR PROGRAMMING AND ACTIVITY ANALYSIS

KEY TERMS

linear programming (*LP*) mathematical technique designed to determine an optimal decision (or an optimal plan) chosen from a large number of possible decisions.

the simplex method linear programming algorithm, which is an iteration method of computation, to move from one corner point solution to another until it reaches the best solution.

the graphical method graphical approach to solving an *LP* problem. It is easier to use but limited to the *LP* problems involving two (or at most three) decision variables.

basic feasible solutions corner point solutions of the feasible region that satisfy all the constraints simultaneously.

primal and dual problems pair of related maximization and minimization problems in linear programming.

shadow prices implicit values or opportunity costs associated with given resources in an *LP* problem.

activity analysis analysis involving the determination of the combination of production processes that maximizes output (or profits), subject to the restrictions on the required resources (inputs).

iso-profit curve curve reflecting the various combinations of products that a firm can sell to earn a given level of profit.

MULTIPLE PRODUCTS AND PRODUCTION PLANNING

Linear programming (*LP*) is a mathematical technique designed to determine an optimal decision (or an optimal plan) chosen from a large number of possible decisions. The optimal decision is the one that meets the specified objective of the company, subject to various restrictions or constraints. It concerns itself with the problem of allocating scarce resources among competing activities in an optimal manner. The optimal decision yields the highest profit, contribution margin (*CM*), or revenue, or the lowest cost. A linear programming model consists of two important ingredients:

1. *Objective function.* The company must define the specific objective to be achieved.

2. *Constraints.* Constraints are in the form of restrictions on availability of resources or meeting minimum requirements. As the name linear programming indicates, both the objective function and constraints must be in *linear* form.

YOU SHOULD REMEMBER

The classical calculus methods, such as the *Lagrangean multiplier technique*, are not well-suited for obtaining optimal solutions to problems with *inequality* constraints. *LP* deals with constrained optimization problems with *linear* objective functions and *linear inequality* constraints, while differential calculus and the Lagrangean multiplier technique deal with problems involving *linear* or *nonlinear* objective functions and *equality* constraints.

Example 1

A firm wishes to find an optimal product mix. The optimal mix would be the one that maximizes its total profit or contribution margin (*CM*) within the allowed budget and production capacity. Or the firm may want to determine a least cost combination of input materials while meeting production requirements, employing production capacities, and using available employees.

APPLICATIONS OF *LP*

Applications of LP are numerous. They include:

1. Selecting least-cost mix of ingredients for manufactured products
2. Developing an optimal budget
3. Determining an optimal investment portfolio (or asset allocation)
4. Allocating an advertising budget to a variety of media
5. Scheduling jobs to machines
6. Determining a least-cost shipping pattern
7. Scheduling flights
8. Gasoline blending
9. Optimal manpower allocation
10. Selecting the best warehouse location to minimize shipping costs

FORMULATION OF *LP*

To formulate an *LP* problem, certain steps are followed. They are as follows:

1. Define what is called *decision variables* that you are trying to solve for.
2. Express the objective function and constraints in terms of these decision variables. All the expressions must be in *linear* form.

In the following example, we will use this technique to find the optimal product mix.

Example 2

The Omni Furniture Manufacturing Company produces two products: desks and tables. Both products require time in two processing departments, assembly department and finishing department. Data on the two products are as follows:

| | Products | | Available |
Processing	Desk	Table	Hours
Assembly	2 per unit	4	100 hours
Finishing	3	2	90
Profit per unit	$25	$40	

The company wants to find the most profitable mix of these two products.

Step 1: Define the decision variables as follows:

x_1 = Number of units of desk to be produced

x_2 = Number of units of table to be produced

Step 2: The objective function to maximize total profit (Z) is expressed as:

$$Z = 25x_1 + 40x_2$$

Then, formulate the constraints as inequalities:

$$2x_1 + 4x_2 \leq 100 \text{ (assembly constraint)},$$
$$3x_1 + 2x_2 \leq 90 \text{ (finishing constraint)}.$$

In addition, implicit in any *LP* formulation are the constraints that restrict x_1 and x_2 to be nonnegative, i.e.,

$$x_1, x_2 \geq 0.$$

Our LP model is

$$\text{Maximize: } Z = 25x_1 + 40x_2,$$
$$\text{Subject to: } 2x_1 + 4x_2 \leq 100,$$
$$3x_1 + 2x_2 \leq 90,$$
$$x_1, x_2 > 0.$$

COMPUTATION METHODS OF *LP*

There are solution methods available to solve *LP* problems. They include:

1. the simplex method

2. the graphical method

The simplex method is the technique most commonly used to solve *LP* problems. It is an algorithm, which is an iteration method of computation, to move from one solution to another until it reaches the best solution.

YOU SHOULD REMEMBER

The simplex method introduces what are referred to as *slack variables* (denoted with, say, s_1 and s_2) to convert *inequalities* to *equalities*, as follows:

$$2x_1 + 4x_2 \leq 100 \qquad \rightarrow \qquad 2x_1 + 4x_2 + s_1 = 100,$$

$$3x_1 + 2x_2 \leq 90 \qquad \rightarrow \qquad 3x_1 + 2x_2 + s_2 = 90,$$

where s_1 and s_2 must not be negative.

If the left-hand side is greater than the right side ($>$), which is usually the case in a *minimization* problem, we say that there is a *surplus*. Then, we need $-s_1$ and $-s_2$ for a conversion to equalities, instead.

The graphical solution is easier to use but limited to the *LP* problems involving two (or at most three) decision variables. The graphical method follows the steps:

Step 1: Change inequalities to equalities.

Step 2: Graph the equalities. To graph the equality, (1) set one variable equal to zero, find the value of the other, and connect those two points on the graph, and (2) mark these intersections on the axes, and connect them with a straight line.

Step 3: Identify the correct side for the original inequalities by shading. Repeat steps 1–3 for each constraint.

Step 4: After all this, identify the feasible region, the area of *feasible solutions*.

Step 5: Solve the constraints (expressed as equalities) simultaneously for the various corner points of the feasible region.

Step 6: Determine the profit or contribution margin at all corners in the region.

YOU SHOULD REMEMBER

Feasible solutions are values of decision variables that satisfy all the constraints simultaneously. They are found on and within the boundary of the feasible region. The graphical approach is based on two important *LP* properties:

1. The optimal solution lies on the boundary of the feasible region, which implies that one can ignore the (infinitely numerous) interior points of the feasible region when searching for an optimal solution.

2. The optimal solution occurs at one of the corner points (basic feasible solutions) of the feasible region.

Example 3

Using the data and the *LP* model from Example 2, and following steps 1 through 4, we obtain the following feasible region (shaded area).

Step 1: Change inequalities to equalities.
$$2x_1 + 4x_2 = 100$$
$$3x_1 + 2x_2 = 90$$

Step 2: Graph the equalities. To graph the equality, set one variable equal to zero, find the value of the other, mark the points on the axes, and connect those two points with a straight line.

For equation 1: If $x_1 = 0$, $x_2 = 25$; if $x_2 = 0$, then $x_1 = 50$, connect $x_2 = 25$ and $x_1 = 50$.
For equation 2: If $x_1 = 0$, $x_2 = 30$; if $x_2 = 0$, then $x_1 = 45$, connect $x_2 = 30$ and $x_1 = 45$.

Step 3: Identify the correct side for the original inequalities. The correct side is the line and the area below it for less-than or equal-to constraints.

Step 4: After all this, identify the feasible region, the area of feasible solutions. The area of feasible solutions is the duplicated area as indicated by the shaded area in Figure 7–1.

Step 5: Solve the constraints (expressed as equalities) simultaneously for the various corner points of the feasible region.

Step 6: Determine the profit or contribution margin at all corners in the feasible region.

We evaluate all of the corner points as follows:

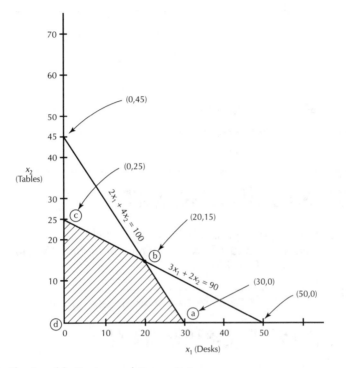

Figure 7–1. The Feasible Region and Corner Points

	Corner Points		Profit
	x_1	x_2	$\$25x_1 + \$40x_2$
(a)	30	0	$\$25(30) + \$40(0) = \$750$
(b)	20	15	$25(20) + 40(15) = 1,100$
(c)	0	25	$25(0) + 40(25) = 1,000$
(d)	0	0	$25(0) + 40(0) = 0$

The corner point (b) ($x_1 = 20$, $x_2 = 15$) produces the most profitable solution ($Z^* = \$1,100$). This point can be found by solving two equations that created it simultaneously, as shown below.

$$2x_1 + 4x_2 = 100 \quad (1)$$
$$3x_1 + 2x_2 = 90 \quad (2)$$

Multiplying the second equation (2) through by 2 and subtract from (1), we obtain

$$2x_1 + 4x_2 = 100 \qquad (1)$$
$$\underline{- 6x_1 + 4x_2 = 180} \qquad (2)$$
$$-4x_1 = -80$$
$$x_1 = \;\; 20$$

Substituting $x_1 = 20$ into (10) or (2) yields $x_2 = 15$.

YOU SHOULD REMEMBER

We can use a computer *LP* software package, such as LINDO (Linear Interactive and Discrete Optimization) and What's Best! to quickly solve an *LP* problem.

THE DUAL PROBLEM IN *LP*

Each *LP* maximization problem has its corresponding dual, a minimization problem and, conversely, a maximization problem. It has the following features:

1. Both the primal and the dual will give the same values for the decision variables in the primal objective functions at their optimal solution points.

2. The optimal value for the primal will equal the optimal value for the dual.

3. The dual is useful since it has many interesting economic interpretations. For example, the dual optimal solutions give the imputed value (or shadow price) of the opportunity cost to the firm of each of the scarce resources.

The following shows how to set up the dual problem:

Primal	Dual
Maximize $Z = \Sigma_j \, c_j x_j$	Minimize $V = \Sigma_i \, b_i u_i$
Subject to: $\Sigma_i \Sigma_j \, a_{ij} x_j \le b_i$	Subject to: $\Sigma_j \Sigma_i \, a_{ji} u_i \ge c_j$
$x_j \ge 0$	$u_i \ge 0$

Where $i = 1, 2, \ldots m$ and $j = 1, 2, \ldots n$

In a 2×2 case,

Primal	Dual
Maximize $Z = c_1x_1 + c_2x_2$	Minimize $V = b_1u_1 + b_2u_2$
Subject to: $a_{11}x_1 + a_{12}x_2 \leq b_1$	$a_{11}u_1 + a_{21}u_2 \geq c_1$
$a_{21}x_1 + a_{22}x_2 \leq b_2$	$a_{12}u_1 + a_{22}u_2 \geq c_2$
$x_1, x_2 \geq 0$	$u_1, u_2 \geq 0$

To begin with, define the dual variables, such as u_1, u_2. The number of dual variables should be the same as the number of the constraints in the primal. And then follow the following rules:

	Primal		Dual
1.	Coefficients in the objective function	↔	The right-hand side in the constraints
2.	The right-hand side in the constraints	↔	Coefficients in the objective function
3.	The constraints are $\leq$	↔	Dual variables ≥ 0
4.	Primal variables ≥ 0	↔	Dual constraints are $\geq$
5.	The matrix of constraints coefficients $\begin{pmatrix} a_{11} & a_{12} \\ a_{21} & a_{22} \end{pmatrix}$	↔	Its transpose $\begin{pmatrix} a_{11} & a_{21} \\ a_{12} & a_{22} \end{pmatrix}$

Example 4

From Example 2, we have

Maximize: $Z = 25x_1 + 40x_2$,

Subject to: $2x_1 + 4x_2 \leq 100$ (for assembly department),

$3x_1 + 2x_2 \leq 90$ (for finishing department),

$x_1, x_2 \geq 0$.

To set up the dual, first introduce the dual variables u_1, u_2. There will be two variables since there are two constraints in the prima. Then the dual can be set up as follows:

Minimize $V = 100u_1 + 90u_2$,

$2u_1 + 3u_2 \geq 25$ (for desk),

$4u_1 + 2u_2 \geq 40$ (for table),

$u_1, u_2 \geq 0$.

Example 5

Solving the dual graphically yields $u_1^* = 8.75$ and $u_2^* = 2.50$. The optimal value $V^* = 1,100$. Figure 7–2 shows graphically the feasible region and the corner points, while Figure 7–3 shows the computer software solution of the example problem.

ECONOMIC INTERPRETATION OF THE DUAL PROBLEM

The dual problem has numerous economic interpretations. They are

1. u_1, u_2 represents a kind of valuation of the resource (capacity) in question. This value is not a market price; rather, it is a value to be imputed to the resource. For this reason, the value of the dual variables is referred to as *shadow price* or *opportunity cost* for the resource. To put it another way, the shadow price is the *maximum price* the firm is willing to pay for an addi-

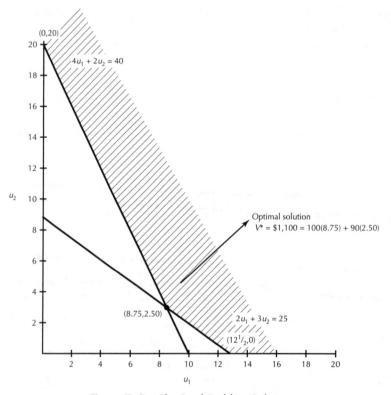

Figure 7–2. The Dual Problem Solutions

VARIABLE	VARIABLE VALUE	ORIGINAL COEFFICIENT	COEFFICIENT SENSITIVITY	
$X1$	20	25	0	Note: $X_1 = 20$
$X2$	15	40	0	$X_2 = 15$

CONSTRAINT NUMBER	ORIGINAL RHS	SLACK OR SURPLUS	SHADOW PRICE	
1	100	0	8.75	Note: $u_1 = \$\ 8.75$
1	90	0	2.50	$u_2 = \$\ 2.50$
				Note: $2 = \$1,100$

OBJECTIVE FUNCTION VALUE: 1,100

SENSITIVITY ANALYSIS

OBJECTIVE FUNCTION COEFFICIENTS

VARIABLE	LOWER LIMIT	ORIGINAL COEFFICIENT	UPPER LIMIT
$X1$	20	25	60
$X2$	16.67	40	50

RIGHT-HAND SIDE

CONSTRAINT NUMBER	LOWER LIMIT	ORIGINAL VALUE	UPPER LIMIT
1	60	100	180
2	50	90	150

Figure 7–3.   Computer Printout For LP

tional unit of a given resource. For example, in Examples 4 and 5, the maximum price the firm is willing to pay for an extra hour of the assembly capacity is $8.75, while it is only $2.50 for an extra hour of the finishing capacity. If the actual price is above the shadow price, the firm will not add an additional unit for that resource.

2. Turn next to the constraint in the dual. Let us examine the first constraint:

$2u_1 + 3\ u_2 \geq 25$. The right-hand-side term 25 denotes the per-unit profit or contribution margin of one desk, while 40 is for one table. Because two hours denotes the amount of time used in the assembly department by a desk and three hours denotes the amount of time required in the finishing department by a desk, the left-hand side represents the total opportunity cost of the production of one desk. Thus, what this constraint requires is that the opportunity costs of producing one desk be imputed at a level at least as large as the per-unit profit for the product.

3. Now look at the dual objective function, $V = 100u_1 + 90u_2$. V simply means the total value imputed to the total opportunity cost of the resources. Thus, the correspondence between the primal and the dual suggest that: to maxi-

mize total profit or contribution by finding the optimal output levels is tantamount to minimizing the total imputed value or opportunity cost of the firm's resources, with the proviso that the opportunity cost of production of each product must be no less than the contribution margin from the product.

4. Notice, however, that if the opportunity cost of production is actually to exceed the profit, the resource allocation must certainly be nonoptimal, because simply by dropping the corresponding product, resources will be released therefrom that can be immediately utilized to better advantage elsewhere. Let us check that.

$$2u_1 + 3\,u_2 \geq 25 \quad \text{(for desk)}$$
$$4u_1 + 2\,u_2 \geq 40 \quad \text{(for table)}$$

We know that the optimal solutions are: $u_1{}^* = 8.75$ and $u_2{}^* = 2.50$. Plugging these numbers into the constraints yields:

$$2(8.75) + 3\,(2.50) = 25 = 25 \text{ (for desk)}$$
$$4(8.75) + 2\,(2.50) = 40 = 40 \text{ (for table)}$$

It shows that the opportunity cost equals the profit for each product, so the resource allocation turns out to be optimal. This results in what we call a *complementary slackness condition.*

In a complementary slackness condition a pair of primal and dual feasible solutions are optimal to the respective problems if and only if, whenever a slackness in one problem is strictly positive, the corresponding nonnegative variable in the other problem is zero. More specifically:

- If a constraint of the primal is not binding (i.e., a slack exists), the shadow price of that constraint will be zero. If a constraint is binding (i.e., no slack exists), the shadow price will be positive.

- If a constraint of the dual is not binding (i.e., opportunity cost is greater than the per-unit profit), the primal variable will be zero. If a constraint is binding (i.e., opportunity cost is equal to the per-unit profit), the primal variable is positive.

Dual constraints	Primal variables
$2(8.75) + 3(2.50) = 25 = 25$ (for desk) $\rightarrow$	$x_1{}^* = 20 > 0$
$4(8.75) + 2(2.50) = 40 = 40$ (for table) $\rightarrow$	$x_2{}^* = 15 > 0$

Also,

Dual variables	Primal constraints
$u_1{}^* = 8.75 > 0 \rightarrow$	$2(20) + 4(15) = 100 = 100$
$u_2{}^* = 2.50 > 0 \rightarrow$	$3(20) + 2(15) = 90 = 90$

YOU SHOULD REMEMBER

1. In this example, both the primal and the dual constraints are binding (no slacks exist or opportunity cost exactly equal to the per-unit profit). Therefore, the optimal values of the primal and the dual are positive.

2. The shadow price is zero if the constraint is not binding, because it would do you no good to expand the capacity in an area where you are not using the full capacity that you already have.

---

5. The optimal solution values for the primal and the dual are the same. To prove: $Z^* = 25(20) + 40(15) = 1,100$ and $V^* = 100(8.75) + 90(2.50) = 1,100$, therefore $Z^* = V^* = \$1,100$.

ACTIVITY ANALYSIS AND SINGLE PRODUCT

The application of *LP* to production discussed in the previous section was concerned with multiple products. The problem dealt with determining the optimal combination of products (i.e., optimal product mix), given restrictions on the resources (inputs) employed in the production process. The focus of the analysis was on *output*—recall that the horizontal and vertical axes of the graphs measured the quantities of the respective products (outputs) and that resources (inputs) were represented only as a series of constraint lines on the outputs.

In what follows, we discuss an activity analysis that involves a single product. It concerns itself with choosing an optimal combination of production processes to be employed to produce the greatest quantity possible of a single product, given fixed amounts of certain inputs. Each of the processes is considered to be an activity. *LP* is also used to find the optimal solution. The focus of the analysis is on *inputs* and the alternative production processes within which the inputs can be employed to obtain the product. *LP* seeks to determine the optimal level of each activity. The theory of production (i.e., process rays, isoquants, and isoprofit curves) can be used to illustrate the alternative production processes and the concept of input substitution. We will first formulate and solve the output-maximization problem. The profit-maximization formulation will be taken up later.

FORMULATION OF THE OUTPUT-MAXIMIZATION PROBLEM

The following example illustrates how to formulate and solve the output-maximization problem.

Example 6

A leather-processing firm employs capital (units) and labor (units) in the dyeing of white suede leather. Three different production processes (A, B, and C) are available for its operation. Each process involves a different combination of labor and capital— process A requires 1 unit of capital and 4 units of labor, process B requires 2 units and 2 units, and process C requires 5 units and 1 unit. The firm's capacity is limited to 5 units of capital and 8 units of labor per day for this dyeing operation.

Define Q_A, Q_B, and Q_C, to be the quantity of dyed leather per day by processes A, B, and C, respectively. Given that the objective is to maximize output subject to the input (capital and labor) constraints, the problem can be formulated as an *LP* problem as follows:

$$\text{Maximize:} \quad Q = Q_A + Q_B + Q_C \qquad \text{(objective function),}$$
$$\text{Subject to} \quad Q_A + 2Q_B + 5Q_C \leq 5 \quad \text{(capital constraint),}$$
$$4Q_A + 2Q_B + Q_C \leq 8 \quad \text{(labor constraint),}$$
$$Q_A, Q_B, Q_C \geq 0 \quad \text{(nonnegativity constraint).}$$

GRAPHICAL APPROACH TO THE OUTPUT-MAXIMIZATION PROBLEM

The *LP* activity problem can be illustrated and solved graphically, using *process rays* to represent the production processes, *production isoquants* to represent the objective function, and a *feasible region* to represent the constraints.

• *PROCESS RAYS*

A production process is one in which the inputs are combined in *fixed proportions* to obtain the output. By this definition, a production process can be represented graphically as a ray through the origin having a slope equal to the ratio of the number of units of the respective resources required to produce one unit of output. In this example, the three production process rays are shown in Figure 7–4. Along ray *A*, the inputs are combined in the ratio of 4 units of labor to 1 unit of capital. Hence, ray *A* has a slope of 4. Similarly, along ray *B* the inputs are combined in the ratio of 2 units of labor to 2 units of capital. Process ray *C* shows the inputs combined in the ratio of 1 to 5.

Each production process is assumed to display constant returns to scale. This means that output along each ray increases proportionately with increases in the inputs. For example, points *D*, *G*, *J* represent the inputs needed to produce one, two, and three units of output.

• PRODUCTION ISOQUANTS

A production isoquant traces out the combinations of any two or more inputs that give rise to the same level of output. The isoquants are constructed by drawing straight lines between the points of equal output on adjacent process rays. Four isoquants, representing output levels *Q* of 1, 2, 3, and 4 respectively, are shown in Figure 7–4. They have parallel line segments between adjacent process rays. For example, line segment *DE* is parallel to *GH*, and line segment *EF* is parallel to *HI*. This occurs since the coefficients of the *Q* variables in the resource constraints are constants.

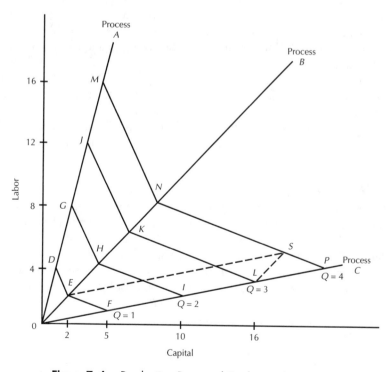

Figure 7–4. Production Rays and Production Isoquants

YOU SHOULD REMEMBER

The segment of an isoquant between two production process rays implies that a *combination* of the two processes is being used to produce that particular level of output.

As was indicated earlier, points along each process ray represent the output obtained if the two inputs (labor and capital) are combined in the ratio of the respective number of units of each resource required to produce a given unit of output. However, the points that lie on isoquants between adjacent process rays have a slightly different interpretation. These points represent a combination of output from each of the adjacent production processes. For example, point S on the "Q = 4" isoquant in Figure 7–4 represents a production combination using both processes B, and C. The quantity of output that is produced by each process can be obtained by constructing a parallelogram, such as the one shown in Figure 7–4. A line is drawn from point J parallel to process ray B, intersecting process ray C at point L. Another line is drawn from point S parallel to process ray B, intersecting process ray C at point D. From the parallelogram OESL, one can determine both the quantity of output produced by each process and the respective amount of inputs used in each process. The firm should produce one unit of output using B, since point E is on the "Q = 1" isoquant and three units of output using process C, since point L is on the "Q = 3" isoquant. This combination will yield the four units of output. At point E, 2 units of capital and 2 units of labor are used in process B; and at point L, 15 units of capital and 3 units of labor are used in process C. Total capital and labor resources used in producing the four units of output are 17 units and 5 units, respectively. All other points that lie between the process rays can be interpreted in a similar manner.

• *FEASIBLE REGION*

The feasible region consists of all the capital and labor input combinations that simultaneously satisfy all constraints of the *LP* problem. The shaded rectangle *OTRW* shown in Figure 7–5 represents the feasible region for the example problem. Since a maximum of 5 units of capital is available per day, only input combinations on or to the left of the *RW* line represent possible solutions to the *LP* problem. Similarly, since a maximum of 8 units of labor is available per day, possible solutions must lie on or below the *TR* line. Finally, the nonnegativity constraints preclude input combinations to the left of the *OT* line and below the *OW* line.

OPTIMAL SOLUTION

The combination of production processes that maximizes output subject to the resource constraints occurs at the point on the boundary of the feasible region that lies on the highest production isoquant. Figure 7–5 indicates that the optimal solution occurs at point R. At point R, three units of output are obtained by using 5 units of capital and 8 units of labor. Constructing the parallelogram $0DRH$ shows that one unit of output should be produced using process $A(Q_A = 1)$ and the remainder, two units in this case, using process B $(Q_B = 2)$.

Alternatively, from the graphical solution we see that output is maximized where $Q_C = 0$, when we substitute this into two constraint equations, we obtain

$$Q_A + 2Q_B = 5,$$
$$4Q_A + 2Q_B = 8,$$

and subtracting the second equation from the first, $-3Q_A = -3$ or $Q_A = 1$. We then can find $Q_B = 2$, which gives us the same solution we found graphically.

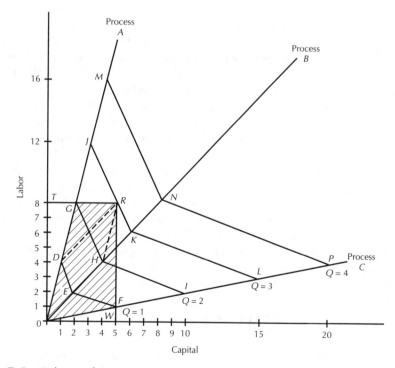

Figure 7–5. Solution of Output-Maximization Problem

PROFIT-MAXIMIZATION PROBLEM

The production problem can also be formulated as a profit-maximization problem.

Example 7

In Example 6, assume that the profit contribution of output produced by processes *A*, *B*, and *C* are $6, $5, and $4 per unit, respectively. Provided that the firm wishes to maximize profits (*Z*) instead of output (*Q*), the objective function becomes

Maximize: $Z = 6Q_A + 5Q_B + 4Q_C$.

An optimal solution to this profit-maximizing *LP* problem can be obtained and illustrated by *isoprofit* curves rather than isoquant curves.

ISOPROFIT CURVES

An isoprofit curve reflects the various combinations of products that a firm can sell to earn a given level of profit. It is constructed by drawing straight lines between the points on adjacent process rays having equal total profits. To illustrate, consider the "*Q* = 1" isoquant from Figure 7–5, which is labeled *MNF* in Figure 7–6. Let us say we want to develop an isoprofit curve corresponding to a profit of $4. Point *F* is clearly on this isoprofit curve, because one unit of output produced by process *C* yields a profit of $4. Point *N* also represents one unit of output. However, each unit of output produced by process *B* yields a profit of $5.

Therefore, the point on process ray *A* having profit of $4 must be $4 ÷ $5 = 80 percent of the distance from the origin (0) to point *N*. This corresponds to point *B*. Similarly, the point on process ray *A* having a profit of $4 must be $4 ÷ $6 = 67 percent of the distance from the origin (0) to point *M*. This occurs at point *D*. By connecting the points on adjacent process rays with straight-line segments, one obtains the "*Z* = $4" isoprofit curve. The profit curves corresponding to profits of $8, $12, and $16 are also shown in Figure 7–6. As with the production isoquants, the isoprofit curves have parallel line segments between adjacent process rays.

OPTIMAL SOLUTION

The combination of production processes that maximizes total profits subject to the resource constraints occurs at the point on the boundary of the feasible

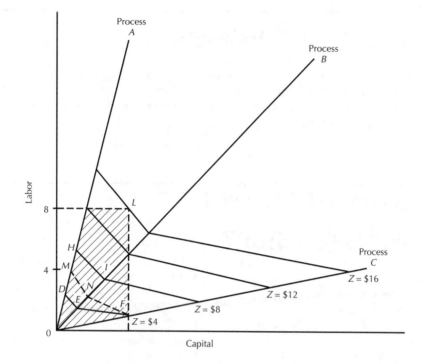

Figure 7–6. Solution of Profit-Maximization Problem

region that lies on the highest isoprofit curve. As shown in Figure 7–6, the optimal solution is a point L, which lies on the "$Z = \$16$" isoprofit curve. Recalling that this solution corresponds to point R in Figure 7–5, the firm should produce one leather using process A and two leathers using process B in order to maximize profits. Substituting these values for Q_A and Q_B, respectively ($Q_C = 0$), into the objective function, we obtain $\$16$ [$6Q_A + 5Q_B + 4Q_C = 6(1) + 5(2) + 4(0) = \$16$]. Alternatively, from the graphical solution we see that output is maximized where $Q_C = 0$, so we substitute this into two constraint equations, we obtain

$$Q_A + 2Q_B = 5,$$
$$4Q_A + 2Q_B = 8,$$

and subtracting the second equation from the first, $-3Q_A = -3$ or $Q_A = 1$. We then can find $Q_B = 2$, which gives us the same solution we found graphically.

YOU SHOULD REMEMBER

The production problem can be set up as a *cost-minimization LP* problem. The procedure for finding an optimal solution is basically the same, except that *isocost* curves are introduced to find the least-cost input combination, rather than isoprofit curves.

KNOW THE CONCEPTS

TERMS FOR STUDY

activity analysis
basic feasible solution
binding constraints
complementary slackness condition
constraints
dual problem
feasible solution
isoprofit curve

linear
linear programming
nonnegativity constraints
objective function
optimal solution
process ray
shadow price
slack variable

DO YOU KNOW THE BASICS?

1. What is linear programming? Why is it called linear?

2. List five popular applications of LP for business decisions.

3. What are the two ingredients of LP?

4. What is the economic meaning of the dual solution?

5. Compare LP, differential calculus, and the Lagrangean multiplier technique.

6. How does activity analysis differ from an optimal product mix problem?

7. What are two major computational methods of LP? Briefly describe the pro and con of each.

8. List three general properties associated with LP.

9. Explain the complementary slackness condition.

PRACTICAL APPLICATION

1. The Carson Company makes two products, X and Y. Their contribution margins are $50 and $90, respectively. Each product goes through three processes: cutting, finishing, and painting. The number of hours required by each process for each product and capacities available are given below:

Product	Hours Required in Each Process Cutting	Finishing	Painting
X	2	4	3
Y	1	6	2
Capacities in Hours	300	500	250

Formulate the objective function and constraints to determine the optimal product mix.

2. A company fabricates and assembles two products, A and B. It takes three minutes to fabricate each unit of A and six minutes to fabricate each unit of B. Assembly time per unit for product A is one minute and for product B, nine minutes. Six hundred minutes of fabrication time and 1,800 minutes of assembly time are available. The company makes a contribution margin of $2 on each unit of A it sells and $1 on each unit of B.

a. Express the problem as an LP model.

b. Solve this problem by the graphical method. What quantities of A and B should be produced in order to maximize profits? What will be the profits earned at these production levels?

3. Given the following primal, formulate its dual:

Maximize: $Z = 13x_1 + 40x_2$

Subject to: $2x_1 + 4x_2 \leq 6$

$x_1 + 2x_2 \leq 10$

$5x_1 + 2x_2 \leq 25$

$x_1, x_2 \geq 0$

4. The Zenico Chemical Company produces an industrial cleaner for carpets. This chemical is made from a mixture of two other chemicals that both contain cleaning agent LIM and cleaning agent LOOM. Their product must contain 175 units of agent LIM and 150 units of agent LOOM, and weigh at least 100 pounds. Chemical A costs $8 per pound, and chemical B costs $6 per pound. Chemical A contains one unit of agent LIM and three units of agent LOOM.

Chemical B contains seven units of agent LIM and one unit of agent LOOM. Set up the problem in the linear programming format, and solve it graphically.

5. Given the following data:

	Products		Available capacity (hours)
	1	2	
Machine 1	3	2	6
Machine 2	1/2	1	4
Revenue	$12	4	

a. Formulate this as an *LP* problem. Use x_1 and x_2 as decision variables.

b. Solve it graphically. What is the maximum revenue?

6. In Problem 5, do the following:

a. Set up the dual problem.

b. Solve the dual graphically.

7. In Problems 5 and 6,

a. Give an economic interpretation of the dual—for both the constraints and the objective function.

b. Illustrate the complementary slackness condition.

8. Given:

Maximize: $Z = \$50A + \$40B$

Subject to: $10A + 5B \leq 100$

$$2B \leq 30$$

$$A,B \leq 0$$

a. Solve the problem graphically.

b. Set up the dual.

c. Determine the shadow prices.

9. In the output-maximization problem (Example 6), assume that production resources are limited to 6 units of capital and 12 units of labor.

a. Formulate the problem algebraically as an *LP* problem.

b. Determine graphically the optimal amount of resources (capital and labor) to use in each of the production processes and the total output obtained.

ANSWERS

KNOW THE BASICS

1. Linear programming (*LP*) is a mathematical technique designed to determine an optimal decision (or an optimal plan) chosen from a large number of possible decisions. The optimal decision is the one that meets the specified objective of the company, subject to various restrictions or constraints. It is linear because we assume both the objective function and constraints are linear.

2. Six popular applications of *LP* are: selecting least-cost mix of ingredients for manufactured products; determining the most profitable mix of products; determining an optimal investment portfolio (or asset allocation); allocating an advertising budget to a variety of media; scheduling jobs to machines; determining a least-cost shipping pattern.

3. Two ingredients of *LP* are objective function and inequality constraints (including nonnegativity constraints).

4. The dual solution represents shadow prices or opportunity costs of resources to the firm. They are the *maximum prices* the firm is willing to pay for an additional unit of given resources. If the actual price is above the shadow price, the firm will not add an additional unit for that resource.

5. *LP* deals with constrained optimization problems with *linear* objective functions and *linear inequality* constraints, while differential calculus and the Lagrangean multiplier technique deal with problems involving *linear* or *nonlinear* objective functions and *equality* constraints.

6. Activity analysis involves a single product. It concerns itself with choosing an optimal combination of production processes to be employed to produce the greatest quantity possible of a single product, given fixed amounts of certain inputs. Each of the processes is considered to be an activity. *LP* is also used to find the optimal solution. The application of *LP* can also involve multiple products. The problem dealt with determining the optimal combination of products (i.e., optimal product mix), given restrictions on the resources (inputs) used in the production process.

7. Two major computational methods of *LP* are (1) the simplex method and (2) the graphical method. The simplex method is the technique most commonly used to solve *LP* problems. It is an algorithm, which is an iteration method of computation, to move from one solution to another until it reaches the best solution. The graphical approach is easier to use but limited to the *LP* problems involving two (or at most three) decision variables.

8. (a). The optimal solution lies on the boundary of the feasible region, which implies that one can ignore the (infinitely numerous) interior points of the feasible region when searching for an optimal solution. (b). The optimal solution occurs at one of the corner points (basic feasible solutions) of the feasible region. (c). The optimal solution values for the primal and the dual are the same.

9. A pair of primal and dual feasible solutions are optimal to the respective problems if, and only if, whenever a slackness in one problem is strictly positive, the corresponding nonnegative variable in the other problem is zero. More specifically, (1) if a constraint of the primal is not binding (i.e., a slack exists), the shadow price of that constraint will be zero. If a constraint is binding (i.e., no slack exists), the shadow price will be positive. (2) If a constraint of the dual is not binding (i.e., opportunity cost greater than the per-unit profit), the primal variable will be zero. If a constraint is binding (i.e., opportunity cost equal to the per-unit profit), the primal variable is positive.

PRACTICAL APPLICATION

1. Let X = Number of units of product X to be produced

Y = Number of units of product Y to be produced

Then, the *LP* formulation is as follows:

Maximize: $Z = \$50X + \$90Y$

Subject to: $2X + 1Y \le 300$

$4X + 6Y \le 500$

$3X + 2Y \le 250$

$X, Y \quad \ge 0$

2a. Let A = Number of units of product A to produce

Let B = Number of units of product B to produce

Maximize: $Z = \$2A + \$1B$

Subject to: $3A + 6B \le 600$ (fabrication)

$1A + 9B \le 1,800$ (assembly)

$A, B \ge 0$

2b. 1. $A = 0$ $B = 100$ $Z = \$100$

     2. $A = 200$ $B = 0$ $Z = \$400$

Thus, 200 units of A should be produced and no units of B. Profit will be $400 at this level.

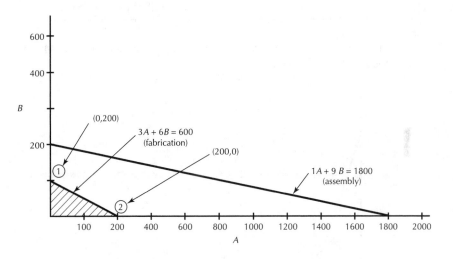

3. There are three dual variables since there are three constraints in the primal, $u_1, u_2,$ and u_3

Minimize $V = 6u_1 + 10u_2 + 25u_3$

Subject to: $2u_1 + u_2 + 5u_3 \geq 13$

             $4u_1 + 2u_2 + 2u_3 \geq 40$

             $u_1, u_2, u_3 \quad\quad \geq 0$

4. Define A = Number of pounds of chemical A to be produced

          B = Number of pounds of chemical B to be produced

Then, the *LP* formulation of this cost minimization problem is

Minimize: $\$8A + \$6B$

Subject to: $A + 7B \geq 175$

           $3A + B \geq 150$

           $A + B \geq 100$

           $A, B \geq 0$

The basic feasible solutions occur at the corner points labeled a, b, c, and d.

Basic Feasible Solutions	Cost = $8A + $6B
a. A = 0, B = 150	($8)(0) + ($6)(150) = $900
b. A = 25, B = 75	($8)(25) + ($6)(75) = $650
c. A = 87.5, B = 12.5	($8)(87.5) + ($6)(12.5) = $775
d. A = 175, B = 0	($8)(175) + ($6)(0) = $1,400

Therefore, the least-cost mixture of the two chemicals A and B is: $A =$ 25 pounds, $B = 75$ pounds.

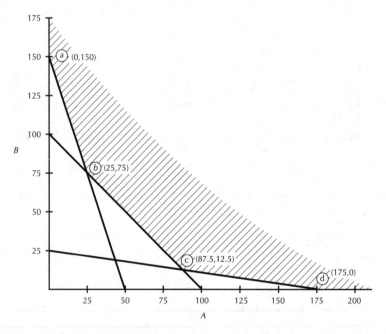

5a. Maximize: $Z = 12x_1 + 4x_2$

Subject to: $3x_1 + 2x_2 \le 6$

$$1/2x_1 + x_2 \le 4$$

$$x_1, x_2 \ge 0$$

5b. The following shows $x_1{}^* = 2$, $x_2{}^* = 0$, and $Z^* = 24$.

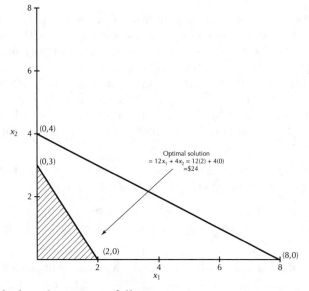

6a. The dual can be set up as follows:

Minimize $V = 6u_1 + 4u_2$

$$3u_1 + 1/2u_2 \geq 12$$

$$2u_1 + u_2 \geq 4$$

$$u_1, u_2 \geq 0$$

6b. The optimal solutions to the dual are: $u_1{}^* = 4$, $u_2{}^* = 0$, and $V^* = 24$.

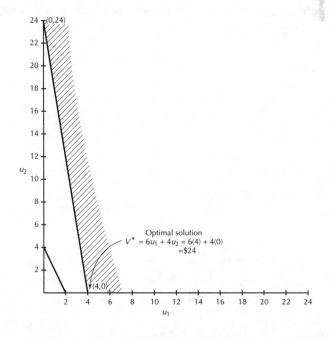

7a. $u_1^* = \$4$, which means an hour of time of Machine 1 has an implicit value of \$4. The actual cost of renting an additional capacity of Machine 1 may be greater or less than \$4. If it is less (say, \$3), the company should consider renting some additional capacity of Machine, since for each additional hour of available capacity that is rented, the return is \$1 (\$4 − \$3), an incremental gain of \$1. (This is true only until the solution mix changes). $u_2^* = 0$, which means time on Machine 2 is like a free good. An additional hour on Machine 2 would not increase revenue of the company. Note also that $Z^* = V^* = \$24$.

7b. We know that the optimal solutions are: $x_1^* = 2$, $x_2^* = 0$, and $Z^* = 24$. Substituting these optimal values into each of the constraints yields

for Machine 1: $3(2) + 2(0) = 6 = 6$. That is, this constraint is binding (or no slack or unused capacity exists, so that the shadow price for this constraint is positive ($u_1^* = 4 > 0$)

for Machine 2: $1/2(2) + (0) = 1 \le 4$, which means there exists three hours of Machine capacity and hence, this constraint is a free good ($u_2^* = 0$).

The complementary slackness condition states:

1. If a constraint of the primal is not binding (i.e., a slack exists), the shadow price of that constraint (u_2 in this problem) will be zero. If a constraint is binding (i.e., no slack exists), the shadow price will be positive ($u_1^* > 0$).

2. If a constraint of the dual is not binding (i.e., opportunity cost greater than the per-unit profit), the primal variable (x_2^* in this problem) will be zero. If a constraint is binding (i.e., opportunity cost equal to the per-unit profit), the primal variable is positive ($x_1^* > 0$).

8a.

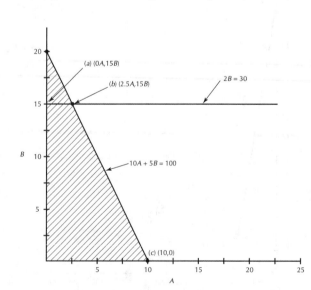

The basic feasible solutions occur at the corner points labeled (*a*), (*b*), and (*c*).

Basic Feasible Solutions	$Z = \$50A + \$40B$
(a) $A = 0$, $B = 15$	$\$50(0) + \$40(15) = \$600$
(b) $A = 2.5$, $B = 15$	$\$50(2.5) + \$40(15) = \$725$
(c) $A = 10$, $B = 0$	$\$50(10) + \$40(0) = \$500$

The point *b* ($A = 2.5$, $B = 15$) is the optimal solution and $Z^* = \$725$

8b. The dual can be set up as follows:

Minimize $V = \quad 100u_1 + 30u_2$

$$10u_1 \geq 50$$

$$5u_1 + 2u_2 \geq 40$$

$$u_1, u_2 \geq 0$$

8c. To find the shadow prices, we solve the dual problem graphically as follows:

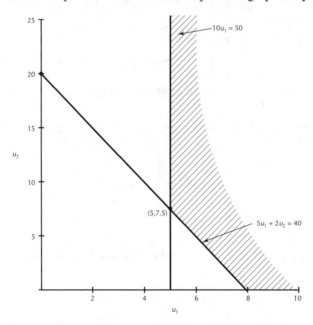

($u_1^* = 5$, $u_2^* = 7.5$) are the shadow prices and $V^* = \$725$.

9a. Maximize: $Q = Q_A + Q_B + Q_C$. (objective function)

Subject to: $Q_A + 2Q_B + 5Q_C \leq 6$ (capital constraint)

$4Q_A + 2Q_B + Q_C \leq 12$ (labor constraint)

$Q_A, Q_B, Q_C \geq 0$ (nonnegativity constraint)

9b.

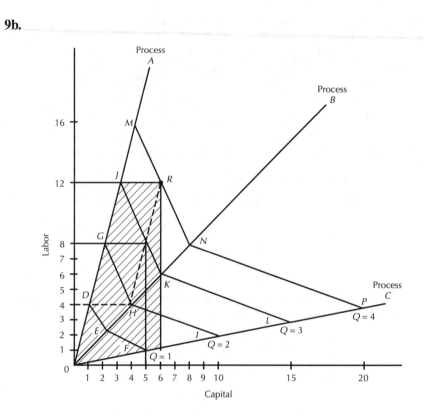

From the graphical solution we see that output is maximized where $Q_C = 0$, so we substitute this into two constraint equations, we obtain

$$Q_A + 2Q_B = 6$$
$$4Q_A + Q_B = 12$$

and subtracting the second equation from the first, $-3Q_A = -6$ or $Q_A = 2$. We then can find $Q_B = 2$, which gives us the same solution we found graphically.

8

COST ANALYSIS

KEY TERMS

short-run cost curves cost curves for which inputs of production are both variable and fixed.

total variable costs costs that vary in total in direct proportion to changes in activity.

total fixed costs costs that remain constant in total regardless of changes in activity.

average variable cost (*AVC*) total variable cost divided by the corresponding number of units of output.

long-run average cost curve curve showing the minimum cost per unit of producing each output when all resource inputs are variable.

planning (envelope) curve locus of points representing the least unit cost of producing the corresponding output.

statistical cost analysis empirical studies that attempt to ascertain the nature of short-run or long-run cost/output relations.

incremental (differential) costs costs associated with any managerial decision. This is equivalent to the marginal cost concept but involves multiple changes in output and discrete output choices, rather than a single-unit change.

sunk costs costs of resources that have already been incurred at some point in the past whose total will not be affected by any decision made now or in the future.

relevant costs expected future costs (and also revenues) that differ between the decision alternatives.

learning curve effect reduction in labor hours as the cumulative production doubles, ranging typically from 10 percent to 20 percent.

break-even point level of total revenue that equals the total of the variable and fixed costs for a given volume of output at a particular capacity use rate.

unit contribution margin selling price minus average variable cost.

operating leverage measure of operating risk; the ratio of a percentage change in operating income to a percentage change in sales volume.

The costs of goods and services derive from the character of the process by which they are produced. The analysis of cost behavior is founded, therefore, upon the principles of production. This chapter translates the relationships among production technology, inputs, and outputs into cost functions. The fundamental starting point in cost analysis is that a functional relationship exists between the costs of production and the rate of output per period of time.

COST FUNCTIONS

A cost function shows the various costs that will be incurred at various output levels, i.e.,

$$\text{Cost} = f(\text{output}).$$

Further, the rate of output is, in turn, a function of the usage of the resource inputs:

$$\text{Output} = f(\text{inputs}).$$

Since the production function displays the relationships between input and output flows, once the prices of the inputs are known, the costs of a specific quantity of output can be determined.

As a result, the level and behavior of costs as a firm's rate of output changes relies heavily on two factors: (1) the characteristic of the underlying production function and (2) the prices paid for the inputs. The first determines the shape of the firm's cost functions, while the second decides the level of costs. In the short run, at least one input is fixed, so a firm may not be able to achieve the best combination of inputs for its desired level of output. Because of the presence of both fixed and variable costs in the short run, we can identify seven different types of short-run cost curves: total fixed cost, total variable cost, total cost, average fixed cost, average variable cost, average total cost, and marginal cost.

THE SET OF TOTAL COST CONCEPTS

Three concepts of total cost are important for analysis of a firm's cost structure in the short run: total fixed cost (*TFC*), total variable cost (*TVC*), and total cost (*TC*).

Total fixed cost (*TFC*) is simply the sum of the quantities of the fixed inputs multiplied by their associated prices. In the short run the level of total fixed costs is a constant. Similarly, total variable cost (*TVC*) is the sum of the amounts a firm spends for each of the variable inputs employed in the production process. Total variable cost is zero when output is zero, because no variable inputs need be employed to produce nothing. However, as output expands, the greater becomes the usage of variable inputs and the greater is total variable cost.

The total cost (*TC*) of a given level of output in the short run is the sum of total variable cost and total fixed cost:

$$TC = TVC + TFC.$$

*TVC*s are costs that vary in total in direct proportion to changes in activity. Examples are direct materials and gasoline expense based on mileage driven. *TFC*s are costs that remain constant in total regardless of changes in activity. Examples are rent, insurance, and taxes.

THE SET OF UNIT COST CONCEPTS

There are four major unit cost concepts: average fixed cost (*AFC*), average variable cost (*AVC*), average total cost (*ATC*), and marginal cost (*MC*). All of these may be derived from the total cost concepts discussed above.

Average variable cost (*AVC*) is total variable cost divided by the corresponding number of units of output, or

$$AVC = \frac{TVC}{Q}.$$

Average fixed cost (*AFC*) is defined as total fixed cost divided by the units of output, or

$$AFC = \frac{TFC}{Q}.$$

Since total fixed cost is a constant amount, average fixed cost declines continuously as the rate of production increases.

Example 1

If TFC = \$1,000, at an output of 10 units AFC = \$1,000/10 = \$100; at an output of 20 units AFC = \$1000/20 = \$50; at an output of 50 units AFC = \$1000/50 = \$20; and so on.

The reduction of AFC by producing more units of output is what businesspeople commonly call spreading the overhead.

Average total cost (ATC) is defined as total cost divided by the corresponding units of output, or

$$ATC = \frac{TC}{Q}.$$

However, since $TC = TFC + TVC$,

$$ATC = \frac{TC}{Q} = \frac{TVC + TFC}{Q} = \frac{TVC}{Q} + \frac{TFC}{Q} = AVC + AFC.$$

Graphically, ATC is U-shaped because the AVC is an increasing function, while the AFC is a continuously decreasing function of output.

MARGINAL COST

Marginal cost (MC) is the cost of producing an additional unit of output. For example, the marginal cost of the 500th unit of output can be calculated by finding the difference in total cost at 499 units of output and total cost at 500 units of output. MC is, thus, the additional cost of one more unit of output. MC is also the change in total variable cost associated with a unit change in output. This is because total cost changes, whereas total fixed cost remains unchanged. MC may also be thought of as the rate of change in total cost as the quantity (Q) of output changes and is simply the first derivative of the total cost (TC) function. Thus,

$$MC = \frac{\Delta TC}{\Delta Q} = \frac{dTC}{dQ}.$$

Economists normally assume firms to be producing at a point at which marginal costs are positive and rising. In managerial applications of this concept, MC is viewed as being equivalent to incremental cost, which is the increment in cost between the two alternatives or two discrete volumes of output.

YOU SHOULD REMEMBER

1. *AFC* is inversely related to the average product (*AP*) of the *fixed* inputs.

2. *AVC* is inversely related to the average product (*AP*) of the *variable* inputs.

3. *MC* is inversely related to the marginal product (*MP*) of added units of *variable* inputs.

If *L* is variable input and *w* = its wage, then $AVC = w/AP_L$; $MC = w/MP_L$.

STAGES OF PRODUCTION AND SHORT-RUN COST CURVES

Figure 8–1 displays the relationship between a production function and the corresponding short-run total and unit cost curves. The shape of the total cost curve is determined entirely by the *TVC* curve, since fixed costs merely shift the total cost curve to a higher level. This means that marginal costs are totally independent of fixed costs.

The *TVC* curve increases at a decreasing rate over the range of output where increasing returns to variable input prevail (0 to Q_1). Over the range of output where decreasing returns to variable input are encountered (Q_1 to Q_2) the *TVC* curve increases at an increasing rate. The explanation for this behavior of *TVC* rests with the principle of diminishing marginal returns (*DMR*). Where the quantity of output increases at an increasing rate, marginal product (*MP*) is also increasing and smaller and smaller increases in variable inputs are required to produce successive units of output. This means that *TVC* will increase by progressively smaller amounts as output rises. But when the point of *DMR* is encountered and *MP* starts to decline, it becomes necessary to use larger and larger amounts of variable input to obtain equal increments of output. *TVC*, therefore, increases at an increasing rate over this output range.

The *AFC* curve decreases continually as the quantity of output increases. Geometrically speaking, the *AFC* curve is a rectangular hyperbola, meaning that the curve approaches the vertical and horizontal axes asymptotically. In addition, were we to pick any point on the *AFC* curve, draw lines perpendicular to the two axes, and calculate the area of the resulting rectangle, this area will be the same irrespective of the point chosen, because this area measures $AFC \times Q$, which is equal to *TFC*, a constant value.

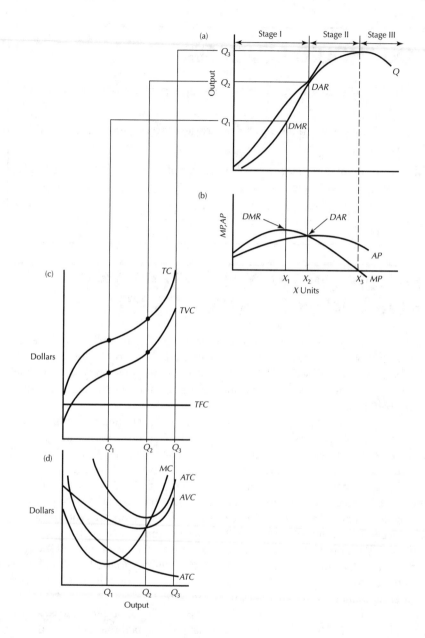

Figure 8–1. Production Functions and Cost Curves

The AVC curve is U-shaped because of its inverse relationship with the average product (AP). When AP is rising, AVC must be falling, and when AP is declining AVC must be rising. Minimum AVC (an output of Q_2) corresponds to the output where AP is maximum (X_2 units of variable input). It is at this output that the point of diminishing average returns (DAR) is encountered and the Stage II phase of production begins. Thus, Stage I levels of output correspond to the output range where AVC is declining, whereas Stage II quantities correspond to the range of output where AVC is rising.

The shape of the ATC curve is obtained by vertically summing the AFC and AVC curves at each output. Because AFC decreases as output expands, the distance between ATC and AVC gets progressively smaller. Thus, the ATC curve is asymptotic to the AVC curve and is U-shaped. ATC continues to fall beyond the output where AVC is minimum, because the continuing declines in AFC more than offset the slight increases in AVC. As output expands further, however, the increases in AVC begin to override the decreases in AFC and ATC turns upward. The minimum point on the ATC curve defines the most efficient output in the short run.

The curvature of the MC function reflects its inverse relationship with MP: So long as MP is rising, MC must be declining. But when diminishing marginal returns set in, MC begins to rise. Hence, assuming a constant price for variable input, increasing returns to variable input result in declining marginal costs and decreasing returns are associated with rising marginal costs. Marginal cost is minimum at the point of DMR where MP is maximum.

Note: In Fig. 8–1, panels (a) and (b) display the set of production function curves corresponding to the three stages of production. Panel (c) represents the corresponding family of total cost functions. Panel (d) shows the shapes of and relationships among various unit cost curves.

Furthermore, the MC curve intersects the AVC and ATC curves at their minimum points—a relationship of mathematical necessity. When the cost of producing an additional unit is less than the average total cost of the previously produced units, the newly computed ATC will fall, being pulled down by the lower MC. Similarly, when the cost of producing an additional unit is greater than the average total cost of the preceding units, the new value of ATC rises, being pulled up by the higher value of MC. It follows that ATC is minimum at the point of intersection of MC and ATC. By analogous reasoning the MC curve must pass through the minimum point of the AVC function. Figure 8–2 illustrates short-run cost curves.

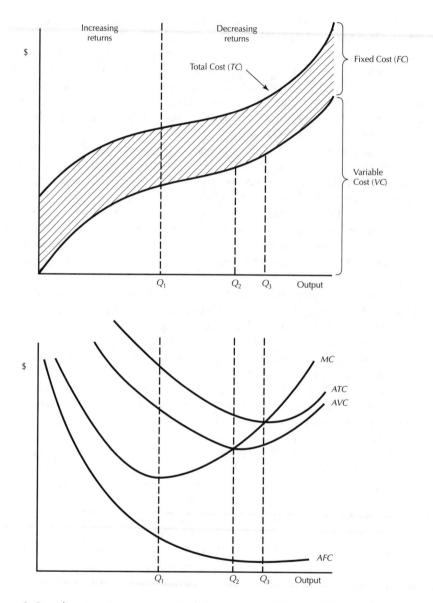

Figure 8–2. Short-Run Cost Curves: Total, Average, and Marginal Costs Relationship

---

YOU SHOULD REMEMBER

1. The average-marginal relationship is the graphical relationship between corresponding average and marginal curves. The relationship is the following: (a) when an average curve (AC) is rising, its corresponding marginal curve (MC) lies above it, (b) when an AC is falling, its corresponding MC lies below, and (c) when an AC is either at a maximum or minimum, its corresponding MC equals AC.

2. Average costs tend to be *U-shaped*.

3. The symbols AC and ATC are used interchangeably.

LONG-RUN COST CURVES— PLANNING CURVES

In the long run, the firm has complete input flexibility; therefore, all resource inputs are variable. There are no total or average fixed costs in the long run since no inputs are fixed, and the discussion of unit costs can be limited to just average costs.

Generally, a firm's long-run cost objective is to be in a position to produce the desired output at the lowest possible cost. This means adjusting its scale of production so as to be "the right size." Sometimes economies can be attained by dividing the production process into smaller production units. Other times, lower unit costs can be achieved by enlarging the scale of production. In examining how efficiency and costs are affected by the scale of production, it is important to distinguish between plants and firms, because the cost efficiency advantages and disadvantages of each are different. Because there are no *TFC* and *AFC* curves, we need look only at the nature and shape of the *long-run average cost (LRAC)* curve.

Suppose technological constraints allow a firm the choice of contracting any one of three plant sizes: small, medium, and large. The *short-run average cost (SRAC)* curve for each of these plant sizes is represented by $SRAC_S$, $SRAC_M$, and $SRAC_L$ in Figure 8–3. Whatever size plant the firm has currently, in the long run it can convert to or construct any one of these three plant scales. Certainly, the firm's choice of plant size is tailored by its perceived need for future production capacity. For example, if the anticipated output rate is $0Q_1$, the firm should elect to build the small-sized plant since it can produce $0Q_1$ units of output per period of time at a cost of AC_1, which is well below either the unit cost of the medium-sized plant (AC_2) or the unit cost of the large-sized plant (AC_3). If the expected output rate is $0Q_2$, the medium-sized plant plainly offers the lowest unit cost. On the other hand, at an output of $0Q_3$ the medium- and large-sized plants are equally efficient from a unit cost standpoint.

The portions of the three short-run average cost curves that are fitting for selecting the optimum plant size are indicated by the solid, scalloped line in Figure 8–3. This line is called the *long-run average cost curve (LRAC)* and shows the minimum cost per unit of producing each output when all resource inputs are variable and any desired scale of plant can be built. The broken line segments of the *SRAC* curves all entail higher unit costs than are capable of being achieved by operating along the *LRAC* curve.

In reality, a firm will have more than just three plant sizes to choose from. When the number of alternative plant sizes approaches infinity, the *LRAC* curve is an "envelope" of the short-run curves and is tangent to each of the short-run average cost curves. This curve is the solid portion of each *SRAC* curve and is called the *envelope* or *planning curve.*

The *LRAC* curve for a firm shows the minimum average cost of producing a product for various firm sizes when the firm has adequate time to adjust any and all of its inputs to optimal levels. By and large, the *LRAC* curves for both plants and firms are U-shaped. The U-shape clearly implies that up to some output, being bigger can mean greater efficiency and lower unit cost, but beyond this output larger plants and firms are less efficient and entail higher unit costs.

The factors causing larger plants to be more efficient than smaller plants include (1) more opportunity for specialization in the use of resource inputs; (2) the fact that the most advanced and efficient technology is practical only when producing large volumes of output; (3) the greater ability of larger plants to take advantage of and utilize by-products; (4) the greater opportunities for larger plants to make volume purchases of raw materials and thereby realize quantity discounts; and (5) the proportionately lower costs of purchasing and installing larger machines and equipment. However, sooner or later economies of scale will be exhausted and increases in plant size will result in diseconomies of scale due to growing difficulties of maintaining efficient supervision and coordination and the bottlenecks and costs of transporting materials, labor, and goods from place to place within the plant.

YOU SHOULD REMEMBER

1. *SRAC* curves relate costs and output for a specified scale of plant, while *LRAC* curves identify optimal scales of plant for each production level.

2. The behavior of long-run costs is a key force in determining the number and size of firms in a particular industry. Generally speaking, where there are significant economies associated with mass-production technologies, the structure of an industry will consist of a small number of large-scale producers. When there are few cost advantages to producing in large quantities and many cost disadvantages, production units will be large in number and small in size.

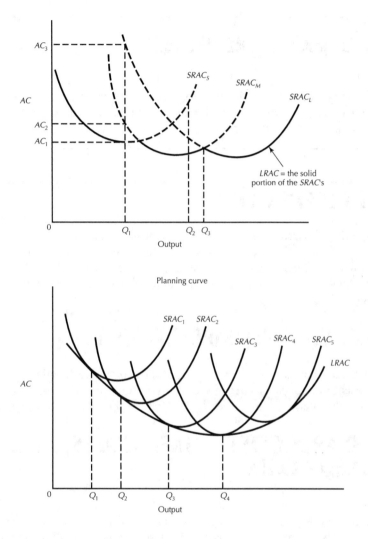

Figure 8–3.   The Long-Run Average Cost Curve (*LRAC*)

STATISTICAL COST ANALYSIS

Firms attempt to ascertain the nature of short-run or long-run cost/output relations. Cost curves are estimated via statistical techniques, such as *regression analysis*, based on *time-series* or *cross-sectional* data. Three types of functions—linear, quadratic, and cubic—especially the first two, have been most commonly employed in fitting statistical cost functions. The choice of one of them depends largely on the extent to which the mathematical properties of the function represent the economics of the particular case.

YOU SHOULD REMEMBER

Although cost and production are clearly related, the nature of input prices must be examined before any cost function can be related to the underlying production function. Input prices and productivity jointly determine cost functions.

TYPES OF COSTS

In accounting, the term "cost" is defined as a measurement, in monetary terms, of the amount of resources used for some purpose. In economics, the term "cost" is used in many different ways. Costs can be classified by criteria such as by behavior. Many of the cost concepts are useful for managerial decision making and planning.

EXPLICIT AND IMPLICIT COSTS

Explicit costs or *out-of-pocket costs* are costs involving cash outlays, while implicit costs or *opportunity costs* are costs that do not involve cash outlays and arise from the alternative use.

VARIABLE COSTS, FIXED COSTS, AND MIXED COSTS

From a managerial standpoint, perhaps the most important way to classify costs is by how they behave in accordance with changes in volume or some measure of activity. By behavior, costs can be classified into the following three basic categories: variable, fixed, and mixed (semivariable) costs. Variable and fixed costs were defined previously. *Mixed* (or *semivariable*) costs are costs that vary with changes in volume but, unlike variable costs, do not vary in direct proportion. In other words, these costs contain both a variable component and a fixed component. Examples are the rental of a delivery truck, where a fixed rental fee plus a variable charge based on mileage is made; and power costs, where the expense consists of a fixed amount plus a variable charge based on consumption. The breakdown of costs into their variable components and their fixed components is important in many areas of economics, such as break-even analysis, and short-term decision making.

OPPORTUNITY COSTS

Opportunity costs are the net revenue foregone by rejecting the best alternative use of resources, such as time, money, or facilities. It is perhaps the most fundamental concept in economics, since it stresses the fact that all resources are generally limited and have alternative uses. For example, assume a company has a choice of using its capacity to produce an extra 10,000 units or renting it out for $20,000. The opportunity cost of using that capacity is $20,000. A further example is the return foregone from having money tied up in accounts receivable for a longer time because of a collection problem. If the extra funds tied up in receivables were $400,000 for a three-month period and the firm could earn 10% per annum, the opportunity cost is $10,000 ($400,000 $\times$ 3/12 $\times$ 10%).

OUT-OF-POCKET (OUTLAY) COSTS

Out-of-pocket (outlay) costs are expenditures by cash to carry on a particular activity. They are the explicit costs that go into a firm's formal accounting records to arrive at a measure of earnings, such as actual cash outlays made during the period for payroll, advertising, and other operating expenses. Depreciation is not an out-of-pocket cost, since it involves no current cash expenditure.

SUNK COSTS

Sunk costs are the costs of resources that have already been incurred at some point in the past whose total will not be affected by any decision made now or in the future. Sunk costs are usually *past* or *historical* costs. Sunk costs are, therefore, not relevant to future decisions. For example, suppose you acquired a machine for $50,000 three years ago that has a book value of $20,000. The $20,000 book value is a sunk cost that does not affect a future replacement decision.

INCREMENTAL (DIFFERENTIAL) COSTS

Incremental (differential) costs are costs associated with any managerial decision. This is equivalent to the marginal cost concept but involves multiple changes in output and discrete output choices rather than a single-unit change.

SHUTDOWN COSTS

Shutdown costs are those costs that would be incurred in the event of a temporary suspension of activities and that could be saved if operations are allowed to continue. The concept is important because of an economic principle that as long as a firm is at least covering its *variable costs,* it will not discontinue operations in the short run since any surplus, known as *contribution margin,* will be applied to the recovery of its *fixed cost.*

INCREMENTAL ANALYSIS VERSUS MARGINAL ANALYSIS

Incremental analysis is frequently used in the practical equivalent of marginal analysis. It relates to a specified managerial decision that can involve a choice between two discrete quantities of output (e.g., 10,000 units vs. 15,000 units). It is the process of examining the impact of alternative choice decisions on revenue, cost, or profit. It focuses attention on changes or differences between alternatives. Managers will have to weigh the incremental cost associated with the decision against the incremental revenue. For this reason, marginal analysis is more appropriately called *incremental analysis.* Not all costs are of equal importance in decision making, and economists must identify these costs that are *relevant* to a decision.

RELEVANT COSTS

In many business decision situations, the ultimate management decision rests on cost data analysis. Cost data are important in many decisions, because they are the basis for profit calculations. Cost data are classified by behavior patterns, and other criteria, as discussed previously.

However, not all costs are of equal importance in decision making, and managers must identify the costs that are relevant to a decision. Such costs are called relevant costs. The relevant costs are the expected future costs (and also revenues) that differ between the decision alternatives. Therefore, sunk costs (past and historical costs) are not considered relevant in the decision at hand. What is relevant are the *incremental* (or *differential*) costs.

Under the concept of relevant costs, which may be appropriately titled the incremental, differential, or relevant cost approach, the decision involves the following steps:

1. Gather all costs associated with each alternative.

2. Drop the sunk costs.

3. Drop those costs that do not differ between alternatives.

4. Select the best alternative based on the remaining cost data.

Example 2

To illustrate the irrelevance of sunk costs and the relevance of incremental costs, let us consider a replacement decision problem. A company owns a milling machine that was purchased three years ago for $25,000. Its present book value is $17,500. The company is contemplating replacing this machine with a new one that will cost $50,000 and have a five-year useful life. The new machine will generate the same amount of revenue as the old one but will substantially cut down on variable operating costs. Annual sales and operating costs of the present machine and the proposed replacement are based on normal sales volume of 20,000 units and are estimated as follows:

	Present Machine	New Machine
Sales	$60,000	$60,000
Variable Costs	35,000	20,000
Fixed Costs:		
Depreciation (straight-line)	2,500	10,000
Insurance, Taxes, etc.	4,000	4,000
Net Income	$18,500	$26,000

At first glance, it appears that the new machine provides an increase in net income of $7,500 per year. The book value of the present machine, however, is a sunk cost and is irrelevant in this decision. Furthermore, sales and fixed costs, such as insurance, taxes, and others, also are irrelevant because they do not differ between the two alternatives being considered. Eliminating all the irrelevant costs leaves us with only the incremental costs, as follows.

Savings in variable costs	$15,000
Less: Increase in Fixed Costs	10,000 *
Net Annual Cash Saving Arising from the New Machine	$5,000
*exclusive of $2,500 sunk cost	

The relevant cost approach assists managers in making important decisions, such as whether to accept a below-normal selling price, which products to emphasize, whether to make or buy, whether to sell or process further, how to formulate a bid price on a contract, and how to optimize utilization of capacity. Table 8–1 summarizes guidelines for typical short-term decisions.

Table 8–1.   Decision Guidelines

Decision	Description	Decision Guidelines
• Special order	Should a discount-priced order be accepted when there is idle capacity?	If regular orders are not affected, accept order when the revenue from the order exceeds the incremental cost. Fixed costs are usually irrelevant.
• Make or buy	Should a part be made or bought from a vendor?	Choose lower-cost option. Fixed costs are usually irrelevant. Often opportunity costs are present.
• Closing a segment	Should a segment be dropped?	Compare loss in contribution margin with savings in fixed costs.
• Sell or process	Should joint products be sold at split off or processed further?	Ignore joint costs. Process further if incremental revenue exceeds incremental cost.
• Scarce resources	Which products should be emphasized when capacity is limited?	Emphasize products with highest contribution margin (CM) per unit of scarce resource (e.g., CM per machine hour).

LEARNING CURVE

In manufacturing, labor hours are often observed to decrease in a definite pattern as labor operations are repeated. More specifically, as the cumulative production doubles, the cumulative average time required per unit will be reduced by some constant percentage, ranging typically from 10 percent to 20 percent. This reduction, and hence related costs, is referred to as the *learning curve effect*.

By convention, learning curves are referred to in terms of the complements of their improvement rates. For example, an 80 percent learning curve denotes a 20 percent decrease in unit time with each doubling of repetitions.

Example 3

Suppose that a project is known to have an 80 percent learning curve. It has just taken a laborer 10 hours to produce the first unit. Then each time the cumulative output doubles, the time per unit for that amount should be equal to the previous time multiplied by the learning percentage. An 80 percent learning curve is shown in Figure 8–4.

Unit	Unit time (hours)
1	10
2	0.8(10) = 8
4	0.8(8) = 6.4
8	0.8(6.4) = 5.12
16	0.8(5.12) = 4.096

The learning curve model is as follows:

$$y_n = a\, n^{-b},$$

where y_n = Time for the nth unit,

a = Time for the first unit (in this example, 10 hours),

b = The index of the rate of increase in productivity during learning (log learning rate %/log 2)

To be able to utilize linear regression, we need to convert this power (or exponential) function form into a linear form by taking a log of both sides, which yields

$$\log y_n = \log a - b \log n.$$

The learning rate, which is indicated by b, is estimated using *least-squares regression* with the sample data on y and n. Note that

$$b = \frac{\log (\text{learning rate})}{\log 2},$$

which means

$$\log (\text{learning rate}) = b \times \log 2.$$

The unit time (i.e., the number of labor hours required) for the nth can be computed using the estimated model:

$$y_n = a\, n^{-b}.$$

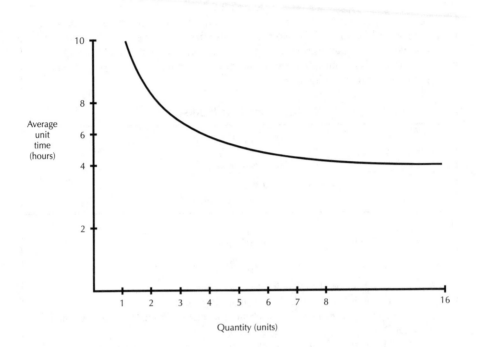

Figure 8–4. An 80% Learning Curve

YOU SHOULD REMEMBER

This learning phenomenon is observed in the behavior of labor and labor driven overhead. Material costs per unit may also be subject to this effect if less scrap and waste occur as a result of learning.

Example 4

For an 80 percent curve with $a = 10$ hours, the time for the third unit would be computed as:

$$y_3 = 10 \, (3^{-log\ 0.8/\ log\ 2}) = 10 \, (3^{-0.3219}) = 7.02.$$

Fortunately, it is not necessary to grid through this model each time a learning calculation is made; values can be found using Table 7 (*Learning Curve Coefficients*) in the Appendix. The time for the nth unit can be quickly determined by multiplying the table value by the time required for the first unit.

Example 5

NB Contractors, Inc. is negotiating a contract involving the production of 20 jets. The initial jet requires 200 labor days of direct labor. Assuming an 80 percent learning curve, we will determine the expected number of labor days for (1) the 20th jet, and (2) all 20 jets as follows:

Using Table 7 with $n = 20$ and an 80 percent learning rate, we find: Unit = 0.381 and Total = 10,485. Therefore,

1. Expected time for the 20th jet = 200 (0.381) = 76.2 labor days.

2. Expected total time for all 20 jets = 200(10.485) = 2,097 labor days.

YOU SHOULD REMEMBER

The learning curve theory has found useful applications in many areas, including:

1. Budgeting, purchasing, and inventory planning
2. Scheduling labor requirements
3. Setting incentive wage rates
4. Pricing new products
5. Negotiated purchasing
6. Evaluating suppliers' price quotations

Example 6 illustrates the use of the learning curve theory for the pricing of a contract.

Example 6

Big Mac Electronics Products, Inc. finds that new product production is affected by an 80 percent learning effect. The company has just produced 50 units of output at 100 hours per unit. Costs were as follows:

Materials—50 units @$20	$1,000
Labor and labor-related costs:	
Direct labor—100 hours @$8	800
Variable overhead—100 hours @$2	200
	$2,000

The company has just received a contract calling for another 50 units of production. It wants to add a 50 percent markup to the cost of materials and labor and labor-related costs. To determine the price for this job, the first step is to build up the learning curve table.

Quantity	Total time (hours)	Average time (per unit)
50	100	2 hours
100	160	1.6 (0.8 × 2 hours)

Thus, for the new 50 unit job, it takes 60 hours in total. The contract price is:

Materials—50 units @$20	$1,000
Labor and labor-related costs:	
Direct labor—60 hours @$8	480
Variable overhead—60 hours @$2	120
	$1,600
50 percent markup	800
Contract price	$2,400

COST-VOLUME-PROFIT AND BREAK-EVEN ANALYSIS

Cost-volume-profit (*CVP*) analysis allows managers to perform many useful analyses. *CVP* analysis deals with how profit and costs change with a change in volume. More specifically, it looks at the effects on profits of changes in such factors as variable costs, fixed costs, selling prices, volume, and mix of products sold. By studying the relationships of costs, sales, and net income, management is better able to cope with many planning decisions. *Break-even analysis*, a branch of *CVP* analysis, determines the break-even sales. Break-even point—the financial crossover point when revenues exactly match costs—does not show up in corporate earnings reports, but managers find it an extremely useful measurement in a variety of ways.

BREAK-EVEN ANALYSIS

The break-even point represents the level of sales revenue that equals the total of the variable and fixed costs for a given volume of output at a particular capacity use rate. For example, you might want to ask the break-even occupancy rate (or vacancy rate) for a hotel or the break-even load rate for an airliner. Generally, the lower the break-even point, the higher the profit and the less the operating risk, other things being equal. The break-even point also provides managers with insights into profit planning.

The *equation approach* is based on the cost-volume-profit equation, which shows the relationships among sales, variable and fixed costs, and net income:

$$TR = TVC + TFC + \text{Net Income}.$$

At the break-even volume, $TR = TVC + TFC + 0$. Defining Q = volume in *units*, the above relationship can be written in terms of Q:

$$P\,Q = AVC \cdot Q + TFC,$$

$$(P - AVC)Q = TFC.$$

Solving for Q yields the following formula for break-even sales volume:

$$Q_{be} = \frac{TFC}{(P - AVC)} = \frac{\text{Total Fixed Costs}}{\text{Unit } CM}$$

The term $(P—AVC)$ is called the *unit contribution margin (CM)*, because it is the profit contribution that each unit sold will make toward covering fixed cost and generating profit. If we multiply both sides of the break-even formula by P and rearrange the terms, we can obtain the formula for break-even sales in *dollars, (S)* as follows:

$$S = PQ = \frac{TFC \cdot P}{(P - AVC)} = \frac{TFC}{(P - AVC)\,/\,P} = \frac{\text{Total Fixed Costs}}{CM \text{ ratio}}$$

The term $(P - AVC)/P$ is called the *contribution margin ratio*, since it is the ratio of the unit CM to price. Notice $S = PQ$.

YOU SHOULD REMEMBER

The break-even analysis assumes: constant price, constant variable cost per unit, and constant sales mix. Strictly speaking, it is *linear* break-even analysis.

Example 7

The Wayne Company manufactures and sells doors to homebuilders. The doors are sold for $25 each. Variable costs are $15 per door, and fixed operating costs total $10,000. The following income (profit/loss) statement is based on a projected sales of 2,000 units:

	Total	Per Unit	Percentage
Sales (2,000 units)	$50,000	$25	100%
Less: Variable costs	30,000	15	60
Contribution margin	$20,000	$10	40%
Less: Fixed costs	5,000		
Net income	$15,000		

Note that $(P-AVC) = (\$25-\$15) = \$10$ and $(P-AVC)/P = (\$25-\$15)/\$25 = 40\%$.
Break-even point in units $= \$5,000/\$10 = 500$ units.
Break-even point in dollars $= 500 \times \$25 = \$25,000$. Alternatively, $\$15,000/40\%$ $= \$12,500$

DETERMINATION OF TARGET INCOME VOLUME

Besides determining the break-even point, *CVP* analysis determines the sales required to attain a particular income level or target net income. The formula is:

$$\text{Target income sales volume} = \frac{\text{Total fixed costs plus Target income}}{\text{Unit } CM}.$$

Example 8

Using the same data given in Example 7, assume that the firm wishes to attain a target income of $15,000. Then, the target income volume would be:

$$\frac{\$5,000 + \$15,000}{\$25 - \$15} = \frac{\$20,000}{\$10} = \$2,000 \text{ units}$$

GRAPHICAL APPROACH IN A SPREADSHEET FORMAT

The graphical approach to obtaining the break-even point is based on the so-called *break-even (B-E) chart* as shown in Figure 8–5. Sales revenue, variable costs, and fixed costs are plotted on the vertical axis while volume, x, is plotted on the horizontal axis. The break-even point is the point where the total sales revenue line intersects the total cost line. The chart can also effectively report profit potentials over a wide range of activity and, therefore, be used as a tool for discussion and presentation.

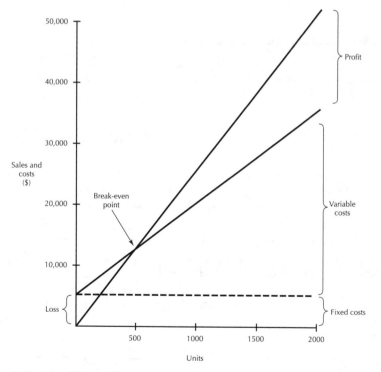

Figure 8–5. Break-Even Chart

OPERATING LEVERAGE

Leverage is that portion of the fixed costs that represents a risk to the firm. Operating leverage, a measure of operating risk, refers to the fixed operating costs found in the firm's income statement. Operating leverage is a measure of operating risk and arises from fixed operating costs. A simple indication of operating leverage is the effect that a change in sales has on operating income.

The formula is:

Operating leverage at a given level of sales (Q)

$$= \frac{\text{Percentage change in operating income}}{\text{Percentage change in sales}}$$

$$= \frac{[(P - AVC)\Delta Q]/[(P - AVC)Q - TFC]}{\Delta Q/Q}$$

$$= \frac{(P-AVC)Q}{(P-AVC)Q-TFC}.$$

Example 9

Assume from Example 7 that the Wayne Company is currently selling 6,000 doors per year. Its operating leverage is

$$\frac{(P - AVC)}{(P - AVC)Q - TFC} = \frac{(\$25 - \$15)(6,000)}{(\$25 - \$15)(6,000) - \$10,000} = \frac{\$60,000}{\$50,000} = 1.2$$

Which means if sales increase (decrease) by 1 percent, the company can expect its net income to increase (decrease) by 1.2 times that amount, or 1.2 percent.

YOU SHOULD REMEMBER

Operating leverage is an elasticity measure, since it is the ratio of a percentage change in operating income to a percentage change in sales.

KNOW THE CONCEPTS

TERMS FOR STUDY

average total cost
break-even point
cost-volume-profit (*CVP*) analysis
implicit vs. explicit costs
incremental (differential) costs
learning curve effect
operating leverage
planning (envelope) curve

relevant costs
shutdown costs
statistical cost analysis
sunk costs
total fixed costs
total variable costs
unit contribution margin

DO YOU KNOW THE BASICS?

1. Describe the graphical relationship between corresponding average cost (*AC*) and marginal cost (*MC*) curves.

2. List the factors causing larger plants to be more efficient than smaller plants.

3. What is the managerial implication of planning curves (long-run cost curves)?

4. What does statistical cost analysis involve?

5. List the basic steps involved in incremental or relevant cost analysis.

6. Distinguish between incremental analysis and marginal analysis.

7. Give some examples of learning curve applications.

8. What is cost-volume-profit (*CVP*) analysis? How is it useful to managers?

9. List some assumptions underlying break-even analysis. What is the distinction between a manager's break-even analysis and an economist's break-even analysis?

10. How do you measure operating risk?

PRACTICAL APPLICATION

1. Given the cost function for your firm: $TC = 40 + 4Q + 2Q^2$

a. What is the average fixed cost (*AFC*) of producing 5 units of output?

b. What is the average variable cost (*AVC*) of producing 5 units of output?

c. What are the average total cost (*ATC*) and marginal cost (*MC*) of producing 5 units of output?

2. Give the following total cost (*TC*) function:

$$200 + 75Q - 1.5Q^2 + 0.01Q^3.$$

a. Calculate the marginal cost (*MC*), average variable cost (*AVC*), average cost (*AC*), and average fixed cost (*AFC*) functions.

b. At what level of output does *MC* reach its minimum? *AVC*? *AFC*?

c. Determine *MC* and *AVC* when *AVC* is at its minimum.

d. Prove that short-run *MC* equals *AVC* when *AVC* is at its minimum.

3. A firm has the following short-run total cost function:

$$TC = 3,000 + 250Q - 7Q^2 + Q^3$$

a. Write the equations for the firm's marginal cost (*MC*), average variable cost (*AVC*), and average total cost (*ATC*).

b. Determine the output level at which *MC* will be minimized.

c. Determine the output level at which *AVC* will be minimized.

4. A firm estimates its selling and administrative costs as

$$TC = \$45,000 + \$60Q + 3Q^2,$$

where Q = sales volume in units.

a. What is the level of fixed selling and administrative costs?

b. Calculate average cost at $Q = 50$.

c. Calculate the level of output at which average costs would be minimized.

5. Janus Costing Inc., a leading maker of coatings, has estimated the following statistical function for its weekly total cost over the past 26 weeks:

$$TC = \$150,000 + \$7Q + 0.006Q^2,$$
$$(70,000) \quad (2) \quad (0.001)$$
$$r^2 = 0.90,$$
$$S_e = 7.888,$$

where Q = gallons of enamel and standard errors of the regression coefficients are in parentheses and S_e = standard error of the estimate.

a. Comment on the result based on the regression statistics given.

b. Calculate the average cost and comment on it.

6. Carson, Inc., uses a learning curve of 80 percent for all new products it develops. A trial run of 500 units of a new product shows total labor-related costs (direct labor, indirect labor, and fringe benefits) of $120,000. Management plans to produce 1,500 units of the new product during the next year.

a. Compute the expected labor-related costs for the year to produce the 1,500 units.

b. Find the unit cost of production for next year for labor-related costs.

7. The Hunt Company has recently purchased a plant to manufacture a new product. The following data pertain to the new operation:

Estimated annual sales	3,500 units @$20
Estimated Costs:	
Direct materials	$6.00/unit
Direct labor	$1.00/unit
Factory overhead (all fixed)	$12,000 per year
Selling expenses	30% sales
Administrative expenses (all fixed)	$16,000 per year

a. Determine the break-even point in units and in dollars.

b. Determine the selling price if profit per unit is $2.04.

c. What is the firm's degree of operating leverage at 5,000 units?

8. The Godberg Zinc Company is one of several suppliers of part X to an automobile manufacturing firm. Orders are distributed to the various die-casting companies on a fairly even basis; however, the sales manager of the company believes that with a reduction in price he could secure another 30 percent increase in units sold. The general manager has asked you to analyze the sales manager's proposal and submit your recommendation. The following data are available:

	Present	Proposed
Unit price	$2.5	$2.00
Unit sales	200,000 units	plus 30%
Variable costs	$350,000	Same unit variable cost
Fixed costs	$120,000	$120,000
Net profit	$ 30,000	?

Calculate (a) the net profit or loss on the sales manager's proposal and (b) the unit sales required under the proposed price to make the original $30,000 profit.

9. Odong Motors has the following cost and other operating data:

Price (P) per car: $8,000,

Total variable costs: $TVC = \$3,500Q + \$10Q^2$,

Total fixed costs: $TFC = \$500,000$.

a. Compute the annual break-even point Q_{be}.

b. Compute the profit-maximizing output Q^*.

10. Norton Rent-Car, Inc. has fixed costs of $250,000 per month and variable costs per car rented per day of $7. If Norton charges $32 per day to rent a car, how many car-rental days must Norton have each month to break even? To make $35,000 per month before taxes?

11. The Norman Company has an annual plant capacity of 25,000 units. Predicted data on sales and costs are given below:

Sales (20,000 units @$50)	$1,000,000
Manufacturing costs:	
Variable	
(materials, labor, and overhead)	$40 per unit
Fixed overhead	$30,000
Selling and administrative expenses;	
Variable	
(sales commission—$1 per unit)	$2 per unit
Fixed	$7,000

A special order has been received from outside for 4,000 units at a selling price of $45 each. The order will have no effect on regular sales. The usual sales commission on this order will be reduced by one-half. Should the company accept the order? Show supporting computations, using incremental analysis based on the concept of relevant cost.

ANSWERS

KNOW THE BASICS

1. The average-marginal relationship between corresponding average and marginal curves is the following: (1) when an average curve (*AC*) is rising, its corresponding marginal curve (*MC*) lies above it; (2) when an *AC* is falling, its corresponding *MC* lies below; and (3) when an *AC* is either at a maximum or minimum, its corresponding *MC* equals *AC*.

2. The factors causing larger plants to be more efficient than smaller plants include (1) more opportunity for specialization in the use of resource inputs; (2) the fact that the most advanced and efficient technology is practical only when producing large volumes of output; (3) the greater ability of larger plants to take advantage of and utilize by-products; (4) the greater opportunities for larger plants to make volume purchases of raw materials and thereby realize quantity discounts; and (5) the proportionately lower costs of purchasing and installing larger machines and equipment.

3. A planning curve is a locus of points representing the least unit cost of producing the corresponding output. Firms determine the size of plant by reference to this curve.

4. Statistical cost analysis is an empirical attempt to ascertain the nature of short-run or long-run cost/output relations. Cost curves are estimated via statistical techniques, such as *regression analysis*, based on *time-series* or *cross-sectional* data. Three types of functions—linear, quadratic, and cubic—especially the first two, have been most commonly employed in fitting statistical cost functions. The choice of one or the other depends largely on the extent to which the mathematical properties of the function represent the economics of the particular case.

5. The incremental, differential, or relevant cost approach involves the following steps:

   1. Gather all costs associated with each alternative.

   2. Drop the sunk costs.

   3. Drop those costs which do not differ between alternatives.

   4. Select the best alternative based on the remaining cost data.

6. Incremental analysis is frequently used in the practical equivalent of marginal analysis. It relates to a specified managerial decision that can involve a choice between two discrete quantities of output (e.g., 10,000 units vs. 15,000 units), while marginal analysis focuses on the impact on revenue or costs of one unit change in volume.

7. The learning curve theory has found useful applications in many areas, including: (a) budgeting, purchasing, and inventory planning, (b) scheduling labor requirements, (c) setting incentive wage rates, (d) pricing new products, and (e) evaluating suppliers' price quotations.

8. Cost-volume-profit (*CVP*) analysis helps managers perform many useful analyses. It allows managers to look at the effects on profits of changes in such factors as variable costs, fixed costs, selling prices, volume, and mix of products sold.

9. A manager's break-even analysis assumes: constant price, constant variable cost per unit, and constant sales mix. Strictly speaking, it is a *linear* break-even analysis. On the other hand, an economist's break-even analysis may produce more than one break-even sales volume.

10. Operating leverage is used to measure operating risk. It tells you how sensitive income is to a change in sales. It is essentially an elasticity measure, since it is the ratio of a percentage change in operating income to a percentage change in sales.

PRACTICAL APPLICATION

1a. $FC = 40, AFC = \dfrac{FC}{Q} = \dfrac{40}{5} = \$8$

1b. $VC = 4Q + 2Q^2, AVC = \dfrac{VC}{Q} = 4 + 2Q = 4 + 2(5) = \$14$

1c. $ATC = AVC + AFC = \$14 + \$8 = \$22,$

$$MC = \dfrac{dTC}{dQ} = 4 + 4Q = 4 + 4 + 4(5) = \$24$$

2a. $MC = \dfrac{dTC}{dQ} = 75 - 3Q + 0.03Q^2$

$$AVC = \dfrac{TVC}{Q} = 75 - 1.5Q + 0.01Q^2$$

$$AC = \dfrac{TC}{Q} = \dfrac{200}{Q} + 75 - 1.5Q + 0.01Q^2$$

$$AFC = \dfrac{200}{Q}$$

2b. $MC = \dfrac{dTC}{dQ} = 75 - 3Q + 0.03Q^2$

$\dfrac{dMC}{dQ} = -3 + 0.06 = 0, Q = 50,$

so MC is minimized at an output level of 50 units.

$AVC = \dfrac{TVC}{Q} = 75 - 1.5Q + 0.01Q^2$

$\dfrac{dAVC}{dQ} = 1.5 + 0.02Q = 0, Q = 75,$

so AVC is minimized at an output level of 75 units.

2c. From part (b), $Q = 75$ when AVC is minimized

$AVC = 75 - 1.5Q + 0.01Q^2 = 75 - 1.5(75) + 0.01(75)^2 = 75 - 112.5 + 56.25 = 18.75$

$MC = 75 - 3Q + 0.03Q^2 = 75 - 3(75) + 0.03(75)^2 = 75 - 225 + 168.75 = 18.75.$

2d. $MC = AVC = 18.75$. This proves that MC equals AVC when AVC is at its minimum in a short-run situation.

3a. $MC = \dfrac{dTC}{dQ} = 240 - 14Q + 3Q^2$

$AVC = \dfrac{TVC}{Q} = 240 - 7Q + Q^2$

$ATC = \dfrac{TC}{Q} = \dfrac{3,000}{Q} + 240Q - 7Q + Q^2$

3b. From part (a), $MC = 240 - 14Q + 3Q^2$

$\dfrac{dMC}{dQ} = -14 + 6Q = 0, Q = 2.33$

3c. From part (a), $AVC = 240 - 7Q + Q^2$

$\dfrac{dAVC}{dQ} = -7 + 2Q = 0, Q = 3.5$

4a. $45,000, which is the intercept term for TC at $Q = 0$.

4b. $ATC = \dfrac{TC}{Q} = \dfrac{45,000}{Q} + 60 + 3Q = \dfrac{45,000}{50} + 60 + 3(50) = \$1,110.$

4c. Set $\dfrac{dATC}{dQ} = 0,$

$$\frac{dATC}{dQ} = \frac{-45,000}{Q^2} + 3 = 0,\ Q^2 = \frac{45,000}{3} = 15,000,\ Q = \sqrt{15,000} = 122.$$

Note

$$\frac{d^2ATC}{dQ^2} = \frac{45,000}{Q^3} > 0, Q = 122 \text{ is at a minimum.}$$

5a. $r^2 = 0.90$ implying that this quadratic cost model accounts for 90 percent of total cost. It is a good fit. t-statistic for each coefficient ($7/2 = 3.5$ and $0.006/.0001 - 6$) exceeds the t-table value $= 2.069$ (at a 5% level and $n - k = 26 - 3 = 23$ degrees of freedom). So these coefficient estimates are reliable.

5b. $ATC = \dfrac{TC}{Q} = \dfrac{150,000}{Q} + 7 + 0.0006Q.$

Thus, we see that AC will first fall, then rise as output expands, and will be U-shaped.

6a. The 80 percent learning theory says that as cumulative quantities double, average time per unit falls to only 80 percent of the previous time. Therefore, the following data can be constructed:

Quantity	Time Cost	Average Cost per Unit
500 units	$120,000	$240 per unit
1,000	192,000	192 (80% × $240)
2,000	308,000	154 (80% × $192)

Thus,

Quantity	Total Cost
2,000	$308,000
500	120,000
1,500	$188,000

6b. Thus expected labor-related costs for the 1,500 units of output is $188,000 and $125.33 per unit ($188,000/1,500 units).

7a.

Variable Costs

Direct materials	$ 6.00
Direct labor	1.00
Selling expenses	6.00
	$13.00 per unit

Fixed Costs

Factory overhead	$12,000
Administrative	16,000
	$28,000

Break-even point in units = $28,000/($20−$13) = 4,000 units

Break-even point in dollars = 4,000 units × $20 = $80,000

7b.

$$TR = TVC + TFC + \text{Net Income}$$

$$\text{Let } P = \text{the selling price}$$

$$\text{then, } 3,500P = \$7(3,500) + 0.3P(3,500) + 28,000 + 2.04(3,500),$$

$$2,450P = \$59,640,$$

$$P = \$24.34.$$

7c. Its operating leverage is:

$$\frac{(P - AVC)}{(P - AVC)Q - TFC} = \frac{(\$20 - \$13)(5,000)}{(\$20 - \$13)(5,000) - \$28,000} = \frac{\$35,000}{\$7,000} = 5,$$

which means if sales increase (decrease) by 1 percent, the company can expect its net income to increase (decrease) by 5 times that amount, or 5 percent.

8a.

Sales (260,000 units @$2.00)	$520,000
Less: Variable costs (@1.75)	455,000
CM	$ 65,000
Fixed costs	120,000
Net income	$(55,000)

8b. Number of unit sales required $= \dfrac{\$120,000 + \$30,000}{\$2.00-\$1.75} = 600,000$ units

9a. The annual break-even point Q_{be} is the output level where $TR = TC$, or total profit $\pi = TR - TC = 0$,

$$TR = PQ = \$8,000Q, \; TC = TVC + TFC = AVC\,Q + TFC$$

$$= \$3,500Q + \$10Q^2 + \$500,000.$$

Thus,

$$\text{total profit} = TR - TC = \$8,000Q - (\$3,500Q + \$10Q^2 + \$500,000)$$

$$= -\$500,000 + \$4,500Q - \$10Q^2 = 0.$$

This is a quadratic equation in the form of $aQ^2 + bQ + c = 0$. Its two roots can be obtained using the following formula:

$$Q = \frac{-b \pm \sqrt{b^2 - 4ac}}{2a}$$

$$= \frac{-4,500 \pm \sqrt{(4,500)^2 - 4(-10)(-500,000)}}{-2(10)}$$

$$= 200 \text{ or } 250 \text{ cars.}$$

There are two break-even points.

9b. To obtain the profit-maximizing output Q^*, we need to take the derivative and set it equal to zero, as follows:

$$\frac{d\pi}{dQ} = \$4,500 - \$20Q = 0, \; Q^* = 225 \text{ cars.}$$

10. $Q = \dfrac{TFC}{(P - AVC)} = \dfrac{TFC}{\text{Unit } CM} = \dfrac{\$250,000}{\$32 - \$7} = 10,000$ car rental units per month.

For $35,000 per month profit before taxes:

$$(\$250,000 + \$35,000)/\$25 = 11,400 \text{ units per month.}$$

11. Note that fixed costs will continue regardless and therefore are irrelevant to this decision.

Incremental revenue (4,000 units @ $45)	$180,000
Less: Incremental costs	
Variable manufacturing	
(4,000 units @$40)	160,000
Variable selling and administrative	
(4,000 @ $1.50*)	6,000
Incremental gain in favor of accepting the order	$14,000

*$1.50 = $2 (variable selling and administrative expenses) − $0.50 (sales commission to be saved)

9

MARKET STRUCTURES AND THE THEORY OF THE FIRM

KEY TERMS

perfect competition market structure possessing the following characteristics: (1) a large number of small firms; (2) homogeneous products; (3) free entry and exit; and (4) perfect communication between buyers and sellers.

Cournot's oligopoly model oligopoly model that assumes that each of the two firms will maximize profits assuming that its competitor's output remains constant.

kinked demand curve "bent" or "kink" industry demand curve with a corresponding discontinuous marginal revenue curve that is found in an oligopolistic industry.

game theory technique that deals with competitive situations where two or more firms have conflicting objectives.

zero-sum game situation in which an economic gain by one company results in an economic loss by another.

value of game payoff at the saddle point.

saddle point equilibrium point at which the maximum of one's own minimum gain is equal to the minimum of the opponent's maximum gain.

four-firm concentration ratio fraction of total industry sales produced by the four largest firms in the industry.

Herfindahl-Hirshman index sum of the squared market shares.

> **Rothschild index** measure of the sensitivity to price of a product group as a whole relative to the sensitivity of the quantity demanded of a single firm to a change in its price.
>
> **Lerner index** measure of the difference between price and marginal cost as a percentage of the product's price.

Market structure refers to such factors as the number of firms in an industry, the relative size of the firms (industry concentration), demand conditions, ease of entry and exit, and technological and cost conditions. Different industries have different structures, and these influence the decisions to be made by the manager. Competition proceeds along different lines, depending on whether there are many or few firms in the industry and whether their products are identical or differentiated. From this standpoint, four main forms of market structure and types of competition exist:

1. *Perfect competition:* many sellers of a standardized product;

2. *Monopolistic competition:* many sellers of a differentiated product;

3. *Oligopoly:* few sellers of either a standardized or a differentiated product;

4. *Monopoly:* a single seller of a product for which there is no close substitute.

PERFECT COMPETITION

Perfect competition is an economic model or market structure possessing the following characteristics: (1) each firm is so small relative to the market that it can exert no perceptible influence on price; (2) the product is homogeneous; (3) there is free mobility of all resources, including free entry and exit of firms into and out of the industry; and (4) all buyers and sellers in the market possess complete and perfect knowledge.

A firm in a perfectly competitive industry operates at an output level where price (or marginal revenue) equals marginal cost and profits are maximized (see Figure 9–1). In reality, there is no industry that is perfectly competitive. Empirical evidence suggests that agricultural and lumber industries provide close approximations to perfect competition.

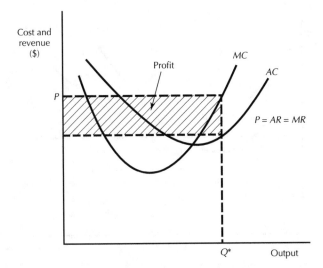

Figure 9–1. Perfect Competition–Short-Run Equilibrium

EXAMPLE 1

If $P = \$10$ then $TR = PQ = \$10Q$ and $MR = \$10$ (Note that this indicates $MR = P$ in a perfectly competitive market). Assuming $TC = 6 + 4Q + Q^2$, then $MC = dTC/dQ = 4 + 2Q$. Note that at a profit-maximizing output Q^*, $MR = P = MC$, $\$10 = 4 + 2Q$. Solve for Q and we get $Q^* = 3$ units. Alternatively, the total profit is

$$\pi = TR - TC = 10Q - (6 + 4Q + Q^2) = -6 + 6Q - Q^2.$$

In order to maximize π, we take the derivative of π with respect to Q, set it equal to zero, and solve for Q: $d\pi/dQ = 6 - 2Q = 0$, $Q^* = 3$ units.

LONG-RUN

In the long-run, all inputs are free to vary. Average cost will tend to be just equal to price and all excessive profits will be eliminated. If P exceeds AC, more firms will enter the market, supply will increase, and price will be driven down to the equilibrium, zero-profit level (see Figure 9–2). It is economic profit that is zero at long-run equilibrium; the accounting profit likely will be positive.

In summary, at the long-run profit-maximizing level of output under perfect competition. equilibrium will be achieved at a point where $P = MR = MC = AC$, and the firm is producing at its most efficient level of output; i.e., where long-run average costs are minimized.

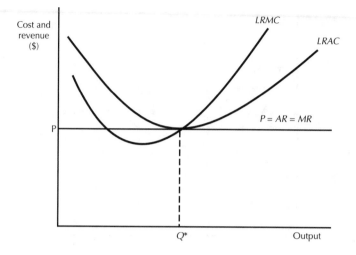

Figure 9–2.   Perfect Competition—Long-Run Equilibrium

MONOPOLISTIC COMPETITION

The distinguishing features of monopolistic competition are that there are (1) many small, owner managed firms selling differentiated, yet similar, products; (2) each firm has the ability to influence its sales by changing its prices; (3) each firm has downsloping, but highly elastic, demand curves; (4) a firm can enter and leave the industry with relative ease; (5) the actions of any one firm have a small effect upon rival firms; and (6) firms behave as if they seek to maximize profits.

The firm in monopolistic competition has three basic strategies for pursuing its principal goal of maximum profits—price changes, variations in its product, and promotional activity. Like every type of firm, a firm in monopolistic competition will maximize short-run profits by producing at the output rate where $MR = MC$.

OLIGOPOLY

Markets are said to be oligopolistic whenever a small number of firms supply the dominant share of an industry's total output. The interdependence among oligopolists extends to all facets of competition: price, output, promotional strategies, innovation, customer service policies, acquisitions and mergers, and so on. Since rival firms may have numerous alternative courses of action, anticipating their actions and reactions introduces a new and exceedingly complex dimension to the firm's decision process. But trying to anticipate the competitive response of rival firms is an exercise no oligopolist can afford to neglect, for the probability is high that a change in a firm's competitive tactics will elicit prompt and pointed reactions from rival firms. The great uncertainty is how one's rivals will react.

For this reason, there is no nice, neat, clear-cut equilibrium position toward which all firms tend to move—such as we found in perfect competition and monopolistic competition. In oligopoly, a wide variety of materially different competitive circumstances can and do exist, no one of which is demonstrably more typical than the others. As a consequence, oligopoly theory consists of dozens of models, each depicting certain facets of oligopolistic conduct and performance but none telling a complete story of competition among the few.

Two popular oligopoly models; Cournot's duopoly model and kinked demand curve, are described below. Both models are based on the assumption that there are just two sellers of a specific product—a case known as *duopoly*. The game theory approach is also briefly outlined.

COURNOT'S DUOPOLY MODEL

Cournot's duopoly model assumes that each of the two firms will maximize profits assuming that the competitor's will keep its output constant. Assume a linear market demand curve, zero cost, and a homogeneous product. Suppose that firm A is initially the only seller in the market. To maximize its profit it sells $0Q*$ units, so marginal revenue equals the zero marginal cost. This will correspond to an output that is exactly one-half of the market demand at a zero price (i.e., $1/2Q*$) where $Q*$ equals market demand at a price of zero (See Figure 9–3). Price is $0P*$ per unit, and profit is $0QCQ*$. The demand curve then facing firm B when it enters the market will be that portion of the curve lying to the right of the point corresponding to $1/2Q*$ ($\overline{AD}$—the unsupplied portion of the market demand curve). Finding that point on the corresponding marginal revenue curve, which equals zero, will yield B's output given A's choice of output. This will correspond to $1/2(1/2)Q*$, given the linear market demand curve. Assuming firm A continues to believe that B will maintain this output level, the new output level chosen by A will correspond to 1/2 of the unsupplied portion of the market demand curve, that is

$$\frac{1}{2}\left(1 - \frac{1}{4}\right)Q* = \frac{3}{8}Q*$$

This action-reaction pattern continues with a convergence on a stable equilibrium in which each firm supplies 1/3 of the total market.

KINKED DEMAND CURVE

One of the key questions that an oligopolistic firm must consider is "How will rival firms respond if we decide to alter our selling price?" A "bent" or

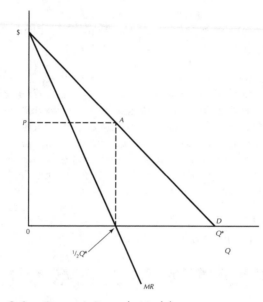

Figure 9–3. Cournot's Duopoly Model

"kink" industry demand curve with a corresponding discontinuous marginal revenue curve is often found in an oligopolistic industry. The theory denotes that, if the firm raises the price above the kink, sales will fall off sharply because other rival firms are not likely to follow suit. If the firm reduces the price below the kink, sales will rise relatively little because other firms are likely to follow the price downward. As a result, the market price tends to become steady at the kink. The matching of price cuts and the ignoring of price increases by rival firms has the effect of making an oligopolist's demand curve highly elastic above the ruling price, but much less elastic or even inelastic below the ruling price.

EXAMPLE 2

California Instruments, Inc., a maker of electronic minicalculators, is operating in a market where management believes that price cutting will only lead to retaliation by other firms but that other firms are unlikely to follow a price increase. (Industry profits are high at the going price.) The firm is currently pricing its machine at $10, but its chief economist has just come up with a new estimate of demand.

Specifically, if all firms change price equally, the monthly demand curve will be Q_1 = 1,500 – 50P. However, if the firm can change its price independently of rival reactions, the monthly demand curve will be Q_2 = 3,000 – 200P. The firm's total cost function is $TC = 1,500 + 3Q + 0.0025Q^2$.

Figure 9–4 shows the two demand curves for the firm's calculators. By solving for the intersection of the two curves ($Q = Q_1 = Q_2$ and $P = P_1 = P_2$), we obtain the maximum quantity the firm can sell without encountering a precipitous drop in MR. (MR will not always be negative for outputs greater than that at the intersection of Q_1 and Q_2.) This occurs at $Q = 1,000$, $P = \$10$, or where $3,000 - 200P = 1,500 - 50P$; $1,500 = 150P$; $P = \$10$.

Using the Q_2 demand function ($Q_2 = 3,000 - 200P$), we can solve for P and obtain $P = 15 - 0.005Q_2$. In this case,

$$TR_2 = PQ_2 = 15Q_2 = 15Q_2 - 0.005Q^2_2,$$

and

$$MR_2 = \frac{dTR_2}{dQ_2} = 15 - 0.01Q_2.$$

Using the Q_1 demand function ($Q_1 = 1,500 - 50P$), we obtain $P = 30 - 0.02Q_1$. For this demand function,

$$TR_1 = PQ_1 = 30Q_1 - 0.02Q^2_1,$$

and

$$MR_1 = \frac{dTR_1}{dQ_1} = 30 - 0.04Q_1.$$

If we substitute 750 for Q_1 in the MR_1 function, we can see that MR_1 will be negative for any level of Q_1 greater than 750. However, MR_1 is not the firm's actual MR function until after the kink in the demand curve.

The kink in the demand curve occurs at $P = \$10$, $Q = 1,000$, and $MR_2 = 5$. However, the firm should only charge \$10 per unit if at $Q = 1,000$ its MC is \$5 per unit or lower. Given management's estimate of the firm's total cost function,

$$TC = 1,500 + 3Q + 0.0025Q^2,$$

$$MC = \frac{dTC}{dQ} = 3 + 0.005Q.$$

At $Q = 1,000$, $MC = \$8$ and $TC = \$7,000$. Since $TR = 1,000(\$10) = \$10,000$, the firm would have an economic profit of ($\$10,000 - \$7,000) = \$3,000$ if it were to continue charging a price of \$10.

For this firm the gap in MR occurs at $Q = 1,000$ where $MR = \$5$. As long as MC is less than \$5 at this output, the firm should charge \$10 per unit for its calculators.

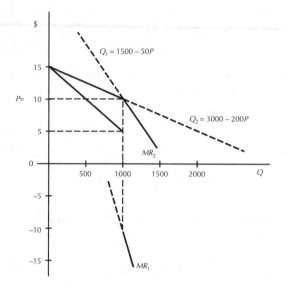

Figure 9–4. Kinked Demand Curve

GAME THEORY

Game theory deals with competitive situations where two or more participants pursue conflicting objectives. The theory attempts to provide optimal strategies for the participants. In games, the participants are competitors; the success of one is usually at the expense of the other. Each company selects and executes those strategies that it believes will result in "winning the game." This theory attempts to explain the price-output decisions of firms in oligopolistic industries and the

---

EXAMPLE 3

A two-person game can be represented in a matrix format. Assume that two rival firms are considering advertising or product differentiation strategies that will have predictable effects on the share of the total market obtained by each.

Payoff Matrix for a Two-Firm, Zero-Sum Game
(Outcomes in terms of Firm A's percentage share of Market)

		B's Strategy			
		B_1	B_2	B_3	Value of game
	A_1	[B]85	60	45[A]	
A's Strategy	A_2	80	[B]70	[B]55[A]	55
	A_3	15[A]	35	50	

labor contract negotiations between management and labor. There are many different types of games that reflect different conflict situations. A two-person, *zero-sum game* is an example. In this game, the participants have exactly opposite interests; that is, one player's gain is the other player's loss.

It has been shown in theory that a two-person, zero-sum game will have a determinate solution as long as a specific rule, known as the *minimax principle*, holds and mixed strategies are permitted. This principle assumes that for each strategy one chooses, the opposition will choose a strategy that maximizes its share of the payoff. Therefore, one chooses a strategy that minimizes the opponent's maximum gain. To illustrate, in the above example,

1. A will choose strategy $A_2B_3 = 55$, which is mathematically

$$\underset{i}{\max}\ \underset{j}{\min}\ \ a_{ij} = A_2B_3 = 55.$$

It indicates that A should choose the strategy which maximizes the minimum payoff associated with each row of the game matrix (places the letter A in the upper right-hand corner).

2. B will choose strategy $A_2B_3 = 55$, which is mathematically

$$\underset{j}{\min}\ \underset{i}{\max}\ \ a_{ij} = A_2B_3 = 55,$$

which indicates B should choose the strategy that minimizes the maximum payoff (placed the letter B in the upper left-hand corner).

3. Whenever A's minimum gain is equal to B's maximum loss or, in other words, when

$$\underset{i}{\max}\ \underset{j}{\min}\ \ a_{ij} = \underset{j}{\min}\ \underset{i}{\max}\ \ a_{ij} = a_{i*j*} = v = A_2B_3 = 55.$$

The game is said to have a *saddle point* or *equilibrium* at $(i*, j*)$ and the *value* of the game (v) is equal to a_{i*j*}. For the example ($i* = 2, j* = 3$) constitutes a saddle point and the value of the game (v) is equal to 55% market share.

MONOPOLY

A key difference between the market situation confronting a pure monopolist and that confronting other enterprises is that the firm's demand curve coincides with the industry demand curve. The firm is the industry. The price-output decision for a profit-maximizing monopolist is illustrated in Figure 9–5.

Just as in the case of perfect competition, profit is maximized at the price output combination where $MR = MC$. Apparently, for a negative-sloping demand curve (e.g., $P = a - bQ$), the MR function is not the same as the demand function. If $P = a - bQ$ then $TR = PQ = aQ - bQ^2$ and $MR = a - 2bQ$. So the slope of the demand function is $-b$, and the MR function $-2b$.

EXAMPLE 4

Assume a monopolist is faced with the demand function,

$$Q = 400 - 2P \text{ (or } P = 200 - 0.5Q)$$

and

$$TC = 35Q + 0.05Q^2.$$

The profit-maximizing output will be at $MR = MC$.
First, $TR = PQ = (200 - 0.5Q)Q = 200Q - 0.5Q^2$. So $MR = 200 - Q$.
Note that $MC = 35 + 0.1Q$
Setting $MR = MC$ yields $200 - Q = 35 + 0.1Q, \ Q = 150$ units
Substituting $Q = 136$ back into the demand function yields:

$$P = 200 - 0.5Q = 200 - 0.5Q(150) = \$125.$$

Hence, the profit-maximizing monopolist would produce 150 units and charge a price of \$125 each. This yields a profit of

$$\pi = TR - TC = PQ - (35Q + 0.05Q^2)$$

$$= (\$125)(150) - [35(150) + 0.05(150)^2] = \$12,375.$$

INDUSTRY CONCENTRATION

Different industries have different market structures, and these influence the decisions to be made by the manager. The following provides an overview of the major structural variables and how they are measured.

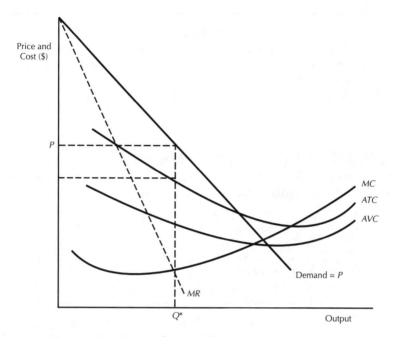

Figure 9–5. Monopolist's Equilibrium

MEASURES OF INDUSTRY CONCENTRATION

There are two common measures used to gauge the degree of concentration in an industry, (1) concentration ratios and (2) Herfindahl-Hirshman index.

• *CONCENTRATION RATIOS*

Concentration ratios measure how much of the total output in an industry is manufactured by the largest firms in that industry. The most popular concentration ratio is the four-firm concentration ratio (C_4). It is the fraction of total industry sales produced by the four largest firms in the industry. The ratio is given by

$$C_4 = \frac{S_1 + S_2 + S_3 + S_4}{S_T}$$

$$= w_1 + w_2 + w_3 + w_4,$$

where S_T = the total sales of all firms in the industry, S_1, S_2, S_3, and S_4 = the sales of the four largest firms, and w_1, w_2, w_3, and w_4 = market shares of the four largest firms.

EXAMPLE 5

An industry is made up of seven firms. Four firms have sales of $1 million each, and two firms have sales of $500,000 each. The four-firm concentration ratio for this industry is 80%, as computed below.

Total industry sales are $S_T =$ $5 million. The sales of the four largest firms = $4 million. The ratio is $4 million/$5 million = 0.8 = 80%

• *HERFINDAHL-HIRSHMAN INDEX*

The Herfindahl-Hirshman index is the sum of the squared market shares multiplied by 10,000 to eliminate the need for decimals:

$$10,000\Sigma w_i^2.$$

By squaring the market shares before adding them up, the index weighs firms with high market shares more heavily.

EXAMPLE 6

Suppose an industry consists of three firms. Two firms have sales of $1million each, and one firm has sales of $3 million. Since total industry sales are $S_T =$ $5 million, the largest firm has a market share of 0.6 = 3/5, and the other two firms have a market share of 0.2 = 1/5 each. Thus, the Herfindahl-Hirshman index for this industry is

$$10,000[(0.3)^2 + (0.2)^2 + (0.2)^2] = 4,400.$$

Note that the four-firm concentration ratio is 1, since the top three firms account for all industry sales.

YOU SHOULD REMEMBER

1. Four-firm concentration ratios are between 0 and 1. Being close to 0 indicates markets in which there are many sellers, giving rise to much competition, while being close to 1 indicates markets in which there is little competition among producers for sales to consumers.

2. The value of the Herfindahl-Hirshman index lies between 0 and 10,000. A value of 10,000 exists when a monopolist exists in the industry. A value of zero results when there are numerous infinitesimally small firms.

MEASURES OF INDUSTRY CHARACTERISTICS

Industries also differ with regard to the underlying demand and market conditions. Presented below are two measures describing industry characteristics: the Rothschild Index and the Lerner Index.

• *THE ROTHSCHILD INDEX*

The elasticity of demand for products tends to vary from industry to industry. Moreover, the elasticity of demand for an individual firm's products generally will differ from the market elasticity of demand for the products. The Rothschild Index (R) provides a measure of how price sensitive an individual firm's demand is relative to the entire market. It is computed as

$$R = e_T/e_I,$$

where e_T is the elasticity of demand for the total market and e_I is the elasticity of demand for the product of an individual firm.

The Rothschild Index takes on a value between 0 and 1.

- When $R = 1$, the individual firm faces a demand curve that has the same sensitivity to price as the market demand curve.

- When R is close to 0, an industry is composed of many firms, each producing similar products.

EXAMPLE 7

The industry elasticity of demand for softwood lumber is 1 and the elasticity of demand for an individual lumber mill is 5. The Rothschild Index for this industry is $1/5 = 0.2$.

• *THE LERNER INDEX*

In addition to structural differences across industries, the conduct, or behavior, of firms also tends to differ across industries. Some industries charge higher markups than other industries. The Lerner Index (L) provides a measure of how much firms in an industry mark up their prices over marginal cost:

$$L = (P-MC)/P.$$

- In industries in which firms rigorously compete for consumer sales by attempting to charge the lowest price in the market, L is close to zero.

- When firms do not rigorously compete for consumers through price competition, L is closer to 1.

EXAMPLE 8

A firm in the lumber industry has a marginal cost of $200 and charges a price of $220. The Lerner Index is ($220–$200)/$220 = 0.09.

KNOW THE CONCEPTS

TERMS FOR STUDY

Cournot's duopoly model
four-firm concentration ratio
game theory
Herfindahl-Hirshman
kinked demand curve
Lerner index
monopolistic competition

oligopoly
perfect competition
Rothschild index
saddle point
value of game
zero-sum game

DO YOU KNOW THE BASICS?

1. List the major determinants of market structure.

2. State the conditions that yield a perfectly competitive market.

3. What is the condition for the long-run profit-maximizing level of output for a perfect competitor?

4. Do the four-firm concentration ratio and the Herfindahl-Hirshman index always provide an accurate evaluation of market power? Explain.

5. Give two good economic examples of game theory application.

6. What is the Cournot's oligopoly model?

7. What is the kinked demand curve? What does this phenomenon denote?

8. List two measures describing industry characteristics and briefly define each.

PRACTICAL APPLICATION

1. Stellar Company is operating under highly competitive market conditions. The going price for its product is $P = \$250$. If the firm's marginal cost function is $MC = -300 + 20Q$, what is the firm's profit-maximizing output?

2. Marie Clothing is operating under highly competitive market conditions and has the following long-run total cost function: $TC = 45Q - 2.5Q + 0.04Q^2$. If the firm's cost function remains stable, what will be the long-run price for Marie's product?

3. Donner Mills, Inc. is a perfectly competitive firm and has the following demand and cost functions:

$$P = MR = \$100,$$

$$TC = 1,000 + 125Q - 0.5Q^2.$$

   If the firm does not operate, it will lose its $1,000 of fixed costs.

   a. What is the profit maximizing output?

   b. Does it make or lose money if it operates where $MR = MC$?

   c. Should the firm operate or temporally shut down?

   d. Determine whether the firm should operate or temporally shut down by comparing MR with average variable cost (AVC).

4. Nolo, Inc. is a monopolist facing the following demand and total cost functions:

$$Q = 25 - 0.5P,$$

$$TC = 50 + 2Q.$$

   a. What is the firm's inverse demand function?

   b. What are the profit-maximizing levels of output and price?

   c. What will be the level of profits?

5. TWO Manufacturing is a monopolist operating two plants at two different locations, producing the same product. The firm has the following demand function:

$$P = 600 - 2Q,$$

   where $Q = Q_1 + Q_2$, and Q_1 and Q_2 = the quantity of output produced at plants 1 and 2, respectively.

The cost functions for the two plants are:

$$TC_1 = 30 + 2Q_1^2,$$

$$TC_2 = 25 + Q_2^2.$$

a. Determine the marginal revenue and marginal cost functions.

b. Determine the profit-maximizing Q_1 and Q_2.

c. What is the price that maximizes profits?

d. What are the maximum profits?

6. Two rival firms, A and B, are considering advertising or product differentiation strategies that will have predictable effects on the share of the total market obtained by each. Assume that two choices are available to each firm in allocating advertising dollars—two-thirds to one market and one-third to the other, or vice versa. The payoff matrix, providing sales increase to Firm A under possible allocations of advertising dollars, is:

Payoff Matrix for a Two-Firm, Zero-Sum Game
(Payoff in terms of sales increase to Firm A)

		B's Strategy	
		B_1	B_2
A's Strategy	A_1	^{B}$700,000	$600,000
	A_2	$900,000	^{B}$400,000

a. Determine the maxmin strategy for Firm A.

b. Determine the minmax strategy for Firm B.

c. Does the game have a saddle point? If so, what is the value of the game, that is, what is the sales increase for Firm A and the sales decrease to Firm B?

7. Anton Mills, Inc. produces and sells lumber in a perfectly competitive industry and has the following cost function:

$$TC = \$600Q - \$20Q^2 + Q^3,$$

where TC = total cost (in thousands of dollars) and Q = output (in thousands of board feet). This function includes a normal profit of 15 percent on invested capital.

a. Determine the price charged by Anton for its product provided that the company and the industry is in equilibrium.

b. Find the value of economic profits, average cost, and marginal cost at this equilibrium price.

c. Graph the *MR*, *MC*, and *AC* curves.

d. Determine the supply function for Anton's output.

8. Hector Industries, Inc., a leading maker of fertilizer chemicals, hired a consulting firm to estimate the industry demand and supply functions. Using Department of Commerce data, they developed the following:

$$Q_S = 3,000P,$$

$$Q_D = 1,000,000 - 2,000P.$$

a. Calculate the equilibrium price/output combination for the industry, assuming the industry is perfectly competitive.

b. Suppose that import restrictions have erased the firm's leading competitors, thereby giving the firm a monopoly position. Calculate the monopoly equilibrium price/output combination for the industry.

c. Comment on the results of (a) and (b).

9. Maintenance Inc. is considering entering the highly competitive Southern California market for monthly property management service. The industry supply and demand functions are given as follows:

$$Q_S = 5,000 + 400P,$$

$$Q_D = 55,000 - 600P.$$

a. Find the industry equilibrium price and output combination.

b. Given the firm's total cost function, $TC = 22,500 + 5Q + 0.0225Q^2$, calculate the firm's profit-maximizing output and profit. Should the firm enter the market?

c. Assuming the market is perfectly competitive, how many firms will there be in the market at long-run equilibrium? What profit will they earn?

10. There are six firms in an industry. Firm A has 40 percent of the market, Firm B has 30 percent, and the remaining firms have 7.5 percent each.

a. Compute the four-firm concentration ratio.

b. Compute the Herfindahl-Hirshman Index.

11. Zessy Industries, Inc. has a product that sells for $30 per unit, and the marginal cost is $10.

a. Determine the Lerner Index.

b. Does the company have market power?

12. Donner Park Products (DPP) faces the following segmented demand curve for its new infant safety seat:

$$P_1 = \$60\text{–}Q \text{ for } Q \le 10{,}000,$$
$$P_2 = \$80\text{–}\$3Q \text{ for } Q \ge 10{,}000.$$

The firm's total cost (TC) function is

$$TC = \$50 + \$20Q + \$0.5Q^2,$$

where Q = output in thousands.

a. Graph DPP's demand, marginal revenue and marginal cost curves.

b. Describe the market structure of DPP's industry.

c. Determine the company's optimal price and quantity, and its profits or losses at this output.

d. How much could marginal costs rise before the optimal price would increase? How much could they fall before the optimal price would decrease?

ANSWERS

KNOW THE CONCEPTS

1. Market structure refers to such factors as the number of firms in an industry, the relative size of the firms (industry concentration), demand conditions, ease of entry and exit, and technological and cost conditions.

2. The conditions for perfect competition include: (1) each firm is so small relative to the market that it can exert no perceptible influence on price; (2) the product is homogeneous; (3) there is free mobility of all resources, including free entry and exit of firms into and out of the industry; and (4) all buyers and sellers in the market possess complete and perfect knowledge.

3. In the long run, equilibrium will be achieved at a point where $P = MR = MC = AC$, and the firm is producing at its most efficient level of output; i.e., where long-run average costs are minimized.

4. These two statistics measure different aspects of market structure and, therefore, may not accurately describe the degree of market power. Both neglect the geographical market and foreign competition.

5. Examples of game theory applications include the price-output decisions of firms in oligopolistic industries and the labor contract negotiations between management and labor.

6. The Cournot's oligopoly model assumes that each of the two firms will maximize profits assuming that its competitor's output remains constant.

7. The kinked demand curve is a "bent" or "kink" industry demand curve with a corresponding discontinuous marginal revenue curve that is found in an oligopolistic industry. The theory denotes that, if the firm raises the price above the kink, sales will fall off sharply since other rival firms are not likely to follow suit. If the firm reduces the price below the kink, sales will rise relatively little since other firms are likely to follow the price downward. As a result, the market price tends to become steady at the kink.

8. They are the Rothschild and the Lerner indexes. The Rothschild Index measures how price sensitive an individual firm's demand is relative to the entire market, while the Lerner Index (L) measures how much firms in an industry markup their prices over marginal cost.

PRACTICAL APPLICATION

1. Profits are maximized where $MR = MC$.

$$MR = P = 250; MC = -300 + 20Q,$$

$$250 = -300 + 20Q; Q^* = 27.5.$$

2. The long-run equilibrium price will be where P = minimum LAC, where

$$LAC = \frac{LTC}{Q} = 45 - 2.5Q + 0.04Q^2.$$

We find minimum LAC where $dLAC/dQ = 0$,

$$\frac{dLAC}{dQ} = -2.5 + 0.08Q = 0,$$

$$Q = 31.25.$$

$$At\ Q = 31.25,$$

$$LAC = 45 - 2.5Q + 0.04Q^2 = 45 - 2.5(31.25) + 0.04(31.25)^2 = \$20.$$

The long-run price for the firm's product will be $20.

3a. Profit is maximized where $MR = MC$,

$$P = MR = \$100,$$

$$MC = MC = \frac{dTC}{dQ} = 125 - Q.$$

So, $100 = 125 - Q$, $Q^* = 25$.

3b. Profits $= TR - TC = PQ - TC = 100(25) - [1000 + 125(25) - 0.5(25)^2]$

$$= 2,500 - (1,000 + 3125 - 312.5) = -\$1,312.5.$$

3c. Since a loss of \$1,312.5 exceeds the fixed cost, the firm should shut down. The firm would be losing less money if it shut down and paid just its fixed costs.

3d. At $Q^* = 25$,

$$AVC = \frac{TVC}{Q} = \frac{125Q + 0.5Q^2}{Q} = 125 - 0.5Q = 125 - 0.5(2.5) = 112.5.$$

As MR of \$100 is below AVC of \$112.5 at the profit maximizing $Q = 25$, the firm should shut down.

4a. $P = 50 - 2Q$

4b. $TR = PQ = (50 - 2Q)Q = 50Q - 2Q^2$

At profit maximizing output, $MR = MC$

$$MR = \frac{dTR}{dQ} = 50 - 4Q, \ MC = \frac{dTC}{dQ} = 2.$$

Hence. $50 - 4Q = 2$; $Q^* = 12$; $P = 50 - 2Q = 50 - 2(12) = \$26$

4c. Profits $= TR - TC = 50Q - 2Q^2 - (50 + 2Q)$

$$= -50 + 48Q - 2Q^2 = -50 + 48(12) - 2(12)^2 = \$238.$$

5a. $TR = PQ = (600 - 2Q)Q = 600Q - 2Q^2,$

$$MR = \frac{dTR}{dQ} = 600 - 4Q = 600 - 4(Q_1 + Q_2),$$

$$MC_1 = \frac{dTC_1}{dQ_1} = 4Q_1, MC_2 = \frac{dTC_2}{dQ_2} = 2Q_2.$$

5b. Profits are maximized when $MR = MC_1 = MC_2$,

$$MR = MC_1; \; 600 - 4(Q_1 + Q_2) = 4Q_1 \rightarrow 8Q_1 + Q_2 = 600,$$

$$MR = MC_2; \; 600 - 4(Q_1 + Q_2) = 2Q_2 \rightarrow 4Q_1 + 3Q_2 = 600.$$

Solving two equations for Q_1 and Q_2 yields: $Q_1 = 60$ and $Q_2 = 120$.

5c. $Q = Q_1 + Q_2 = 60 + 120 = 180$,

$P = 600 - 2Q = 600 - 2(180) = \$240$.

5d. Maximum profits are

$$\pi = TR - TC_1 - TC_2 = 600Q - 2Q^2 - (30 + 2Q_1^2) - (25 + Q_2^2)$$

$$= 600(180) - 2(180)^2 - 30 - 2\,(60)^2 - 25 - (120)^2 = \$21,545.$$

PAYOFF MATRIX FOR A TWO-FIRM, ZERO-SUM GAME

(Payoff in terms of sales increase to Firm A)

B's Strategy

A's Strategy		B_1	B_2	Value of the game
	A_1	\$700,000	[B]\$600,000[A]	\$600,000
	A_2	[B]\$900,000	\$400,000	

6a. A will choose the maximin strategy $A_1B_2 = \$600,000$ (placed the letter A in the upper right-hand corner).

6b. B will choose the minimax strategy $A_1B_2 = \$600,000$ (placed the letter B in the upper left-hand corner).

6c. The game has a saddle point or equilibrium and the *value* of the game (v) is \$600,000, which represents a \$600,000 sales increase to Firm A and the same amount of decrease to Firm B.

7a. If the company and the industry is in equilibrium, then $P = AC$ where AC is at a minimum. To determine the point of minimum AC, set $dAC/dQ = 0$,

$$AC = \frac{TC}{Q} = \frac{\$600Q - \$20Q^2 + Q^3}{Q} = 600 - 20Q + Q^2,$$

$$\frac{dAC}{dQ} = -20 + 2Q = 0, \; Q = 10.$$

At $Q = 10$,

$$AC = 600 - 20Q + Q^2 = 600 - 20(10) + (10)^2 = 500.$$

Since $P = AC = \$500$.

7b. In equilibrium, economic profits $= 0$, and $AC = MC$.

$$\text{Profits} = TR - TC = PQ - (\$600Q - \$20Q^2 + Q^3)$$

$$= (500)(10) - 600(10) + 20(10)^2 - (10)^3$$

$$= 0,$$

$$AC = 600 - 20Q + Q^2 = 600 - 20(10) + (10)^2 = 500,$$

$$MC = \frac{dTC}{dQ} = 600 - 40Q + 3Q^2 = 600 - 40(10) + 3(10)^2 = 500.$$

7c.

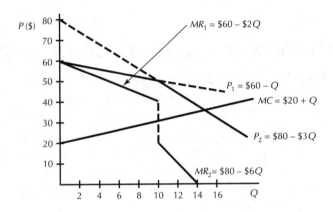

Figure 9–6.

7d. A competitive firms' supply function is the portion of the *MC* curve lying above the *AVC* curve (or above the *AC* curve). Note that Anton does not have fixed costs in its total cost function,

$$AC = AVC.$$

8a. The industry equilibrium price is

$$Q_S = Q_D,$$

$$3{,}000P = 1{,}000{,}000 - 2{,}000P,$$

$$P = \$200.$$

At $P = \$200$, the industry equilibrium output is

$$Q_S = 3{,}000P = 3{,}000(200) = 600{,}000.$$

8b. The profit-maximizing output for the monopoly is: $MR = MC$. Note that the industry supply curve represents the horizontal sum of the MC curves for individual firms. Hence, when the industry is converted into a monopoly, the industry supply curve represents the relevant MC curve:

$$Q_S = 3{,}000P \rightarrow P = 0.00033Q = MC.$$

From the demand curve, $Q_D = 1{,}000{,}000 - 2{,}000P$, $P = 500 - 0.0005Q$,

$$TR = PQ = (500 - 0.0005Q)Q = 500Q - 0.0005Q^2,$$

$$MR = \frac{dTR}{dQ} = 500 - 0.001Q.$$

At the profit maximizing output,

$$MR = MC,$$

$$500 - 0.001Q = 0.00033Q,$$

$$Q = 375{,}940,$$

$$P = 500 - 0.0005Q = 500 - 0.0005(375{,}940) = \$312.$$

8c. From parts (a) and (b), we see that monopolists offer consumers too little output (from 600,000 down to 375,940) at too high a price ($200 up to $312).

9a.
$$Q_S = Q_D,$$

$$55{,}000 - 600P = 5{,}000 + 400P,$$

$$P = 50,$$

$$Q_D = 5{,}000 + 400P = 5{,}000 + 400(50) = 25{,}000.$$

9b. Since the industry is competitive, $P = MR = 50$,

$$TC = 22{,}500 + 5Q + 0.0225Q^2,$$

$$MC = \frac{dTC}{dQ} = 5 + 0.045Q$$

Set $MR = MC$,

$$50 = 5 + 0.045Q, Q = 1{,}000$$

$$\text{Profit} = TR - TC = PQ - (22{,}500 + 5Q + 0.0225Q^2)$$

$$= 50(1{,}000) - 22{,}500 - 5(1{,}000) - 0.0225(1{,}000)^2,$$

$$= 50{,}000 - 22{,}500 - 5{,}000 - 22{,}500 = 0.$$

The firm would be indifferent between entering and not entering this market.

9c. With perfect competition, there will be n identical firms producing $1/n$ of total output. Each firm would be earning zero profit.

10a. The four-firm concentration ratio $= 0.4 + 0.3 + 0.075 + 0.075 = 0.85 = 85\%$.

10b. The Herfindahl-Hirshman index $= 10{,}000[(0.4)^2 + (0.3)^2 + (0.075)^2 + (0.075)^2 + (0.075)^2 + (0.075)^2] = 2{,}725$

11a. The Lerner Index is

$$\frac{P - MC}{P} = \frac{30 - 10}{30} = 0.67.$$

11b. Since the index is close to one, there is evidence of market power.

12a.

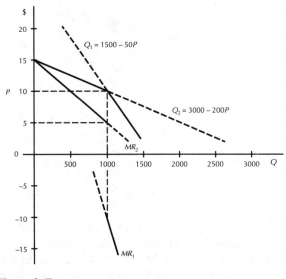

Figure 9–7.

12b. DDP is in an oligopolistic industry. As shown in the graph (a), it faces a kinked demand curve implying that competitors will react to price reductions by cutting their own prices, thereby causing the segment of the demand curve below the kink to be relatively inelastic. Price increases are not followed, causing the portion of the demand curve above the kink to be relatively elastic.

12c. As shown in part (a), the *MC* curve passes through the gap in the *MR* curve. Graphically, this indicates that optimal $P = \$50$ and $Q = 10(000)$.

Analytically,

$$MR_1 = \$60\text{--}\$2Q, Q \le 10,000,$$

$$MR_2 = \$80\text{--}\$6Q, Q \ge 10,000,$$

$$MC = 20 + Q.$$

Solving for the output levels where $MR = MC$ indicates that $MR_1 > MC$ over the range $Q < 10$, and $MR_2 < MC$ for the range $Q > 10$. Therefore, we know DPP will produce 10(000) units of output and market them at $P = \$50$. And finally,

$$\text{Profit} = TR - TC = PR - TC$$

$$= 50(10) - [\$50 + \$20(10) + \$0.5(10)^2]$$

$$= \$200(000).$$

12d. At $Q = 10(000)$,

$$MR_1 = 60 - 2Q$$

$$= 60 - 2(10)$$

$$= \$40,$$

$$MR_2 = 80 - 6Q$$

$$= 80 - 6(10)$$

$$= \$20.$$

This implies that if marginal costs at $Q = 10(000)$ exceed \$40, the optimal price would increase. On the contrary, if marginal costs at $Q = 10(000)$ fall below \$20, the optimal price would decrease. So long as marginal costs at $Q = 10(000)$ are in the range of \$20 to \$40, DPP will have no incentive to change its price.

10 PRICING IN PRACTICE

In this chapter, we examine a number of pricing methods used in practice. We begin with the most popular pricing approach, cost-plus pricing. We also take a look at how to utilize economic theory to reach a profit-maximizing pricing decision. The marginal cost concept and demand elasticity play key roles in achieving profit maximization. Further, we examine various pricing strategies for firms that may yield even greater profits, such as price discrimination, two-part pricing, block pricing, and peak-load pricing. The price discrimination method is also analyzed as a way for firms with market power to deal with pricing problems posed by multiple products. Two common pricing policies—skimming and penetrating—are also presented.

COST-BASED PRICING

Cost-based pricing is a widely used pricing technique that involves:

a. Defining an appropriate cost base, typically the average unit cost of producing and marketing a product or service, and

b. Adding a percentage markup. The markup on cost formula is

$$\text{Markup on cost} = \frac{\text{Price} - \text{Cost}}{\text{Cost}}$$

EXAMPLE 1

A firm's unit cost is $3.00 and the unit price is $3.90, the 30 percent markup is calculated as

$$\frac{\$3.90 - \$3.00}{\$3.00} = 30\%.$$

Solving the markup on cost formula for price provides the expression that determines price in a cost-plus pricing system, i.e.,

Price = Cost (1 + Markup on Cost) = $3.00(1 + 03) = $3.90.

Despite its popularity, a cost-plus pricing system is subject to some criticisms: (a) it fails to take into account demand as measured in terms of buyers' desires and purchasing power, and (b) it does not reflect competition in terms of rivals' reactions and the possible entry of new firms.

OPTIMAL PRICING POLICY AND PRICE ELASTICITY

We note, without a mathematical derivation, the relationship between the point price elasticity of demand, marginal revenue, and price:

$$MR = P\left(1 + \frac{1}{e_p}\right).$$

This follows directly from the mathematical definition of marginal revenue (*MR*). This formula is useful in setting a firm's pricing policy. From the profit-maximizing condition $MR = MC$, we can derive the formula for determining the profit-maximizing price level, which is shown below.

$$MC = MR,$$

$$MC = P\left(1 + \frac{1}{e_p}\right).$$

Solving for the optimal or profit-maximizing *P**, yields

$$P^* = \frac{MC}{\left(1 + \dfrac{1}{e_p}\right)}.$$

EXAMPLE 2

ABC summer catalog of outdoor sporting shoes features $5 off the regular $40 price on a popular Z model. Customer response was more than enthusiastic, with sales rising from 10,000 to 20,000 units. The company buys shoes from a local wholesale distributor for $28, and incurs $4 in marginal marketing costs per unit. The price elasticity of demand is:

$$e_p = \frac{\%\text{ change in } Q}{\%\text{ change in } p} = \frac{\dfrac{20,000 - 10,000}{10,000}}{\dfrac{35 - 40}{40}} = \frac{1}{0.125} = -8.$$

The profit-maximizing price is then

$$P = \frac{\$32}{1 + \frac{1}{-8}} = \$36.6.$$

MARKUP PRICING AND PROFIT MAXIMIZATION

Most firms differentiate markups for different products on the basis of price elasticities and competitive pressure. This section tries to identify the precise relation between the price elasticity and the optimal markups on cost and price. First, recall that

$$P^* = MC \frac{1}{\left(1 + \dfrac{1}{e_p}\right)}.$$

The formula implies that the profit-maximizing price is obtained by multiplying *MC* by

$$\frac{1}{\left(1 + \dfrac{1}{e_p}\right)}.$$

Recall that price = cost (1 + markup on cost). Substituting this into the left-hand side of the formula, we obtain:

$$MC\,(1 + \text{markup on cost}) = MC \left(\frac{1}{1 + \dfrac{1}{e_p}}\right).$$

Simplifying the expression and solving for "markup on cost" yields:

$$\text{Markup on cost} = \left(\frac{1}{1 + \dfrac{1}{e_p}}\right) - 1 = \frac{-1}{e_p + 1}.$$

The optimal markup on cost = $OMC^* = -1/(e_p + 1)$.

EXAMPLE 3

In Example 2 , we note $e_p = -2.5$. The optimal markup on cost is:

$$OMC^* = \frac{-1}{e_p + 1} = \frac{-1}{(-2.5 + 1)} = -1/-1.5 = 0.6667 \text{ or } 66.67\%$$

Note that the more elastic the demand for a product (the more "price sensitive" it is), the smaller the optimal margin. Products with relatively price-insensitive demand will be optimally priced with higher markups.

STRATEGIES THAT YIELD EVEN GREATER PROFITS

The analysis in the previous section demonstrated how a manager can implement the familiar $MR = MC$ rule for setting the profit-maximizing price. Given estimates of demand and cost functions, such a price can be computed directly. Alternatively, given publicly available estimates of demand elasticities, a manager can implement the rule by using the appropriate markup formula.

In some markets, managers can enhance profits above those they would earn by simply charging a single per unit price to all consumers. Several pricing strategies can be used to yield profits above those earned by simply charging a single price where $MR = MC$.

Pricing strategies are price discrimination, two-part pricing, block pricing, and commodity bundling, which are strategies appropriate for firms with various cost structures and degrees of market interdependence. Thus, these strategies can enhance profits of firms in industries with monopolistic, monopolistically competitive, or oligopolistic structures.

PRICE DISCRIMINATION

Price discrimination is defined as the act of selling the same good or service, produced under a single control (i.e., by a monopolist), at different prices to different buyers. Price discrimination exists when a multiproduct firm prices closely related products in such a manner that the differences in their prices are not proportional to the differences in their marginal costs of production and distribution.

Price discrimination can be encountered in the:

a. *First degree*: Separate prices for each consumer. This creates maximum profits for sellers.

b. *Second degree*: Block rates or quantity discounts based on usage.

c. *Third degree:* Different prices for each customer class defined on the basis of age, sex, income, etc. This is the most common type of price discrimination. Examples are: (1) stores offer "student discounts," (2) hotels and restaurants offer senior citizen discounts, and (3) telephone companies charge lower rates on weekends than during the day, implying that businesses may pay a higher price for telephone services than households.

YOU SHOULD REMEMBER

1. If the following conditions are satisfied, a firm can enhance profits by engaging in price discrimination:

   a. There is no resale market for the product.

   b. The firm has a good idea of identifying who belongs to which consumer type.

   c. Consumers are divided into two or more types, with one type having a more elastic demand than the others.

2. A firm that can segment its market will maximize profits by operating in such a way that $MR = MC$ in each market segment.

EXAMPLE 4

Suppose the demand and total cost (TC) functions facing a monopolist are given by

$$P_1 = 10 - Q_1 \text{ (or } Q_1 = 10 - P_1),$$

$$P_2 = 6 - Q_2 \text{ (or } Q_2 = 6 - P_2),$$

$$TC = 4 + (Q_1 + Q_2).$$

Total combined profit in the two markets equals:

$$\pi = TR - TC = P_1 Q_1 + P_2 Q_2 - [4 + (Q_1 + Q_2)]$$

$$= (10 - Q_1)Q_1 + (6 - Q_2)Q_2 - [4 + (Q_1 + Q_2)]$$

$$= -4 + 9Q_1 - Q^2_1 + 5Q_2 - Q^2_2.$$

In order to maximize profits, we find partial derivatives of profit with respect to Q_1 and Q_2, set them equal to zero, and solve for them:

$$\frac{\partial \pi}{\partial Q_1} = 9 - 2Q_1 = 0, Q_1 = 4.5,$$

$$\frac{\partial \pi}{\partial Q_2} = 5 - 2Q_2 = 0, Q_2 = 2.5.$$

Substituting Q_1 and Q_2 into the demand and profit functions yields

$$P_1 = \$5.5, P_2 = \$3.5, \text{ and } \pi = \$22.5$$

YOU SHOULD REMEMBER

The general profit maximizing rule for the firm seeking price discriminations is that the firm should produce and sell in each market until marginal revenue in each market is equal to the firm's marginal cost, i.e., $MR_1 = MR_2 = MC$. Otherwise, consumers in the higher price market will be able to buy the product in the lower price market.

TWO-PART PRICING

Companies with market power can magnify profits using *two-part pricing*. With two-part pricing, a firm charges a fixed fee for the right to buy its products or services, plus a per unit charge for each unit purchased. This pricing strategy is commonly used by such establishments as athletic clubs, golf courses, and health clubs. They typically charge a fixed "initiation fee" plus a charge (either per month or per visit) to use the facilities. Buying clubs are another good example. By paying a membership fee in these clubs, members get to buy products at "wholesale cost."

BLOCK PRICING

Block pricing is another way a firm with market power can increase profits. An example is the purchase of toilet paper in packages of three rolls or cans of soft drink in a six pack. By packaging units of a product and selling them as one package, the firm earns more than by posting a simple per unit price. Block pricing enhances profits by forcing consumers to make all-or-none decisions to purchase units of a good.

COMMODITY BUNDLING

Commodity bundling reflects the practice of bundling two or more different products together and selling them at a single "bundle price." For example, travel agencies often sell "package deals" that include airfare, hotel, and meals at a bundled price instead of pricing each component of a vacation separately. PC makers bundle computers, monitors, and software and sell them at a bundled price. Many car dealers bundle options, such as air conditioning, power steering, and automatic transmission, and sell them at a "special package price."

STRATEGIES FOR SPECIAL COST AND DEMAND STRUCTURES

There are pricing strategies available to firms with special cost and demand structures to maximize profits. They include peak-load pricing and cross subsidization.

PEAK-LOAD PRICING

When demand is higher at some times of the day than at other times, a firm may enhance profits by *peak-load pricing*. This practice involves charging a higher price during peak times than is charged during off peak times. Many markets have periods in which demand is high and periods in which demand is low. Toll roads, utility companies, and airlines all tend to have this feature. When the demand during peak times is so high that the capacity of the firm cannot serve all customers at the same price, the firm can use peak load pricing to enhance its profits.

YOU SHOULD REMEMBER

Peak-load pricing is similar to price discrimination but, due to capacity limitations, the firm is unable to fully equate the marginal revenues of those who purchase at different times.

CROSS SUBSIDIZATION

Whenever the demand for two products made by a company are interrelated through costs or demand, the firm may increase profits by *cross subsidization*. It involves selling one product at or below cost and the other product above cost. This way, the company's profits made with one product are used to subsidize sales of another product. Consider a firm that sells two different types of computer software. One type is a Windows system, and the other is an application that runs on the window (say, a spreadsheet). Clearly there are economies of scope and cost complementarities in making the two products jointly; cost savings arise due to designing the software within the firm. Furthermore, the demand for the two products is likely to be interdependent; the spreadsheet is valuable to a consumer only to the extent that it runs on a version of the window. In such instances, a firm may find it profitable to sell one of the products at (or below) cost and charge a relatively higher price for the other product. For instance, the firm may price the Windows system at (or below) cost to induce numerous consumers to use it to run their computers. Once consumers commit to the company's version of Windows, the firm can charge a higher price for its applications software.

YOU SHOULD REMEMBER

The advantage of cross subsidization is that it allows the company to sell multiple products, which leads to cost savings in the presence of economies of scope. If the two products have demands that are interdependent, the firm can induce consumers to buy more of each product than they would otherwise.

PRICING POLICIES

Many firms use two pricing tactics, depending upon the type of goal they wish to accomplish with pricing. They are skimming and penetrating pricing policies.

SKIMMING PRICING

Skimming pricing is the method of pricing that involves setting a high initial price for a new product, with a progressively lowering of the price as time passes and as the market broadens and matures. The objective of this pricing method is to maximize short-term profits.

PENETRATING PRICING

Penetrating pricing is a pricing policy that involves setting low initial prices in order to gain quick acceptance in a broad portion of the market. It calls for the sacrifice of some short-term profits in order to gain a better long-term market share. The lower price is then often raised as the product moves into its growth stage. One objective is to obtain a committed customer. This policy is also used by a firm when consumer demand is price-elastic.

KNOW THE CONCEPTS

TERMS FOR STUDY

block pricing	peak-load pricing
commodity bundling	penetrating pricing
cost-based price	price discrimination
markup pricing	skimming pricing
optimal pricing	two-part pricing

DO YOU KNOW THE BASICS?

1. What criticisms is cost-plus pricing subject to?

2. Explain the difference between markup on cost and markup on price.

3. What is the role of sunk costs in short-run managerial decision making?

4. State three important conditions for price discrimination to work well.

5. A local family doctor read an article published by AMA estimating that elasticity of demand for the representative family practice is −2. How much should the family doctor markup her price over marginal cost?

6. Explain why theaters sometimes give senior citizen discounts.

7. Many restaurants offer free appetizers with a two-drink minimum during a limited number of hours. Is this profit-maximizing behavior?

8. Give some examples of firms using peak-load pricing. Can they enhance their profits using this pricing practice?

9. Give some examples of firms using two-part pricing.

PRACTICAL APPLICATION

1. A monopolist is profit maximizing when the price elasticity of demand is −2 and price is $5. What is the monopolist's marginal cost?

2. As an owner of a local market, you sell a gallon of milk for $2. If your elasticity of demand for milk sold at your store is -2.5, what are your profit-maximizing markup and price?

3. Carlos Service Stations is contemplating selling mugs imprinted with its logo. Preliminary estimates suggests the following demand function: $Q = 10,000-2,000P$

   a. How many mugs could Carlos sell at $1.50 each; at $2.00 each?

   b. What price must Carlos charge to sell 8,000 mugs?

   c. At what price would quantity be zero?

   d. How many mugs should Carlos have ready if it decides to give the mugs away for promotional purposes?

   e. Calculate the point elasticity of demand at a price of $1.50.

   f. At what price is the elasticity of demand equal to -1 (i.e., unitary)?

4. Suppose the demand function for Stacy Flowers is given by $P(Q) = 10-2Q$ and the cost function is $TC(Q) = 2Q$. What is the profit-maximizing level of output and price for this firm?

5. Yumi summer catalog of outdoor sporting shoes features $3 off the regular $36 price on a popular Z model. Customer response was more than enthusiastic, with sales rising from 15,000 to 25,000 units. The company buys shoes from a local wholesale distributor for $28 and incurs $3.5 in marginal marketing costs per unit.

   a. Determine the point price elasticity of demand.

   b. Is the regular $36 price optimal in the sense of maximizing Yumi's profits on the shoes?

6. Donjovi Corporation is an insulation contractor serving both residential and commercial customers in Oregon. Demand functions have been estimated as:

$$Q_1 = 400,000 - 400P_1 \text{ (Residential demand)},$$

$$Q_2 = 1,200,000 - 1,600P_2 \text{ (Commercial demand)}$$

where Q is tons of insulation installed and P is dollars. Each ton of installed insulation results in $600 of marginal labor and materials expense.

   a. Calculate profit-maximizing price and output levels, assuming price discrimination between its two types of customers.

   b. Calculate the maximum profit earned by the firm.

   c. Calculate point price elasticities for each type of customer at the activity levels identified in part (a). Comment on these results.

7. Suppose the demand and total cost (TC) functions facing a monopolist are given by

$$P_1 = 12 - Q_1 \text{ (or } Q_1 = 12 - P_1),$$

$$P_2 = 8 - Q_2 \text{ (or } Q_2 = 8 - P_2),$$

$$TC = 5 + 2(Q_1 + Q_2).$$

Total combined profit in the two markets equals

$$\pi = TR - TC = P_1Q_1 + P_2Q_2 - [5 + 2(Q_1 + Q_2)]$$

$$= (2 - Q_1)Q_1 + (8 - Q_2Q_2) - [5 + 2(Q_1 + Q_2)]$$

$$= -5 + 10Q_1 - Q^2_1 + 6Q_2 - Q^2_2.$$

   a. Determine profit-maximizing price and output levels and total profit at these levels.

   b. Prove that at the profit maximizing output, MR_1 equals MR_2.

   c. Determine what profits would be if the firm did not discriminate between the two markets.

ANSWERS

KNOW THE CONCEPTS

1. A cost-plus pricing system suffers from some criticisms: (a) it fails to take into account demand as measured in terms of buyers' desires and purchasing power, and (b) it does not reflect competition in terms of rivals' reactions and the possible entry of new firms.

2. Markup on cost is the profit margin for a product expressed as a percentage of unit cost, while markup on price is the profit margin expressed as a percentage of price, rather than unit cost.

3. Sunk costs are unaffected by decisions made now or in the future and are therefore irrelevant in the short-run decision making.

4. If the following conditions are satisfied, a firm can enhance profits by engaging in price discrimination: (a) there is no resale market for the product, (b) the firm has a good idea of identifying who belongs to which consumer type, and (c) consumers are divided into two or more types, with one type having a more elastic demand than the others.

5. $P* = \dfrac{MC}{\left(1 + \dfrac{1}{e_p}\right)} = \dfrac{MC}{1 + \dfrac{1}{-2}} = 2MC.$

The doctor should charge her price twice over the marginal cost.

1. Since seniors have a more elastic demand than nonsenior citizens, a lower price is charged to them to maximize the profits.

2. It may be an example of cross subsidization. The appetizers are typically salty, leading customers to buy more drinks than would otherwise be the case.

3. Toll roads, utility companies, and airlines are good examples. When the demand during peak times is so high that the capacity of the firm cannot serve all customers at the same price, the firm can use peak-load pricing to enhance its profits.

4. This pricing strategy is commonly used by such establishments as athletic clubs, golf courses, and health clubs.

PRACTICAL APPLICATION

1.

$$MC = P\left(1 + \dfrac{1}{e_p}\right) = \$5\left(1 + \dfrac{1}{-2}\right) = \$2.5$$

2.

$$P* = \dfrac{MC}{\left(1 + \dfrac{1}{e_p}\right)} = \dfrac{\$2}{1 + \dfrac{1}{-2.5}} = \$3.33$$

3a. At $1.50, $Q = 10{,}000 - 2{,}000(1.5) = 7{,}000$

At $2.00, $Q = 10{,}000 - 2{,}000(2) = 6{,}000$

3b. Set $Q = 8{,}000$ and solve for P

$8{,}000 = 10{,}000 - 2{,}000P$; $P = \$1.00$

3c. Set $Q = 0$ and solve for P

$0 = 10{,}000 - 2{,}000P$, $P = \$5.00$

3d. Set $P = 0$ and solve for Q

$Q = 10{,}000 - 2{,}000(0)$, $Q = 10{,}000$

3e. We know from (a) that at $1.50, $Q = 10{,}000 - 2{,}000(1.5) = 7{,}000$

$$e_p = \frac{\% \text{ change in } Q}{\% \text{ change in } P} = \frac{dQ/Q}{dP/P} = \frac{dQ}{dP}\frac{p}{Q} = (-2000)\frac{1.50}{7{,}000} = -0.43$$

3f. Demand is unit elastic where $MR = 0$. To find MR, write the demand curve in inverse form:

$$Q = 10{,}000 - 2{,}000P \text{ or } P = 5 - 0.0005Q,$$

$$TR = PQ = (5 - 0.0005Q)Q = 5Q - 0.0005Q^2.$$

Set $MR = 0$ and solve for Q:

$$MR = \frac{dTR}{dQ} = 5 - 0.001Q = 0, \quad Q = 5{,}000.$$

Substitute to solve for P:

$$P = 5 - 0.0005Q = 5 - 0.0005(5{,}000) = \$2.50$$

The demand elasticity is unitary at a price of $2.50.

4.

$$TR = PQ = (10 - 2Q)Q = 10Q - 2Q^2 \quad MR = 10 - 4Q$$

and

$$TC = 2Q. \quad MC = 2.$$

Setting $MR = MC$ yields, $10 - 4Q = 2$.

So $Q^* = 2$. Substituting this into the demand function yields the profit-maximizing price:

$$P = 10 - 2Q = 10 - 2(2) = \$6.$$

5a. The price elasticity of demand is

$$e_p = \frac{\% \text{ change in } Q}{\% \text{ change in } p} = \frac{(25,000 - 15,000)/15,000}{(33 - 36)/36} = 8.$$

5b. The profit-maximizing price is

$$P = \$31.5(1 + 1/\!-\!8) = \$36.$$

The answer is yes; the regular $36 is the profit-maximizing price.

6a. With price discrimination, profits are maximized by setting $MR = MC$ in each market, where $MC = \$600$.

<u>Residential</u>

$$Q_1 = 400,000 - 400P_1, \text{ so } P_1 = 1,000 - 0.0025Q_1$$

$$TR_1 = (1,000 - 0.0025Q_1)Q_1$$

$$= 1,000Q_1 - 0.0025Q^2_1$$

$$MR_1 = dTR_1/dQ_1 = 1,000 - 0.005Q_1$$

$$MR_1 = MC$$

$$1,000 - 0.0005Q_1 = 600$$

$$0.005Q_1 = 400$$

$$Q_1 = 80,000$$

$$P_1 = 1,000 - 0.0025(80,000) = \$800 \text{ per ton}$$

<u>Commercial</u>

$$Q_2 = 1,200,000 - 1,600P_2.$$

So

$$P_2 = 750 - 0.000625Q_2$$

$$TR_2 = (750 - 0.000625Q_2)Q_2$$

$$= 750Q_2 - 0.000625Q^2{}_2$$

$$MR_2 = \frac{dTR_2}{dQ_2} = 750 - 0.000125Q_2$$

$$MR_2 = MC$$

$$750 - 0.00125Q_2 = 600$$

$$0.00125Q_2 = 150$$

$$Q_2 = 120,000$$

$$P_2 = 750 - 0.000625(120,000)$$

$$= \$675 \text{ per ton}$$

6b. The profit earned by the firm is

$$\text{Profit} = TR - TC = P_1Q_1 + P_2Q_2 - AVC(Q_1 + Q_2)$$

$$= 800(80,000) + 675(120,000) - 600(80,000 + 120,000)$$

$$= 25,000,000$$

6c.

Residential

$$e_p = \frac{dQ_1}{dP_1} \times \frac{P_1}{Q_1}$$

$$= -400 \times (800/80{,}000) = -4$$

Commercial

$$e_p = \frac{dQ_2}{dP_2} \times \frac{P_2}{Q_2}$$

$$= -1{,}600 \times (675/120{,}000) = -9$$

A higher price for residential customers is consistent with the lower degree of price elasticity observed in that market.

7a. In order to maximize profits, we find partial derivatives of profit with respect to Q_1 and Q_2, set them equal to zero, and solve for them:

$$\frac{\partial \pi}{\partial Q_1} = 10 - 2Q_1 = 0;\ Q_1 = 5$$

$$\frac{\partial \pi}{\partial Q_2} = 6 - 2Q_2 = 0;\ Q_2 = 3$$

Substituting Q_1 and Q_2 into the demand and profit functions yields:

$P_1 = \$7$, $P_2 = \$5$, and $\pi = \$29$

7b. To see if $MR_1 = MR_2$, we find the TR function,

$TR = P_1Q_1 + P_2Q_2 = (12-Q_1)Q_1 + (8-Q_2)Q_2 = 12Q_1 - Q^2_1 + 8Q_2 - Q^2_2.$

Determining MR_1 and MR_2 and substituting the solution values $Q_1 = 5$ and $Q_2 = 3$:

$$MR_1 = \frac{\partial TR}{\partial Q_1} = 12 - 2Q_1 = 12 - 2(5) = 2$$

$$MR_2 = \frac{\partial TR}{\partial Q_2} = 8 - 2Q_2 = 8 - 2(3) = 2$$

7c. We add up Q_1 and Q_2 to obtain a total demand function:

$$P_1 = 12 - Q_1 \text{ (or } Q_1 = 12 - P_1)$$

$$P_2 = 8 - Q_2 \text{ (or } Q_2 = 8 - P_2)$$

$$Q = Q_1 + Q_2 = 12 - P_1 + 8 - P_2 = 20 - P_1 - P_2$$

Since price discrimination is no longer possible, P_1 and P_2 must be identical, i.e.,

$$Q = 20 - P_1 - P_2 = 20 - 2P \text{ or } P = 10 - Q/2$$

Total profit is now

$$\pi = TR - TC = PQ - TC = 10Q - Q^2/2 - 5 - 2Q = 8Q - Q^2/2 - 5$$

$$\frac{d\pi}{dQ} = 8 - Q = 0, Q = 8$$

Substituting yields: $P = \$6$ and $\pi = \$27$.

Note that price discrimination yields more profit ($29 versus $27).

11

ANALYSIS OF PROJECT DECISIONS (CAPITAL BUDGETING)

Capital budgeting is the process of planning for and evaluating long-term capital expenditure decisions. There are many investment decisions that the firm may have to make in order to grow. Examples of capital budgeting applications are product line selection, keep or sell a business segment, lease or buy, and which asset to invest in.

WHAT ARE THE TYPES OF INVESTMENT PROJECTS?

There are typically two types of long-term investment decisions:

1. *Expansion decisions* in terms of obtaining new facilities or expanding existing ones. Examples include:

   a. Investments in property, plant, and equipment, as well as other types of assets.

   b. Resource commitments in the form of new product development, market research, introduction of a computer network, refunding of long-term debt, and so on.

   c. Mergers and acquisitions in the form of buying another company to add a new product or service line.

2. *Replacement decisions* replacing obsolete assets with new ones. Examples include replacing an old machine with a high-tech machine.

WHAT ARE THE FEATURES OF INVESTMENT PROJECTS?

Long-term investments have three important features:

1. They typically involve a large amount of initial cash outlays that tend to have a long-term impact on the firm's future profitability. Therefore, this initial cash outlay needs to be justified on a cost-benefit basis.

2. There are expected recurring cash inflows (for example, increased revenues, savings in cash operating expenses, and so on) over the life of the investment project. This frequently requires considering the *time value of money*.

3. Corporate income taxes could make a difference in the accept or reject decision. Therefore, income tax factors must be taken into account in every capital budgeting decision.

UNDERSTANDING THE CONCEPT OF TIME VALUE OF MONEY

A dollar now is worth more than a dollar to be received later. This statement sums up an important principle: money has a time value. The reason is that you could invest the dollar now and have more than a dollar at the specified later date.

Time value of money is an important consideration in making business decisions. For example, compound interest computations are required to calculate future sums of money emanating from an investment. Discounting (present value) is the opposite of compounding. It is used to appraise the future cash flow of capital budgeting proposals. Many applications of time value of money exist in accounting, economics, finance, and other business areas.

HOW DO YOU CALCULATE FUTURE VALUES—HOW MONEY GROWS?

A dollar in hand today has more of a worth than a dollar to be received in the future due to the interest it could generate from putting the funds in an investment. Compounding interest means that interest earns interest. Let us define:

F_n = future value: the amount of money at the end of year n,

P = principal,

i = annual interest rate,

n = number of years.

Then,

F_1 = the amount of money at the end of year 1

= principal and interest = $P + iP = P(1 + i)$,

F_2 = the amount of money at the end of year 2

= $Fi(1 + i) = P(1 + i)(1 + i) = P(1 + i)^2$.

The future value of an investment compounded annually at rate i for n years is

$$F_n = P(1 + i)^n = P \cdot T1(i,n),$$

Where $T1(i,n)$ is the compound amount of $1 and can be found in Table 1 in Appendix V.

Note: $(1+i)^n = T1(i,n)$ is the future value interest factor, *FVIF.*

EXAMPLE 1

You place $100,000 in a bank account earning 10 percent interest compounded annually. How much money will be accumulated after 6 years? Note that $F_n = P(1+i)^n$

$$F_6 = \$100,000 \, (1 + 010)^6 = \$100,000 \, T1(10\%, 6 \text{ years})$$

From Table 1, the *T1* for 6 years at 10 percent is 1.772.
Therefore, $F_6 = \$100,000 \, (1.772) = \$177,720.$

FUTURE VALUE OF AN ANNUITY

An annuity is defined as a series of payments (or receipts) of a fixed amount for a stated number of periods. We assume period-end payments. The future value of an annuity is a compound annuity of depositing or investing equal amounts of money at year-end for specified time periods.

Let S_n = the future value of an n-year annuity,

A = the amount of the annuity.

Then we can write

$$S_n = A(1 + i)^{n-1} + A (1 + i)^{n-2} + \ldots + A(1 + i)^0$$

$$= A[(1 + i)^{n-1} + (1 + i)^{n-2} + \ldots + (1 + i)^0]$$

$$= A \cdot \sum_{t=0}^{n-1} (1 + i)^t = A\left(\frac{(1 + i)^{n-1}}{i}\right) = A \cdot T2(i,n),$$

Where $T2(i,n)$ represents the future value of an annuity of $1 for n years compounded at i percent and can be found in Table 2 in Appendix V.

Note: $T2(i,n)$ is the future value interest factor for an annuity, *FVIFA.*

EXAMPLE 2

You want to know how much you will have in a bank account after 10 years by depositing $20,000 at the end of each year for the next 10 years. The annual interest rate is 12 percent. The $T2(12\%,10$ years$)$ is given in Table 2 as 7.548. Therefore,

$$S_{10} = \$20,000 \; T2(12\%, \; 10) = \$20,000 \; (7.548) = \$350,960.$$

WHAT IS PRESENT VALUE—HOW MUCH IS MONEY WORTH NOW?

Present value is the value today of future cash flows. The computation of present values (discounting) is the opposite of determining the compounded future value. The interest rate i is referred to as the <u>discount rate</u>. The discount rate we use is more commonly called the <u>cost of capital</u>, which is the minimum rate of return required by the investor. Recall that

$$F_n = P(1 + i)^n.$$

Therefore,

$$P = \frac{F_n}{(1 + i)^n} = F_n\left(\frac{1}{(1 + i)^n}\right) = F_n \cdot T3(i,n),$$

where $T3(i,n)$ represents the present value of $1 and is given in Table 3 in the Appendix.

Note: $T3(i,n)$ is the present value interest factor, PVIF.

EXAMPLE 3

You have the option of receiving $60,000 6 years from now. If you earn 15 percent on your money, how much should you pay for this investment? To answer this query, you need to compute the present value of $60,000 to be received 6 years from now at a 15 percent rate of discount. F_6 is $60,000, i is 15 percent, and n is 6 years. $T3(15\%,6)$ from Table 3 is 0.432.

$$P = \$60,000 \left(\frac{1}{(1 + 0.15)^6}\right) = \$60,000 \; T3(15\%,6) = \$60,000(0.432) = 25,920.$$

This means that you can earn 15 percent on your money, and you would be indifferent to receiving $25,920 now or $60,000 6 years from today because the amounts are time equivalent. Stated another way, you could invest $25,920 today at 15 percent and have $60,000 in 6 years.

PRESENT VALUE OF AN ANNUITY

Interest received from notes, bonds, pension funds, and insurance contracts involve annuities. To compare these financial instruments, the present value of each must be determined. The present value of an annuity (P_n) is solved as follows:

$$P_n = A + A\frac{1}{(1+i)^1} + A\frac{1}{(1+i)^2} \cdots + A\frac{1}{(1+i)^n}$$

$$= A\left(\frac{1}{(1+i)^1} + \frac{1}{(1+i)^2} + \cdots + \frac{1}{(1+i)}\right)^n$$

$$= A\sum_{t=1}^{n}\frac{1}{(1+i)^t} = A\frac{1}{i}\left(1 - \frac{1}{(1+i)}\right) = A \cdot T4(i,n),$$

where A = the amount of an annuity and $T4(i,n)$ represents the present value of an annuity of \$1 discounted at i percent for n years and is found in Table 4 in the Appendix.

Note: $T4(i,n)$ is the present value interest factor for an annuity, *PVIFA*.

EXAMPLE 4

Assume an annuity of \$10,000 for 3 years. Then the present value is

$$P_n = A \cdot T4\ (i,n),$$

$$P_3 = \$10,000\ T4(10\%, 3\ years) = \$10,000\ (2.487) = \$24,870.$$

YOU SHOULD REMEMBER

There are many financial calculators that contain preprogrammed formulas to perform many present value and future value applications. Furthermore, spreadsheet software, such as Microsoft's Excel, Quattro, and Lotus 1–2–3 have built-in financial functions to perform many such applications.

A BASIC FRAMEWORK FOR CAPITAL BUDGETING

The economic theory of the firm suggests that to maximize its profit, a firm should operate at the point where the marginal cost of an additional unit of output just equals the marginal revenue derived from that output. This rule may be equally applicable to the capital budgeting process. The marginal cost may be thought as the firm's cost of capital—that is, the cost of successive increments of capital acquired by the firm, while the marginal revenue may be regarded as the rates of return earned on succeeding investments. Figure 11–1 illustrates this concept.

The projects are indicated by lettered bars on the graph. For example, Project A requires an outlay of $2 million and is expected to generate a 24 percent return. Project B will cost $1 million ($3 million minus $2 million on the horizontal axis) and generate a 22 percent return, and so on. The marginal cost of capital (*MCC*) line represents the cost of each additional dollar raised in the capital markets.

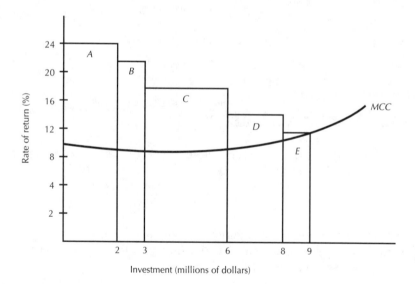

Figure 11–1. Simplified Capital Budgeting Process

Graphically, the projects are arranged in descending order by their rates of return, indicating that no firm has an unlimited number of investment opportunities, which all generate lofty returns. As new products are made, new markets entered, and cost-saving high tech adopted, the number of highly profitable projects tends to diminish. Using this basic framework, the firm should embark on *A, B, C, D,* and *E,* since their returns exceed the firm's *MCC.*

The remainder of this chapter takes up some practical, analytical tools that are helpful in making capital budgeting decisions.

HOW DO YOU MEASURE INVESTMENT WORTH?

Three popular methods of evaluating investment projects are as follows:

1. Net present value (*NPV*)

2. Internal rate of return (*IRR*)

3. Profitability index (Benefit/cost ratio)

The *NPV* method and the *IRR* method are called *discounted cash flow (DCF)* methods. Each of these methods is discussed below.

NET PRESENT VALUE

Net present value (*NPV*) equals the present value (*PV*) of cash inflows from a proposal less the initial investment (*I*):

$$NPV = PV - \mathrm{I}.$$

The present value of future cash flows is determined using the *cost of capital* (or minimum required rate of return) as the discount rate. When cash inflows are equal, the present value would be

$$PV = A \cdot T4 \ (i,n),$$

where *A* is the amount of the annuity.

Decision rule: If *NPV* is positive, accept the project. Otherwise, reject it.

EXAMPLE 5

Consider the following investment:

Initial investment	$37,910
Estimated life	5 years
Annual cash inflows after taxes	$10,000
Cost of capital (minimum required rate of return)	8%

Present value of the cash inflows is:

$PV = A \cdot T4(i,n)$

$\quad = \$10,000. \; T4(8\%,5 \text{ years})$

$\quad = \$10,000 \, (3.993)$	$39,930
Initial investment (I)	37,910
Net present value ($NPV = PV\text{-}I$)	$ 2,020

Since the *NPV* of the investment is positive, the investment should be accepted.

The advantages of the *NPV* method are that it obviously recognizes the time value of money and it is easy to compute whether the cash flows from an annuity or vary from period to period.

YOU SHOULD REMEMBER

If cash inflows are different from year to year, you should compute the present value separately year by year using Table 3 in the Appendix.

INTERNAL RATE OF RETURN

Internal rate of return (*IRR*), a project's yield or real return, is defined as the rate of interest that equates *I* with the *PV* of future cash inflows.

In other words, at *IRR*

$$I = PV \quad \text{or} \quad NPV = 0$$

<u>Decision rule</u>: Accept the project if the *IRR* exceeds the cost of capital. Otherwise, reject it.

EXAMPLE 6

Assume the same data given in Example 5, and set the following equality ($I = PV$):

$$\$37{,}910 = \$10{,}000 \cdot T4(i,5\ years),$$

$$T4(i,5\ years) = \frac{\$37,910}{\$10,000} = 3.791,$$

which is right on 10% in the 5-year line of Table 4 in the Appendix.

Since the *IRR* of the investment is greater than the cost of capital (8 percent), accept the project.

The advantage of using the *IRR* method is that it does consider the time value of money and, therefore, it gives a more exact and realistic yield on the project.

The shortcomings of this method are that (1) it is time-consuming to compute, (2) it fails to recognize the varying sizes of investment in competing projects, and (3) it is not unusual for the project with nonconventional patterns of cash flows (i.e., negative cash flows in some periods) to have *multiple IRRs*.

YOU SHOULD REMEMBER

It is extremely tedious to compute the *IRR*, especially when the cash inflows are not even. Most financial calculators and spreadsheet programs can be used in making *IRR* calculations. For example, Lotus 1–2–3 has a function @IRR(guess, range). 1–2–3 considers negative numbers as cash outflows, such as the initial investment and positive numbers as cash inflows. Suppose you want to calculate the *IRR* of a $12,950 investment (the value -12,950 entered in cell A1) that is followed by 10 monthly cash inflows of $3,000 (B1.K1). Using a guess of 12% (the value of 0.12), which is in effect the cost of capital, your formula would be @IRR (0.12, A1...K1) and 1–2–3 would return 19.14.

PROFITABILITY INDEX

The profitability index, also called *benefit/cost ratio*, is the ratio of the total *PV* of future cash inflows to the initial investment, that is, *PV/I*. This index is used as a means of ranking projects in descending order of attractiveness.

Decision rule: If the profitability index is greater than 1, accept the project.

EXAMPLE 7

Using the data in Example 5, the profitability index is

$$\frac{PV}{I} = \frac{\$39,930}{37,910} = 1.05.$$

Since this project generates $1.05 for each dollar invested (i.e., its profitability index is greater than 1), accept the project.

The profitability index has the advantage of putting all projects on the same relative basis regardless of size.

CAPITAL RATIONING—PROJECT RANKING WITH A LIMITED BUDGET

Many companies set a ceiling on the capital spending budget. Capital rationing deals with choosing the combination of acceptable projects that generate the highest overall *NPV*. The profitability index is used to rank projects when funds are limited.

EXAMPLE 8

The Westmont Company has a fixed budget of $250,000. It wants to select a mix of acceptable projects from the following:

Projects	I($)	PV($)	NPV($)	Profitability Index	Ranking
H	70,000	112,000	42,000	1.6	1
I	100,000	145,000	45,000	1.45	2
J	115,000	126,500	11,500	1.10	5
K	80,000	100,000	20,000	1.25	3
L	60,000	57,000	-3,000	0.95	6
M	82,000	95,000	13,000	1.16	4

The ranking resulting from the profitability index shows that the company should select projects H, I, and K:

	I	PV
H	$70,000	$112,000
I	100,000	145,000
K	80,000	100,000
	$250,000	$357,000

Therefore,

$$NPV = \$357 - \$250,000 = \$107,000.$$

HOW DO INCOME TAXES AFFECT INVESTMENT DECISIONS?

Income taxes have to be considered in capital budgeting decisions. The project looks good on a before-tax basis may have to be rejected on an after-tax basis and vice versa. Income taxes usually impact both the amount and the timing of cash flows. Because net income, not cash inflows, is subject to tax, after-tax cash inflows are different from after-tax net income. To calculate after-tax cash flows, depreciation, which is not a cash outlay, must be added to profits after taxes.

After-tax cash inflows = after-tax net income + depreciation.

EXAMPLE 9

The Navistar Company estimates that it can generate sales of $67,000 and incur annual cost of operations of $52,000 for the next ten years if it buys a special-purpose machine at a cost of $100,000. No residual value is expected. Depreciation is by straight-line. Assume that the income tax rate is 30%, and the after-tax cost of capital (minimum required rate of return) is 10%. After-tax cash inflows can be calculated as follows:

Note that depreciation by straight-line is $100,000/10 = $10,000 per year. Thus,

$$\text{After-tax cash inflows} = \text{after-tax net income} + \text{depreciation}$$

$$= (\$67,000 - \$52,000)(1 - 0.3) + \$10,000$$

$$= \$15,000 \ (0.7) + \$10,000$$

$$= \$10,500 + \$10,000 = 20,500.$$

To see if this machine should be purchased, the net present value can be calculated.

$$PV = \$20{,}500 \; T4(10\%, \; 10 \text{ years}) = \$20{,}500 \; (6.145) = \$125{,}972.50.$$

Thus,

$$NPV = PV - I = \$125{,}972.50 - \$100{,}000 = \$25{,}972.50$$

Since *NPV* is positive, the machine should be bought.

EXAMPLE 10

The treasurer of a small appliance maker estimates the cash inflows, outflows, and net cash flows before taxes shown in columns 1, 2, and 3 of the table below, if it buys a high-tech machine at a cost of $1,000,000. No residual value is expected. Life is 5 years. Depreciation is by straight-line. Assume that the income tax rate is 35%, and the after-tax cost of capital (minimum required rate of return) is 10%. The process of arriving at net cash flow after taxes are shown in columns 4, 5, 6, 7, and 8.

Year (1)	Cash Inflow (1)	Cash Outflow (2)	Net Cash Flow Before Taxes (3) = (1) − (2)	Depreciation (Noncash) Expense) (4) = 0.2 x 1,000,000	Net Income Before Taxes (5) = (3)−(4)	Income Taxes (6) = 0.35 x (5)	Net Income After Taxes (7) = (5)−(6)	Net Cash Flow After Taxes (8) = (7) + (4)
1	$1,000,000	$625,000	$375,000	$200,000	$175,000	$61,250	$113,750	$313,750
2	$ 900,000	$610,000	$290,000	$200,000	$ 90,000	$31,500	$ 58,500	$258,500
3	$ 925,000	$635,000	$290,000	$200,000	$ 90,000	$31,500	$ 58,500	$258,500
4	$ 930,000	$605,000	$325,000	$200,000	$125,000	$43,750	$ 81,250	$281,250
5	$ 825,000	$557,000	$268,000	$200,000	$ 68,000	$23,800	$ 44,200	$244,200

EXAMPLE 11

The *NPV* of the machine can be calculated using Table 3 in the Appendix, as shown below.

Year	Cash Flow After Taxes	T3 at 10% Table value	Present Value
0	$(1,000,000)	$ 1.000	$(1,000,000)
1	$ 313,750	$ 0.909	$ 285,199
2	$ 258,500	$ 0.826	$ 213,521
3	$ 258,500	$ 0.751	$ 194,134
4	$ 281,250	$ 0.683	$ 192,094
5	$ 244,200	$ 0.621	$ 151,648
			NPV = $ 36,596

THE POSTAUDIT

The last step in capital budgeting is a postaudit review that should be performed by an individual independent of the decision. Actual operating costs and cash receipts from sales should be determined and compared with the costs and revenues estimated when the project was originally reviewed and accepted. The postaudit review performs functions including:

1. Informs management about the accuracy of projections of cash flows.

2. Identifies additional factors that might have been forgotten in a particular project.

3. Sees how effectively and efficiently the process is working.

COST OF CAPITAL AND THE DISCOUNT RATE

The cost of capital is defined as the return rate required to maintain the company's market value (or market price of stock). Project managers must know the cost of capital (*minimum required rate of return*). It was used either as a discount rate under the *NPV* method or as a hurdle rate under the *IRR* method earlier in the chapter. The cost of capital is a weighted average cost of a company's financing instruments, including bonds, preferred stock, common stock, and retained earnings.

COST OF DEBT

The cost of debt is stated on an after-tax basis, because the interest on the debt is tax deductible. However, the cost of preferred stock is the stated annual dividend rate. This rate is not adjusted for income taxes because the preferred dividend, unlike debt interest, is not a deductible expense in computing corporate income taxes.

EXAMPLE 12

Assume that the Hume Company issues a $1,000, 7 percent, 10-year bond whose net proceeds are $960. The tax rate is 40 percent. Then, the after-tax cost of debt is

$$7.00\% \ (1 - 0.4) = 4.2\%.$$

EXAMPLE 13

The Hume company has preferred stock that pays a $12 dividend per share and has a market price per share of $100. The cost of preferred stock is

$$\frac{\text{Dividend per share}}{\text{Price per share}} = \frac{\$12}{\$100} = 12\%.$$

COST OF COMMON STOCK

The cost of common stock is the rate of return investors demand on a company's common stock. One way to measure the cost of common stock is to use the *Gordon's growth model*. The model is

$$P_o = \frac{D_1}{r - g},$$

where

P_o = value (or market price) of common stock

D_1 = dividend to be received in 1 year,

r = investor's required rate of return,

g = rate of growth (assumed to be constant over time)

Solving the model for r results in the formula for the cost of common stock:

$$r = \frac{D_1}{P_o} + g.$$

EXAMPLE 14

The market price of the Hume Company's stock is $50. The current year dividend will be $6 per share. The anticipated annual growth rate in dividends is 8 percent. The cost of common stock equals

$$\frac{D_1}{P_o} + g = \frac{\$6}{\$50} + 8\% = 20\%.$$

COST OF RETAINED EARNINGS

The cost of retained earnings is closely tied to the cost of common stock, because the cost of equity obtained by retained earnings is the same as the rate of return investors demand on the company's common stock.

COMPUTING THE OVERALL COST OF CAPITAL

The company's overall cost of capital is the weighted average of the individual financing costs. The weights are the proportion of each type of financing to the total financing.

Σ (percentage of the total capital structure by each source of financing $\times$ cost of capital for each source)

The computation of overall cost of capital is illustrated in the following example.

EXAMPLE 15

Assume that the capital structure at the latest statement date is indicative of the proportions of financing that the company intends to use over time:

		Cost
Mortgage bonds ($1,000 par)	$20,000,000	4.20% (from Example 12)
Preferred stock ($100 par)	5,000,000	12.00 (from Example 13)
Common stock ($40 par)	20,000,000	20.00 (from Example 14)
Retained earnings	5,000,000	20.00
Total	$50,000,000	

These proportions would be applied to the assumed individual explicit after-tax costs below:

Source	Weights	Cost	Weighted Cost
Debt	40%(a)	4.20%	1.68%(b)
Preferred stock	10	12.00%	1.20
Common stock	40	20.00%	8.00
Retained earnings	10	20.00%	2.00
	100%		12.88%

(a) $20,000,000/$50,000,000 = 0.40 = 40%
(b) 4.20% $\times$ 40% = 1.68%
   Overall cost of capital is 12.88%.

By computing a company's cost of capital, we can determine its minimum rate of return, which is used as the discount rate in present value calculations. A company's cost of capital is also an indicator of risk. For example, if your company's cost of financing increases, it is being viewed as more risky by investors and creditors, who are demanding higher return on their investments in the form of higher dividend and interest rates.

KNOW THE CONCEPTS

TERMS FOR STUDY

after-tax cash inflows	discount rate
annuity	internal rate of return
capital budgeting	net present value
capital rationing	profitability index
cost of capital	time value of money

DO YOU KNOW THE BASICS?

1. Define the term *capital budgeting*.

2. What is the profitability index, and of what value is it?

3. How would you define the internal rate of return of a capital project?

4. What is the definition of the net present value (*NPV*) of a project? What is the decision rule under the *NPV* method?

5. How would you define the cost of capital?

6. What role does the cost of capital play in the *IRR* method and in the *NPV* method?

7. What is the purpose of a postaudit?

PRACTICAL APPLICATION

1. The following data are given for Barron's Aluminum Company:

Initial cost of proposed equipment	$80,000
Estimated useful life	7 years
Estimated annual savings in cash operating expenses (after taxes)	$20,000
Predicted residual value at the end of the useful life	$ 4,000
Cost of capital after taxes	12%

Compute the following:

a. Present value of estimated annual savings

b. Present value of estimated residual value

c. Total present value of estimated cash inflows

d. Net present value (*NPV*)

e. Internal rate of return (*IRR*)

2. The Travis Company is considering a capital outlay of $75,000. Net annual cash inflows after taxes are estimated at $15,000 for 10 years. Straight-line depreciation is to be used, with no residual value. Compute the items listed below.

a. Net present value (*NPV*), assuming a cost of capital after tax of 12 percent.

b. Internal rate of return (*IRR*)

3. Fill in the blanks for each of the following independent cases. Assume an investment useful life of 10 years.

	Annual Cash Inflow	Investment	Cost of Capital	IRR	NPV
1.	$200,000	$898,800	14%	(a)	(b)
2.	$140,000	(c)	14%	20%	(d)
3.	(e)	$200,000	(f)	14%	$35,624
4.	(g)	$300,000	12%	(h)	$39,000

4. Horn Corp. invested in a four-year project. Horn's cost of capital after taxes is 8 percent. Additional data about the project follows:

Year	Cash Inflow from Operations, After Taxes	Present Value of $1 at 8%
1	$3,000	0.926
2	$3,500	0.857
3	$2,400	0.794
4	$2,600	0.735

Assuming a positive net present value of $500, what was the amount of the original investment?

5. Gene, Inc., bought equipment with a useful life of eight years and no residual value. Straight-line depreciation is used. It was anticipated to result in cash inflow from operations, net of income taxes, of $4,000. The present value of an ordinary annuity of $1 for eight periods at 10 percent is 5.335. The present value of $1 for eight periods at 10 percent is 0.467. Assume Gene used an internal rate of return of 10 percent. How much was the amount of the initial investment?

6. UCB Corporation is considering five different investment opportunities. The company's cost of capital is 12 percent. Data on these opportunities under consideration are given below:

Project	Investment	PV at 12%	Profitability Index (rounded)
(a)	$70,000	$80,000	1.14
(b)	40,000	46,000	1.15
(c)	25,000	27,453	1.10
(d)	20,000	21,000	1.05
(e)	18,000	17,000	0.94

Rank these five projects in descending order of preference, based to profitability index. Which projects should be chosen if $110,000 is the spending limit?

7. Two new machines are being evaluated for possible purchase. Forecasts related to the two machines are:

	Machine 1	Machine 2
Purchase price	$50,000	$60,000
Estimated life (straight-line depreciation)	4 years	4 years
Estimated scrap value	None	None
Annual cash benefits before income tax:		
Year 1	$25,000	$45,000
Year 2	25,000	19,000
Year 3	25,000	25,000
Year 4	25,000	25,000
Income tax rate	40%	40%

Compute the net present value of each machine. Assume a cost of capital after taxes of 8%.

8. The Nomo Company estimates that it can generate sales of $70,000 and incur annual cost of operations of $50,000 for the next ten years if it buys a special-purpose machine at a cost of $90,000. No residual value is expected. Depreciation is by straight-line. Assume that the income tax rate is 30%, and the after-tax cost of capital (minimum required rate of return) is 10%. Should the company buy the machine? Use the *NPV* method.

9. The *JS* Company is considering buying a machine at a cost of $800,000, which has the following cash flow pattern. No residual value is expected. Depreciation is by straight-line. Assume that the income tax rate is 40%, and the after-tax cost of capital (minimum required rate of return) is 10%. Should the company buy the machine? Use the *NPV* method.

Year	Cash Inflow (1)	Cash Outflow (2)
1	$ 800,000	$ 550,000
2	$ 790,000	$ 590,000
3	$ 920,000	$ 600,000
4	$ 870,000	$ 610,000
5	$ 650,000	$ 390,000

10. The Henley Company issues a $1,000, 6 percent, 20-year bond whose net proceeds are $960. The tax rate is 40 percent. What is the company's after-tax cost of debt?

11. The market price of the Henley Company's stock is $50. The dividend to be paid at the end of the coming year is $5 per share and is expected to grow at a constant annual rate of 5 percent. What is the cost of this common stock?

ANSWERS

KNOW THE CONCEPTS

1. Capital budgeting is the process of evaluating alternative capital projects and selecting alternatives that provide the most profitable return on available funds.

2. The profitability index is the present value of the expected after-tax cash inflows of investment divided by the initial cash outlay. The higher the index, the more profitable the project per dollar of investment.

3. The internal rate of return is the rate of return that equates the present value of future expected cash inflows from an investment with the cost of the investment; it is the rate at which the net present value of the project is zero.

4. The *NPV* of a project is given by the present value of the expected cash inflows that it will generate minus the initial cost. Projects are acceptable if their *NPV*s are greater than zero.

5. The cost of capital is the minimum return that is necessary for a firm to maintain its value and grow.

6. Under the *IRR* method, the cost of capital is a cutoff point for deciding which projects are acceptable for further consideration. Under the *NPV* method, the cost of capital is the discount rate used to calculate the present value of the cash inflows.

7. The purpose of a postaudit is to determine whether or not a project is living up to its expectations by comparing actual costs and benefits with estimated costs and benefits.

PRACTICAL APPLICATION

1a. $20,000 $\times$ *PV* factor of an annuity of $1 at 12% for 7 years = $20,000 T4 (12%, 7 years) = $20,000 $\times$ 4.564 = $91,280

1b. $4,000 $\times$ *PV* factor of $1 = $4,000 T3(12%, 7 years) = $4,000 $\times$ 0.452 = $1,808

1c. Total *PV* = $91,280 + 1,808 = $93,088

1d. *NPV* = *PV*−*I* = $93,088−$80,000 = $13,088

1e. At *IRR*, *I* = *PV*.

Thus,

$$\$80,000 = \$20,000 \times T4 \ (i, \ 7 \ \text{years})$$

$$T4(i, 7 \ \text{years}) = \frac{\$80,000}{\$20,000} = 4.00,$$

which is, in the seven-year line, somewhere between 16% and 18%.

2a. Net present value (*NPV*) = *PV* of cash inflows after taxes

[discounted at the cost of capital (12%)] − Initial investment

$= \$15,000 \times T4 \ (12\%, \ 10 \ \text{years}) - \$75,000 = \$15,000 \ (5.650) - \$75,000 = \$9,750$

2b. Internal rate of return (*IRR*) = Rate which equates the amount invested with the present value of cash inflows generated by the project.

Therefore, we set the following equation:

$$\$75,000 = \$15,000 \ T4 \ (i, \ 10 \ \text{years})$$

$$T4(i, 10 \ \text{years}) = \frac{\$75,000}{\$15,000} = 5,$$

which stands between 14 percent and 16 percent.

	Table Value	
14%	5.216	5.216
True rate		5,000
16%	4,833	
Difference	0.383	0.216

Using interpolation,

$$IRR = 14\% + [(5.216 - 5.0000)/(5.216 - 4.833)] \ (16\% - 14\%)$$

$$= 14\% + [(0.216)/(0.383)] \ (2\%)$$

$$= 14\% + (0.564)(2\%) = 14\% + 1.13\% = 15.13\%$$

3.

1a. 18% ($898,800/$200,000 = 4.494, the present value factor for 18% and 10 years)

1b. $144,400; ($200,000 × 5.216 = $1,043,200, so *NPV* = $1,043,200−$898,800 = $144,400)

2c. $586,880; ($140,000 × 4.192, the present value factor for 20% and 10 years; at *IRR*, *PV* = *I*)

2d. $143,360; ($140,000 × 5.216 = $730,240, so *NPV* = $730,240−$568,880 = $143,360)

3e. $38,344; ($200,000/5.216 factor for 14% and 10 years)

3f. 10%; *NPV* = *PV*−*I*; *PV* = *NPV* + *I*;

Total *PV* = $35,624 + $200,000; $235,624/$38,344

= 6.145, the present value factor for 10%

4g. $60,000; (Total *PV* = $39,000 + $300,000 = $339,000/5.650 factor for 12% = $60,000)

4h. About 15%; ($300,000/$60,000 = 5, which stands halfway between 14% and 16%)

4. Since *NPV* = *PV*−*I*, *I* = *PV*−*NPV*:

Year	Cash Inflow	Present Value T3 of $1	Total *PV*
1	$3,000	0.926	$2,778
2	3,500	0.857	3,000
3	2,400	0.794	1,906
4	2,600	0.735	1,911
Present value of future inflows (*PV*)			$9,595
Net present value (*NPV*)			500
Initial outlay (1)			$9,095

5. By definition, at *IRR*, *PV* = *I* or *NPV* = 0. To determine the amount of initial investment, all that is needed is to compute the present value of $4,000 a year for 8 periods.

$$PV = \$4,000 \times 5.335 = \$21,340$$

6.

	Order of Preference Profitability Index
(a)	2
(b)	1
(c)	3
(d)	4
(e)	5

Projects (a) and (b) should be selected, where combined *NPV* would be $16,000 ($6,000 + $10,000) with the limited budget of $110,000.

7. After-tax cash benefit:

Yr.	Cash Benefit (a)	Depreciation	Taxable Income	Income Tax (b)	Net After-Tax Cash Inflow (a)−(b)
Machine 1					
1	$25,000	$12,500	$12,500	$5,000	$20,000
2	25,000	12,500	12,500	5,000	20,000
3	25,000	12,500	12,500	5,000	20,000
4	25,000	12,500	12,500	5,000	20,000
Machine 2					
1	$45,000	$15,000	$30,000	$12,000	$33,000
2	19,000	15,000	4,000	1,600	17,400
3	25,000	15,000	10,000	4,000	21,000
4	25,000	15,000	10,000	4,000	21,000

Net present value:

Year	Cash(Outflow) Inflow	Present Value of $1 8 Percent	Net Present Value of Cash Flow
Machine 1			
0	$(50,000)	1.000	$(50,000)
1–4	20,000	3.312	66,240
		Net present value	$ 16,240
Machine 2			
0	$(60,000)	1.000	$(60,000)
1	33,000	0.926	30,558
2	17,400	0.857	14,912
3	21,000	0.794	16,674
4	21,000	0.735	15,435
		Net Present Value	$17,579

8. After-tax cash inflows can be calculated as follows:

Note that depreciation by straight-line is $90,000/10 = $9,000 per year. Thus,

After-tax cash inflows = after-tax net income + depreciation

$= (\$70,000-\$50,000)(1-0.3) + \$9,000$

$= \$20,000\ (0.7) + \$9,000 = \$14,000 + \$9,000 = 23,000.$

To see if this machine should be purchased, the net present value can be calculated.

$$PV = \$23,000\ T4(10\%,\ 10\ \text{years}) = \$23,000\ (6.145) = \$141,335.$$

$$\text{Thus, } NPV = PV - I = \$141,335 - \$90,000 = \$51,335$$

Since *NPV* is positive, the machine should be bought.

9. Net Cash Flow After Taxes Calculation

Year	Cash Inflow (1)	Cash Outflow (2)	Net Cash Flow Before Taxes (3) = (1) – (2)	Depreciation (noncash expense) (4) = 0.2 x 800,000	Net Income Before Taxes (5) = (3)–(4)	Income Taxes (6) = 0.4 x (5)	Net Income After Taxes (7) = (5)–(6)	Cash Flow After Taxes (8) = (7) + (4)
1	$ 800,000	$ 550,000	$ 250,000	$ 160,000	$ 90,000	$ 36,000	$ 54,000	$214,000
2	$ 790,000	$ 590,000	$ 200,000	$ 160,000	$ 40,000	$ 16,000	$ 24,000	$184,000
3	$ 920,000	$ 600,000	$ 320,000	$ 160,000	$ 160,000	$ 64,000	$ 96,000	$256,000
4	$ 870,000	$ 610,000	$ 260,000	$ 160,000	$ 100,000	$ 40,000	$ 60,000	$220,000
5	$ 650,000	$ 390,000	$ 260,000	$ 160,000	$ 100,000	$ 40,000	$ 60,000	$220,000

The Net Present Value (*NPV*) is computed as follows:

Year	Cash Flow After Taxes	T3 at 10% Table value	Present Value
0	$ (800,000)	$ 1.000	$(800,000)
1	$ 214,000	$ 0.909	$ 194,526
2	$ 184,000	$ 0.826	$ 151,984
3	$ 256,000	$ 0.751	$ 192,256
4	$ 220,000	$ 0.683	$ 150,260
5	$ 220,000	$ 0.621	$ 136,620
		NPV =	$ 25,646

The company should buy the machine, since *NPV* is positive ($25,646).

10. The after-tax cost of debt is

$$6.00\% \ (1 - 0.4) = 3.6\%$$

11. The cost of this common stock is

$$\frac{D_1}{P_o} + g = \frac{\$5}{\$50} + 5\% = 15\%.$$

12
RISK ANALYSIS

KEY TERMS

risk variability of actual cash flow around the expected cash flows.

expected value weighted average using the probabilities as weights.

standard deviation square root of the mean of the squared deviations from the expected value. An absolute measure of risk.

coefficient of variation ratio of the standard deviation to the expected value. A relative measure of risk.

risk aversion displaying a diminishing marginal utility of income or wealth.

expected utility weighted average of utilities using the probabilities as weights.

certainty equivalent approach approach that converts cash flows from individual projects into risk-adjusted certainty equivalent cash flows.

risk-adjusted discount rate riskless rate plus a risk premium.

decision tree graphical method of showing the sequence of possible outcomes.

Risk analysis is the process of measuring and analyzing the risks associated with managerial and investment decisions. It is important especially in making capital investment decisions because of the large amount of capital involved and the long-term nature of the investment being considered. The higher the risk associated with a proposed project, the greater the return that must be earned to compensate for that risk.

RISK

Risk refers to the variability of cash flow (or earnings) around the expected value (return). Risk can be measured in either absolute or relative terms. Statistics such as standard deviation and coefficient of deviation are used to measure risk.

EXPECTED VALUE

Expected value is a weighted average using the probabilities as weights. For decisions involving uncertainty, the concept of expected value provides a rational means for selecting the best course of action.

The expected value ($\bar{r}$) is found by multiplying the profit outcome for ith possible event by the probability of each profit outcome:

$$\bar{r} = \Sigma r_i p_i,$$

where r_i is the profit outcome for ith possible event and p_i is the probability of occurrence of that profit outcome.

EXAMPLE 1

Consider two investment proposals, A and B, with the following probability distribution of cash flows in each of the next five years:

Cash Inflows

Probability	(0.2)	(0.6)	(0.2)
A	$200	300	400
B	$100	300	500

The expected value of the cash inflow in proposal A is

$$\$200(0.2) + 300(0.6) + 400(0.2) = \$300.$$

The expected value of the cash inflow in proposal B is

$$\$100(0.2) + 300(0.6) + 500(0.2) = \$300.$$

STANDARD DEVIATION

Whenever we talk about the expected value, one statistic that goes with it is standard deviation. Standard deviation is a statistic that measures the tendency of data to be spread out or is also a measure of the dispersion of a probability distribution. The smaller the deviation, the tighter the distribution, and thus, the lower the riskiness of the project. It is intuitively a margin of error associated with a given expected value. Economists can make important inferences from past data with this measure. It is the square root of the mean of the squared deviations from the expected value ($\bar{r}$) The standard deviation, denoted with the Greek letter σ, read as *sigma*, is calculated as follows:

$$\sigma = \sqrt{\Sigma(r - \bar{r})^2 p_i},$$

where

$$\bar{r} = \Sigma r_i p_i$$

To calculate σ, we proceed as follows:

Step 1. First compute the expected rate of return ($\bar{r}$)

Step 2. Subtract each possible return from $\bar{r}$ to obtain a set of deviations $(r - \bar{r})$

Step 3. Square each deviation, multiply the squared deviation by the probability of occurrence for its respective return, and sum these products to obtain the variance (σ^2):

$$\sigma^2 = \Sigma (r - \bar{r})^2 p.$$

Step 4. Finally, take the square root of the variance to obtain the standard deviation (σ).

EXAMPLE 2

In Example 1, the standard deviations of proposals A and B are computed as follows:

For A: $\sigma_A = \sqrt{(\$200 - 300)^2(0.2) + (300 - 300)^2(0.6) + (400 - 300)^2(0.2)} = \$63.25,$

For B: $\sigma_B = \sqrt{(\$100 - 300)^2(0.2) + (300 - 300)^2(0.6) + (500 - 300)^2(0.2)} = \$126.49.$

Proposal B is more risky than proposal A, since its standard deviation is greater.

The standard deviation can be used to measure the variation of such items as the expected profits, expected contribution margin, or expected cash flows. It can also be used to assess the risk associated with investment projects.

COEFFICIENT OF VARIATION

Coefficient of variation is a popular measure of relative risk. It represents the degree of risk per unit of return. It is computed by dividing the standard deviation by the expected value:

$$\frac{\sigma}{\bar{r}}.$$

EXAMPLE 3

Consider two projects with the following data:

Proposal	Expected Value	Standard Deviation
A	$230	$107.7
B	250	208.57

The coefficient of variation for each proposal is:

$$\text{For } A: \quad \frac{\$107.7}{\$230} = 0.47,$$

$$\text{For } B: \quad \frac{\$208.57}{\$250} = 0.83.$$

Therefore, because the coefficient is a relative measure of risk, *B* is considered more risky than *A*.

YOU SHOULD REMEMBER

Risk can be measured in either absolute or relative terms. Standard deviation is a measure of absolute risk, while the coefficient of variation is used to measure relative risk.

UTILITY THEORY AND RISK

In theory, three possible profiles in risk tolerance or attitudes toward risk exist. They are: aversion to risk, neutrality to risk, and preference for risk. Each decision maker's attitude toward risk is determined by his utility of income or wealth.

1. A risk-averse decision maker displays a diminishing marginal utility of income or wealth. This is a common, but not universal, attitude.

2. A risk-indifferent decision maker has a constant marginal utility of income or wealth.

3. A risk-seeker's marginal utility of income or wealth increases.

Managerial decisions cannot be based solely on expected outcomes, but must incorporate an analysis of risk attitudes. Figure 12–1 shows the relations between money and its utility for three types of decision makers: (a) a risk averter, (b) risk-neutral manager, and (c) risk seeker.

TYPES OF RISKS

Any investment project is susceptible to risk (uncertainty). Risk refers to the fluctuation in profit as well as to the possibility of loss associated with a given managerial decision. The company faces different types of risks when selecting a project. The irony is that they could produce unexpected returns. Risks include

1. *Liquidity risk.* The chance that corporate assets or investments cannot be sold on short notice for its market value.

YOU SHOULD REMEMBER

The utility function can take various mathematical forms: for example,

1. $U = 30 + 2X$ (X = money or income) indicates a constant marginal utility of income (i.e., risk neutral).

2. $U = 30X - X^2$ indicates a diminishing marginal utility of income (i.e., risk aversion).

3. $U = 20X + X^2$ indicates an increasing marginal utility of income (i.e., risk seeking).

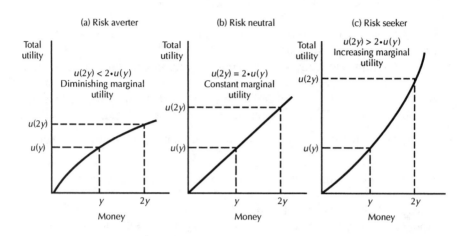

Figure 12–1. Risk Profiles and Money/Utility Relations

EXAMPLE 4

You are considering two investment choices, each costing $5,000. Cash inflows of possible outcomes and their associated probabilities are:

Investment A		Investment B	
Cash inflows	Probability	Cash inflows	Probability
$ 6,000	0.25	$ 5,000	0.3
8,000	0.50	9,000	0.5
10,000	0.25	10,000	0.2

Assume that your utility function is given by the following table:

Money	$5,000	6,000	7,000	8,000	9,000	10,000
Utility (Utils)	125	144	161	176	189	200

First. the expected value of the cash inflow in Investment A is

$$\$6,000(0.25) + 8,000(0.5) + 10,000(0.25) = \$8,000.$$

The expected value of the cash inflow in Investment B is

$$\$5,000(0.3) + 9,000(0.5) + 10,000(0.2) = \$8,000.$$

Second, the standard deviations of Investments A and B are computed as follows:

For A: $\sigma_A = \sqrt{(\$6,000 - 8,000)^2(0.25) + (8,000 - 8,000)^2(0.5) + (10,000 - 8,000)^2(0.25)} = \$1,414.21$,

For B: $\sigma_B = \sqrt{(\$5,000 - 8,000)^2(0.3) + (9,000 - 8,000)^2(0.5) + (10,000 - 8,000)^2(0.2)} = \$2,000$.

Investment B is more risky than Investment A.
Third, the expected utility, $E(U)$, of each investment is computed as follows:
For Investment A:

$$E(U_A) = 144(0.25) + 176(0.5) + 200 (0.25) = 174 \text{ utils},$$

For Investment B:

$$E(U_B) = 125(0.3) + 189(0.5) + 200(0.2) = 172 \text{ utils}.$$

Based on the expected utility, you should choose Investment A. Since you are a risk averter, having a diminishing marginal utility of money, you would prefer the investment with less risk, with equal expected dollar returns. Note that your utility does not increase by 19 (144 minus 125) as your income increases by $1,000.

---

2. *Inflation (purchasing power) risk.* The failure of corporate agreements involving a fixed payment (such as leases and corporate bonds) to earn a return to keep up with increasing price levels.

3. *Interest rate risk.* The variability in the value of an asset due to changing interest rates and money conditions. For example, if interest rates increase (decrease), bond (stock) prices decrease (increase).

4. *Business risk.* The risk associated with changes in a firm's sales. This may be due to operating difficulties, such as a strike and technological obsolescence.

5. *Market risk.* The change in the price of a portfolio of investments arising from changes in the overall stock market, irrespective of the fundamental financial condition of the company. For instance, stock prices of companies may be impacted by bull or bear markets.

6. *Default risk.* The risk that the issuing company may be unable to pay interest and/or principal when due. An example is a financially unsound company.

7. *Financial risk.* A type of investment risk associated with excessive debt.

8. *Industry risk.* The uncertainty of the inherent nature of the industry, such as high-technology, product liability, and accidents.

9. *International and political risks.* The risks stemming from foreign operations in politically unstable foreign countries. An example is a U.S. company having a location and operations in a hostile country.

10. *Economic risk.* The negative impact of a company from economic slowdowns. For example, airlines have lower business volume in recession.

11. *Currency risk.* The risk arising from the fluctuation in foreign exchange rates.

12. *Social risk.* Problems facing the company due to ethnic boycott, discrimination cases, and environmental concerns.

Risk levels vary among investments. For example, stocks experience less inflation risk than fixed income securities. Money market investments have less liquidity risk than real estate.

RISK ANALYSIS IN CAPITAL BUDGETING

Risk analysis is important in making capital investment decisions because of the large amount of capital involved and the long-term nature of the investments being considered. The higher the risk associated with a proposed project, the greater the rate of return that must be earned on the project to compensate for that risk.

Since different investment projects involve different risks, it is important to incorporate risk into the analysis of capital budgeting. There are several methods for incorporating risk, including:

1. Probability distributions

2. Risk-adjusted discount rate

3. Certainty equivalent

4. Simulation

5. Sensitivity analysis

6. Decision trees (or probability trees)

PROBABILITY DISTRIBUTIONS

Expected values of a probability distribution may be computed. Before any capital budgeting method is applied, compute the expected cash inflows, or in some cases, the expected life of the asset.

EXAMPLE 5

A firm is considering a $30,000 investment in equipment that will generate cash savings from operating costs. The following estimates regarding cash savings and useful life, along with their respective probabilities of occurrence, have been made:

Annual Cash Savings	Probability	Useful Life	Probability
$6,000	0.2	4 years	0.2
$8,000	0.5	5 years	0.6
$10,000	0.3	6 years	0.2

Then, the expected annual saving is

$$\begin{aligned} \$6,000\ (0.2) &= \$1,200 \\ \$8,000\ (0.5) &= 4,000 \\ \$10,000\ (0.3) &= \underline{3,000} \\ &\ \$8,200 \end{aligned}$$

The expected useful life is

$$\begin{aligned} 4\ (0.2) &= 0.8 \\ 5\ (0.6) &= 3.0 \\ 6\ (0.2) &= \underline{1.2} \\ &\ 5 \text{ years} \end{aligned}$$

The expected *NPV* is computed as follows (assuming a 10 percent cost of capital):

$$NPV = PV - I = \$8,200\ T4(10\%,\ 5 \text{ years}) - \$30,000$$

$$= \$8,200\ (3.7908) - \$30,000 = \$31,085 - \$30,000 = \$1,085.$$

The expected *IRR* is computed as follows: By definition, at *IRR*,

$$I = PV,$$

$$\$30,000 = \$8,200\ T4\ (i,\ 5 \text{ years}),$$

$$T4(i, 5 \text{ years}) = \frac{\$30,000}{\$8,200} = 3.6585,$$

which is about halfway between 10 percent and 12 percent in Table 4 in the Appendix, so we can estimate the rate to be about 11 percent. Therefore, the equipment should be purchased, since (1) *NPV* = $1,085, which is positive, and/or (2) *IRR* = 11 percent, which is greater than the cost of capital of 10 percent.

RISK-ADJUSTED DISCOUNT RATE

This method of risk analysis adjusts the cost of capital (or discount rate) upward as projects become riskier, i.e., a risk-adjusted discount rate is the riskless rate plus a risk premium. Therefore, by increasing the discount rate from 10 percent to 15 percent, the expected cash flow from the investment must be relatively larger or the increased discount rate will generate a negative *NPV*, and the proposed acquisition/investment would be turned down. The expected cash flows are discounted at the risk-adjusted discount rate and then the usual capital budgeting criteria, such as *NPV* and *IRR*, are applied.

YOU SHOULD REMEMBER

The use of the risk-adjusted discount rate is based on the assumption that investors demand higher returns for riskier projects.

EXAMPLE 6

A firm is considering an investment project with an expected life of 3 years. It requires an initial investment of $35,000. The firm estimates the following data in each of the next 4 years:

After-Tax Cash Inflow	Probability
– $ 5,000	0.2
$10,000	0.3
$30,000	0.3
$50,000	0.2

Assuming a risk-adjusted required rate of return (after taxes) of 20 percent is appropriate for the investment projects of this level of risk, compute the risk-adjusted *NPV*. First, the present value is

$PV = - \$5,000(0.2) + \$10,000(0.3) + \$30,000(0.3) + \$50,000(0.2) = \$21,000.$

The expected $NPV = \$21000 \ T4(20\%,3) - \$35,000$

$$= 21,000 \ (2.107) - \$35,000 = \$44,247 - \$35,000 = \$9,247.$$

CERTAINTY EQUIVALENT APPROACH

The certainty equivalent approach to risk analysis is to convert cash flows from individual projects into risk-adjusted certainty equivalent cash flows. The approach is drawn directly from the concept of utility theory. This method forces the decision maker to specify at what point the firm is indifferent to the choice between a certain sum of money and the expected value of a risky sum.

Under this approach, first determine a *certainty equivalent adjustment factor*, α, as:

$$\alpha = \frac{\text{Certain sum}}{\text{Equivalent risky sum}}.$$

Once α's are obtained, they are multiplied by the original cash flow to obtain the equivalent certain cash flow. Then, the accept-or-reject decision is made using the normal capital budgeting criteria. The risk-free rate of return is used as the discount rate under the *NPV* method and as the cutoff rate under the *IRR* method.

EXAMPLE 7

XYZ, Inc., with a 14 percent cost of capital after taxes is considering a project with an expected life of 4 years. The project requires an initial certain cash outlay of $50,000. The expected cash inflows and certainty equivalent coefficients are as follows:

Year	After-Tax Cash Flow	Certainty Equivalent Adjustment Factor
1	$10,000	0.95
2	15,000	0.80
3	20,000	0.70
4	25,000	0.60

Assuming that the risk-free rate of return is 5 percent, the *NPV* and *IRR* are computed as follows.

First, the equivalent certain cash inflows are obtained as follows:

Year	After-Tax Cash Inflow	α	Equivalent Certain Cash Inflow	PV at 5%	PV
1	$10,000	0.95	$ 9,500	0.9524	$9,048
2	15,000	0.80	12,000	0.9070	10,884
3	20,000	0.70	14,000	0.8638	12,093
4	25,000	0.60	15,000	0.8227	12,341
					44,366

NPV = $44,366 - $50,000 = -$5,634.

By trial and error, we obtain 4 percent as the *IRR*. Therefore, the project should be rejected, since (1) *NPV* = -$5,634, which is negative, and/or (2) *IRR* = 4 percent is less than the risk-free rate of 5 percent.

SIMULATION

This risk analysis method is frequently called Monte Carlo simulation. It requires that a probability distribution be constructed for each of the important variables affecting the project's cash flows. Since a computer is used to generate many results using random numbers, project simulation is expensive.

SENSITIVITY ANALYSIS

Forecasts of many calculated *NPV*s under various alternative functions are compared to see how sensitive *NPV* is to changing conditions. It may be found that a certain variable or group of variables, once their assumptions are changed or relaxed, drastically alters the *NPV*. This results in a much riskier asset than was originally forecast.

DECISION TREES

Some firms use decision trees (probability trees) to evaluate the risk of capital budgeting proposals. A decision tree is a graphical method of showing the sequence of possible outcomes. A capital budgeting tree shows the cash flows and *NPV* of the project under different possible circumstances. The decision tree method has the following advantages: (1) it visually lays out all the possible outcomes of the proposed project and makes management aware of the adverse possibilities, and (2) the conditional nature of successive years' cash flows can be expressly depicted. The disadvantages are that: (1) most problems are too complex to permit year-by-year depiction, and (2) it does not recognize risk.

EXAMPLE 8

Assume *XYZ* Corporation wishes to introduce one of two products to the market this year. The probabilities and present values (*PV*) of projected cash inflows are given below:

Product	Initial investment	PV of cash inflows	Probabilities
A	$225,000		1.00
		$450,000	0.40
		200,000	0.50
		−100,000	0.10
B	80,000		1.00
		320,000	0.20
		100,000	0.60
		−150,000	0.20

A decision tree analyzing the two products is given in Figure 12–2.

Based on the expected *NPV*, choose product *A* over product *B*. This analysis fails to recognize the risk factor in project analysis.

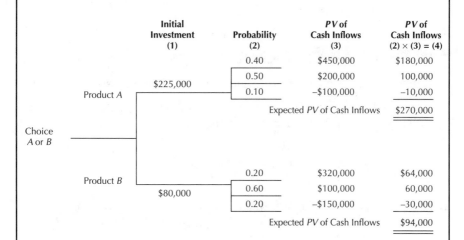

	Initial Investment (1)	Probability (2)	PV of Cash Inflows (3)	PV of Cash Inflows (2) × (3) = (4)
		0.40	$450,000	$180,000
Product A	$225,000	0.50	$200,000	100,000
		0.10	−$100,000	−10,000
			Expected PV of Cash Inflows	$270,000
Choice A or B				
		0.20	$320,000	$64,000
Product B	$80,000	0.60	$100,000	60,000
		0.20	−$150,000	−30,000
			Expected PV of Cash Inflows	$94,000

For Product A: Expected *NPV* = expected *PV* − *I* = $270,000 − $225,000 = $45,000
For Product B: Expected *NPV* = $94,000 − $80,000 = $14,000

Based on the expected *NPV*, choose product *A* over product *B*.

Figure 12–2. A Decision Tree

KNOW THE CONCEPTS

TERMS FOR STUDY

certainty equivalent	risk
coefficient of variation	risk-adjusted discount rate
decision tree	simulation
expected value	standard deviation

DO YOU KNOW THE BASICS?

1. What is risk analysis in capital budgeting?

2. How do you define risk?

3. What is meant by the term *expected value*?

4. What kinds of attitudes toward risk exist?

5. List five common categories of risk.

6. How does the standard deviation differ from the coefficient of variation?

7. What is a risk-adjusted discount rate?

8. Define a certainty equivalent adjustment factor. How is it used?

9. What is a decision tree? Explain how is it used, and discuss the problem inherent in its application to capital project analysis.

PRACTICAL APPLICATION

1. Assume likely rate of return (including dividends and price changes), depending upon the economic climate (i.e., prosperity, normal, and stagflation).

State of economy	Return (r)	Probability (p)
Prosperity	20%	0.5
Normal	10	0.3
Stagflation	–5	0.2

   a. Compute the expected return.

   b. Compute the standard deviation.

2. The Stat Company has the following information concerning the demand for one of its products:

Units Demanded	Probability of Unit Demand	Contribution Margin of Units Demanded
0	0.10	$0
1	0.15	1
2	0.20	2
3	0.40	3
4	0.10	4
5	0.05	5

Compute the expected contribution margin.

3. The owner of the Delicious Donut Shop must decide between the rental of two types of donut-making machines. Machine A, an inexpensive economy model, rents for $1,000 per month, but the variable production cost is $0.25 per donut. Machine B rents for $3,000 per month, but the variable production cost is only $0.01 per donut. Monthly demand varies between 100,000 and 190,000 donuts according to the following probabilities:

Demand	Probability
100,000	0.12
120,000	0.17
150,000	0.41
170,000	0.24
190,000	0.06

Make a cost comparison of the two machines. Which machine should he rent?

4. The probabilities and net cash inflows of an investment are

Probability	Net Cash Inflows
0.2	$ 60
0.1	80
0.3	90
0.2	115
0.2	150

a. Calculate the expected value, standard deviation, and coefficient of variation.

b. Is this investment considered relatively risky or riskless? Why?

5. The sales manager of the Electronic Toy Company is considering two toys: a doll and a game. The toys have discrete probability distributions of cash inflows in each of the next three years.

Event	Doll	Probability	Game
Prosperity	$20,000	0.2	$42,000
Normal	15,000	0.5	20,000
Recession	9,000	0.3	(5,000)

a. For each toy item, compute

    1. The expected value of the cash inflows in each of the next three years

    2. The standard deviation

    3. The coefficient of variation

b. Which toy would you select, and why?

6. You are considering two investment choices, each costing $8,000. Cash inflows of possible outcomes and their associated probabilities are as follows:

Investment A		Investment B	
Cash inflows	Probability	Cash inflows	Probability
$ 9,000	0.2	$ 22,000	0.5
11,000	0.5	4,000	0.5
12,000	0.3		

Assume that your utility function is given by the following table:

Money	$4,000	9,000	10,000	11,000	12,000	22,000
Utility (Utils)	31	63	68	73	78	109

a. Calculate the expected value of each investment alternative.

b. Calculate the standard deviation of each investment alternative.

c. Calculate the coefficient of variation.

d. Which investment should you choose?

e. Suppose you have an option to buy a risk-free government bond yielding $10,000. Should you pick this one over either investment alternative?

7. Handu, Inc. is contemplating a capital investment project with an expected useful life of 10 years that requires an initial cash outlay of $225,000. The company estimates the following data:

Annual Cash Inflows ($)	Probabilities
0	0.10
50,000	0.20
65,000	0.40
70,000	0.20
90,000	0.10

  a. Assuming a risk-adjusted required rate of return of 25 percent is appropriate for projects of this level of risk, calculate the risk-adjusted *NPV* of the project.

  b. Should the project be accepted?

8. Moore Corporation is considering the purchase of a new machine that will last 5 years and require a cash outlay of $300,000. The firm has a 12 percent cost of capital rate, and its after-tax risk-free rate is 9 percent. The company has expected cash inflows and certainty equivalents for these cash inflows, as follows:

Year	After-Tax Cash Inflows ($)	Certainty Equivalent
1	100,000	1.00
2	100,000	0.95
3	100,000	0.90
4	100,000	0.80
5	100,000	0.70

  a. Calculate the unadjusted *NPV* and the certainty equivalent *NPV*.

  b. Determine if the machine should be purchased.

9. Based on the industry supply and demand analysis, Madden Corporation wishes to build a full-scale manufacturing facility. It is considering:

  A. Build a large plant, costing $5 million.

  B. Build a small plant, costing $2 million.

The probabilities of various demands and present values of projected cash inflows for these demand situations are given below.

Action	Demand Conditions	PV of Cash Inflows ($)	Probabilities
A	High	$8.0 million	0.5
	Medium	4.0 million	0.3
	Low	1.5 million	0.2
B	High	$2.5 million	0.5
	Medium	2.0 million	0.3
	Low	1.5 million	0.2

a. Construct a decision tree to analyze the two options.

b. Which option would you choose? Comment on your decision.

ANSWERS

KNOW THE CONCEPTS

1. Risk analysis is the process of measuring and analyzing the risks associated with managerial and investment decisions.

2. Risk refers to the variability of cash flow (or earnings) around the expected value (return).

3. Expected value is a weighted average using the probabilities as weights. For decisions involving risk or uncertainty, the concept of expected value provides a rational means for selecting the best course of action.

4. (a) a risk averter, (b) risk-neutral manager, and (c) risk seeker.

5. (1) *Liquidity risk*. The chance that corporate assets or investments may not be sold on short notice for its market value. (2) *Inflation (purchasing power) risk*. The failure of corporate agreements involving a fixed payment (such as leases and corporate bonds) to earn a return to keep up with increasing price levels. (3) *Interest rate risk*. The variability in the value of an asset to changing interest rates and money conditions. For example, if interest rates increase (decrease), bond (stock) prices decrease (increase). (4) *Business risk*. The risk associated with changes in a firm's sales. This may be due to operating difficulties, such as strike and technological obsolescence. (5) *Market risk*. The change in the price

of a portfolio of investments arising from changes in the overall stock market, irrespective of the fundamental financial condition of the company. For instance, stock prices of companies may be impacted by bull or bear markets.

6. Risk can be measured in either absolute or relative terms. Standard deviation and coefficient of variation are used to measure risk. Standard deviation is a measure of absolute risk, while the coefficient of variation is used to measure relative risk.

7. This method of risk analysis adjusts the cost of capital (or discount rate) upward as projects become riskier, i.e., a risk-adjusted discount rate is the riskless rate plus a risk premium.

8. A certainty equivalent adjustment factor, α, is defined as:

$$\alpha = \frac{\text{Certain sum}}{\text{Equivalent risky sum}}.$$

Once α's are obtained, they are multiplied by the original cash flow to obtain the equivalent certain cash flow. Then, the accept-or-reject decision is made, using the normal capital budgeting criteria.

9. A decision tree is a graphical method of showing the sequence of possible outcomes. A capital budgeting tree shows the cash flows and *NPV* of the project under different possible circumstances. The disadvantages are: (1) most problems are too complex to permit year-by-year depiction, and (2) it fails to recognize risk.

PRACTICAL APPLICATION

1a. The expected rate is:

$$\bar{r} = (20\%)(0.5) + (10\%(0.3) + (-5\%)(0.2) = 12\%.$$

On average, your annual return is 12%, ranging from a 5 percent loss to a 20 percent gain.

1b.

Return   Probability

(r)	(p)	rp	($r - \bar{r}$)	$(r - \bar{r})^2$	$(r - \bar{r})^2 p$
20%	0.5	10%	8%	64	32
10	0.3	3	−2	4	1.2
−5	0.2	−1	−17	289	57.8
		$\bar{r}$ = 12%			91

$$\sqrt{91} = 9.54\%$$

The expected annual return has an average variation of 9.54 percent.

2.

Unit Demanded	Probability of Unit Demand	Contribution Margin of Units Demanded	Expected Contribution Margin
0	0.10	$ 0	$ 0
1	0.15	$1.00	$0.15
2	0.20	$2.00	$0.40
3	0.40	$3.00	$1.20
4	0.10	$4.00	$0.40
5	0.05	$5.00	$0.25
Expected contribution margin			$2.40

3.

Machine A:

Variable Production Cost	Machine Rental	Total	Probability	Expected Cost
$2,500	$1,000	$3,500	0.12	$420.00
$3,000	$1,000	$4,000	0.17	$680.00
$3,750	$1,000	$4,750	0.41	$1,947.50
$4,250	$1,000	$5,250	0.24	$1,260.00
$4,750	$1,000	$5,750	0.06	$345.00
Expected cost				$4,652.50

Machine B:

Variable Production Cost	Machine Rental	Total	Probability	Expected Cost
$1,000	$3,000	$4,000	0.12	$480.00
$1,200	$3,000	$4,200	0.17	$714.00
$1,500	$3,000	$4,500	0.41	$1,845.00
$1,700	$3,000	$4,700	0.24	$1,128.00
$1,900	$3,000	$4,900	0.06	$294.00
Expected cost				$4,461.00

Machine B promises the lower expected cost. (Machine B has a lower cost for demands of 150,000 units and greater, although machine A affords a lower estimated cost at the two lower demand levels.) Therefore, the owner of the shop should rent machine B.

4a. Expected value $\bar{r}$ = ($60)(0.2) + ($80)(0.1) + ($90)(0.3) + ($115)(0.2) + ($150)(0.2) = $100

Standard deviation σ =

$$\sqrt{(0.2)(\$60)-\$100)^2+(0.1)(\$80-\$100)^2+(0.3)(\$90-\$100)^2+(0.2)(\$115-\$100)^2+(0.2)(\$150-\$100)^2}$$

$= \$30.58$

Coefficient of variation = $30.58/$100 = 0.3

4b. The investment is relatively riskless because the coefficient of variation is low.

5a. (1) For the doll:

Expected value = ($20,000)(0.2) + ($15,000)(0.5) + ($9,000)(0.3)

$$= \$4,000 + \$7,500 + \$2,700 = \$14,200$$

For the game:

Expected value = ($42,000)(0.2) + ($20,000)(0.5) + (5,000)(0.3)

$$= \$8,400 + 10,000 + \$1,500 = \$19,900$$

5a. (2) For the doll:

$$\sqrt{(\$20,000-14,200)^2(0.2)+(\$15,000-14,200)^2(0.5)+(\$9,000-14,200)^2(0.3)} = \$3,893.58$$

For the game:

$$\sqrt{(\$42,000-16,900)^2(0.2)+(\$20,000-16,900)^2(0.5)+(\$5,000-16,900)^2(0.3)} = \$16,573.77$$

5a. (3) The coefficient of variation is

$$\text{For the doll } \frac{\$3,893.58}{\$14,200} = 0.274,$$

$$\text{For the game } \frac{\$16,573.77}{\$19,900} = 0.833.$$

5b. Since the coefficient is a relative measure of risk, the game is said to have a greater degree of risk than the doll. Therefore, the doll is the better choice.

6a. The expected value of the cash inflow in Investment A is:

$$\bar{r} = \$9,000(0.2) + 11,000(0.5) + 12,000(0.3) = \$10,900$$

The expected value of the cash inflow in Investment B is

$$\bar{r} = \$22,000(0.5) + 4,000(0.5) = \$13,000$$

6b. The standard deviations of Investments A and B are computed as follows:

For A: $\sigma_A = \sqrt{\$9,000 - 10900)^2(0.2) + (11,000 - 10,900)^2(0.5) + (12,000 - 10,900)^2(0.3}} = \$1,044.03$

For B: $\sigma_B = \sqrt{(\$22,000 - 13,000)^2(0.5) + (4,000 - 13,000)^2(0.5)} = \$9,000$

Investment B is more risky than Investment A.

6c.

Investment	Expected Value	Standard Deviation
A	$10,900	$1,044.03
B	13,000	9,000.00

The coefficient of variation for each proposal is:

$$\text{For } A: \$1,044.03/\$10,900 = 0.096$$

$$\text{For } B: \$9,000/\$13,000 = 0.692.$$

Therefore, because the coefficient is a relative measure of risk, B is considered more risky than A.

6d. The expected utility, $E(U)$, of each investment is computed as follows:

For Investment A:

$$E(U_A) = 63(0.2) + 73(0.5) + 78(0.3 = 72.5 \text{ utils}$$

For Investment B:

$$E(U_B) = 31(0.5) + 109(0.5) = 70 \text{ utils}$$

Based on the expected utility, you should choose Investment A.

6e. You should pick Investment A giving an expected utility of 72.5 utils compared to 68 for the government bond.

7a.

$$r = \$0(0.10) + \$50,000(0.2) + \$65,000(0.4) + \$70,000(0.2) + \$90,000(0.1)$$

$$= \$0 + \$10,000 + \$26,000 + \$14,000 + \$9,000 = \$59,000$$

Expected $NPV = PV - I$

$$= \$59,000 \ T4(25\%, 10) - \$225,000 = \$210,689 - \$225,000 = -\$14,311$$

7b. Reject the project, since the expected NPV is negative.

8a.

$$NPV = PV - I = \$100,000 \ T4(12\%,5) - \$300,000$$

$$= \$100,000(3,605) - \$300,000 = \$360,500 - \$300,000 = \$60,500$$

Year	After-Tax Cash Inflows	Certainty Equivalents ($)	Certain Cash Inflows	($) PV at 9%	PV ($)
1	100,000	1.00	100,000	0.917	91,700
2	100,000	0.95	95,000	0.842	79,990
3	100,000	0.90	90,000	0.772	69,480
4	100,000	0.80	80,000	0.708	56,640
5	100,000	0.70	70,000	0.650	45,500
					343,310

Certainty equivalent $NPV = \$343,310 - \$300,000 = \$43,310$

8b. Because of a positive *NPV*, the machine should be purchased.

9a. Expected *NPV*s for A and B are as follows:

Action	Demand Conditions	PV of Cash Inflows ($) (1)	Probabilities (2)	(1)× (2)
A	High	$8 million	0.5	$4 million
	Medium	4 million	0.3	1.2 million
	Low	1.5 million	0.2	0.3 million
			PV	$5.5 million
			I	5 million
			Expected *NPV* =	0.5 million
B	High	$3 million	0.5	$1.5 million
	Medium	2 million	0.3	0.6 million
	Low	1.5 million	0.2	0.3 million
			PV	$2.4 million
			I	2 million
			Expected *NPV* =	0.4 million

9b. Choose Option *A* since its expected *NPV* is greater than Option *B*'s. This approach, however, does not tell us how risky each option is.

13
LEGAL AND REGULATORY ENVIRONMENT OF THE FIRM

An important element of the competitive environment is the growing importance of government involvement in the market economy. Recent changes in the method and scope of government regulation, including moves toward deregulation, affect the entire spectrum of economic activity, from industrials, to financial institutions (banks, savings and loans, insurance, etc.), to power and transportation utilities. Both state and federal regulation and antitrust policy constitute important constraints on many managerial decisions. As a result, their analysis constitutes an important aspect of managerial economics. This chapter presents the role of government in the market economy, including:

1. economic and political rationale for regulation,

2. direct regulation of firms possessing substantial market power,

3. antitrust policy designed to maintain a "workable" level of competition in the economy, and

4. public expenditure decisions and cost-benefit analysis.

THE RATIONALE FOR REGULATION

Government regulation is sometimes justified on the basis of its ability to correct various market imperfections or market failures that lead to inefficiency and waste. Most often, market failure is thought to be caused by:

a. Structural problems: too few buyers or sellers.

b. Incentive problems: externalities such as pollution.

Government regulation is sometimes justified on the basis of political considerations. Primary among such considerations are desires to:

a. Preserve Consumer Choice: A wide variety of production enhances personal freedom.

b. Limit Economic and Political Power: Unchecked economic and political power could threaten basic liberties.

ANTITRUST POLICY: GOVERNMENT REGULATION OF MARKET CONDUCT AND STRUCTURE

Antitrust policy is a set of legislations aimed at prohibiting monopolies, restraints of trade, price fixing and discrimination, exorbitant quantity discounts to large buyers, and conspiracies to suppress competition. Federal statutes include the Sherman Antitrust Act, Clayton Antitrust Act, Robinson-Patman Act, and Celler-Kefauver Act.

SHERMAN ANTITRUST ACT (1890)

The cornerstone of U.S. antitrust policy is contained in Sections 1 and 2 of the *Sherman Antitrust Act* of 1890:

Section 1: Every contract, combination in the form of trust or otherwise, or conspiracy, in restraint of trade or commerce among the several states, or with foreign nations, is hereby declared to be illegal. Every person who shall make any such contract or engage in any such combination or conspiracy shall be deemed guilty of a felony, and, on conviction thereof shall be punished by a fine not exceeding five thousand dollars (one million dollars if a corporation, or, if any other person, one hundred thousand dollars) or by imprisonment not exceeding one (three) years, or by both said punishments, in the discretion of the court.

Section 2: Every person who shall monopolize, or attempt to monopolize, or combine or conspire with any person or persons, to monopolize any part of the trade or commerce among the several States, or with foreign nations, shall be deemed guilty of a felony, and, on conviction thereof, shall be punished by a fine not exceeding five thousand dollars (one million dollars if a corporation, or, if any other person, one hundred thousand dollars) or by imprisonment not exceeding one (three) years, or by both said punishments, in the discretion of the court.

CLAYTON ACT (1914)

The Clayton Act was designed to overcome some of the ambiguity of the Sherman Act by explicitly prohibiting certain behavior. The Clayton Antitrust Act is one of three major antitrust laws, passed as an amendment to the Sherman Antitrust Act in 1914. The act listed four illegal practices in restraint of competition. It outlawed price discrimination, tying contracts and exclusive dealerships, and horizontal mergers. It also outlawed *interlocking directorates* (the practice of having the same people serve as directors of two or more competing firms).

Section 2: Forbade price discrimination between firms which tended to lessen competition. This section was later amended by the Robinson-Patman Act (1936). It is important to remember that price discrimination between consumers, such as senior citizen discounts for bus service, is legal.

Section 3: Made leases or any sales contracts which lessened competition illegal. This provision was aimed at so-called tying contracts.

Section 7: Forbade stock mergers for monopoly purposes.

ROBINSON-PATMAN ACT (1936)

The *Robinson-Patman Act* (1936) is an amendment to strengthen Section 2 of the Clayton Act regarding price discrimination. For example, Section 2(a) of the Robinson-Patman Act amends Section 2 of the Clayton Act and makes price discrimination illegal if it is designed to lessen competition or create a monopoly:

Section 2 (a): That it shall be unlawful for any person engaged in commerce, in the course of such commerce, either directly or indirectly, to discriminate in price between different purchasers of commodities of like grade and quality, . . . where such discrimination may be substantially to lessen competition or tend to create a monopoly in line of commerce, or to injure, destroy, or prevent competition.

Price discrimination that arises because of cost or quality differences is permitted under the act, as is price discrimination when it is necessary to meet a competitor's price in a market. Still, there is considerable ambiguity regarding whether a particular type of price discrimination is illegal under the law.

CELLER-KEFAUVER ACT (1950)

The *Cellar-Kefauver Act* (1950) strengthened Section 7 of the Clayton Act by making it more difficult for firms to engage in mergers and acquisitions without violating the law:

Section 7: That no corporation engaged in commerce shall acquire, directly or indirectly, the whole or any part of the stock or other share capital and no corporation subject to the jurisdiction of the Federal Trade Commission shall acquire the whole or any part of the assets of another corporation engaged also in commerce, where in any line of commerce in any section of the country, the effect of such acquisition may be substantially to lessen competition, or to tend to create a monopoly.

ENFORCEMENT

The *Antitrust Division of the Department of Justice (DOJ)* and the *Federal Trade Commission (FTC)* are charged with the task of enforcing antitrust regulations. The FTC has limited judicial power; taking violators to court falls almost exclusively on the Antitrust Division of the DOJ. Instead, the FTC issues cease-and-desist orders based on information gathered in a specific case. If the cease-and-desist order is not followed, the FTC may levy a fine of up to $10,000 on the guilty party. If further noncompliance occurs, the FTC usually enjoins the DOJ for further prosecution.

RESOURCE ALLOCATION AND THE SUPPLY OF PUBLIC GOODS

The resource allocation question applies both to privately produced goods and to public sector output. In theory, the amount of any good that should be supplied at a point in time is that quantity that equates the marginal social cost (MSC) of the good with its marginal social benefit (MSB).

First, the marginal *private* economic cost of a good includes all explicit and implicit costs of its production that are borne by the producer. A product's marginal *social* cost differs from its marginal private cost by the amount of external costs (third-party costs) that accompany the production of an incremental unit of output. This cost includes the value to consumers of any alternative product or products whose production is reduced or eliminated.

In a similar fashion we can define marginal social benefit as the sum of marginal private benefits and marginal external, or third-party, benefits. The private benefits accrue to those who directly pay a price for the good, while the external benefits are enjoyed by either the purchaser or the nonpurchasers but are not accounted for in the product's market price.

A good should be provided up to the quantity where $MSC = MSB$. A theoretically optimal allocation of society's resources exists when for all goods the condition that $MSB = MSC$ is attained.

EXAMPLE 1

Assume a two-good case, where a and b are the goods, where both costs and benefits are measured in dollars, and where initially we have

$$MSB_a = MSC_a = 20,$$

$$MSB_b = MSC_b = 40.$$

Thus, the social cost of producing the marginal or last unit of a is $20, while that of producing the marginal unit of b is $40. Obviously, it is also true that

$$\frac{MSB_a}{MSC_a} = \frac{MSB_b}{MSC_b} = 1.$$

First, for a given income distribution, efficient resource allocation will take place when, for n goods,

$$\frac{MSB_a}{MSC_a} = \frac{MSB_b}{MSC_b} = \cdots = \frac{MSB_n}{MSC_n} = 1.$$

This condition simply means that a dollar's worth of social benefit is received for an additional dollar spent on the production of each good. Any deviation from this condition would result in a situation where too much of some good (or goods) and too little of some other good (or goods) is produced.

YOU SHOULD REMEMBER

1. The optimal quantity of a public good (Q^*) is produced where the MSB of the good equals its MSC. At Q^*, net social benefit—the difference between total social benefit *t* and total social cost—is maximized. Production beyond Q^* would add more to social cost than to social benefit.

2. No incremental activity (j) should be undertaken where $MSC_j > MSB_j$

PUBLIC PROJECT ANALYSIS AND COST-BENEFIT ANALYSIS

In public project analysis, we seek to evaluate investments from the point of view of society as a whole. This means that we need to determine social benefits deriving from public projects and social costs incurred to launch those projects. A social benefit is any gain in utility and a social cost is any loss of utility as measured by the opportunity cost of the project in question.

We use *cost-benefit analysis*, which is simply the extension of capital project analysis, as discussed in Chapter 11, to public sector microeconomic decisions. The steps usually taken in the construction of a cost-benefit analysis for a public-sector undertaking are as follows:

1. Specify objectives and identify constraints.

2. Formulate alternative means of meeting objectives.

3. Estimate costs of each alternative.

4. Estimate benefits attributable to each alternative.

5. Select the best alternative.

The *benefit-cost (B/C) ratio* or *profitability index* is widely used for public expenditure decisions.

CLASSIFICATION OF GOODS

Most goods originate with private sectors. They are categorized as private goods, and those that are governmental in origin are public goods. Public goods are nonrival and nonexclusionary in consumption and, therefore, benefit persons other than those who buy the goods. A good is *nonrival* in consumption if the consumption of the good by one person does not preclude other people from also consuming the good. A good is *nonexclusionary* if, once provided, no one can be excluded from consuming it. Examples of public goods are radio signals, lighthouses, national defense, and clean air.

In order to determine which public goods or projects are worthwhile, and their optimal magnitude, we have to quantify the expected stream of costs and the value of the benefits and determine whether revenues can be collected or not. Since any public project involves expected future flows of costs and benefits, we need to deal with the issue of appropriate discounting. What is a proper *social discount rate* is an unresolved issue.

YOU SHOULD REMEMBER

Whether market interest rates adequately reflect the time preferences of society or the productivity of public projects is always subject to debate.

SOCIAL GOODS AND EXTERNALITIES

When goods are public or social goods, there are always nonmarket interactions in which people are forced to provide resources to others while receiving full compensation or in which people receive benefits without having to make appropriate payments. These nonmarket flows of burdens and benefits are known as *externalities*. Externalities are third-party *spillover*, or *neighborhood*, effects. Externalities are the positive (external economies) or negative (external diseconomies) effects that market exchanges have on people who do not participate directly in those exchanges. Positive externalities include the social benefits conferred by a firm in training workers who become available to work for other firms that incur no training costs. Negative externalities are costs of producing, marketing, consuming a product that is not borne by the product's manufacturers or consumers. These types of externalities include traffic congestion and air pollution. The term *technological* externalities is often used and is distinguished from *pecuniary* externalities. Quantifying these externalities and including them in estimates of social benefits and social costs may not be an easy task.

EXAMPLE 2

State Senator Dan Smith has proposed a new state supported convention facility in the state's capitol. The convention facility would provide the state with annual social benefits $500,000 (in lease receipts and in positive externalities) and would cost $4,000,000. The project has a 15-year life. The state planning board normally uses a 9% discount rate when evaluating capital projects. To determine if the state legislature should adopt Smith's proposal, we can calculate the benefit-cost (B/C) ratio. The present value of the benefit is: $500,000 at 9% for 15 years = $50,000 $T4$ (9%, 15 years) = $500,000 $\times$ 8.061= $4,030,500. B/C = 4,030,500/4,000,000 = 1.008, thus, the state should accept Smith's proposal because it has a B/C ratio greater than 1.

KNOW THE CONCEPTS

TERMS FOR STUDY

antitrust policy

benefit-cost ratio

Clayton Antitrust Act

positive and negative externalities

public goods

Robinson-Patman Act

Sherman Antitrust Act

DO YOU KNOW THE BASICS?

1. Compare the application of the marginality concept in the private and public sectors.

2. Give an example of a public good. Explain why it is a public good.

3. Give four reasons why free markets may fail to provide the socially efficient output of goods or services.

4. Explain the implications of the Robinson-Patman Act for business decisions.

5. List the basic steps used in cost-benefit analysis.

6. Describe the importance of externalities in the analysis of public goods? Do market prices of private goods adequately reflect externalities?

7. What principle determines the optimal allocation of public goods? Discuss why this principle equally applies to privately produced goods.

PRACTICAL APPLICATION

1. City Council member Norm Henteleff has proposed a new airport facility. The facility would provide the state with $300,000 in net cash flow (lending fees, rent, etc.) and would cost $1,800,000. The project has a 20-year life. The City's planning board normally uses a 10% discount rate when evaluating capital projects. Should the city council adopt Smith's proposal? Use the benefit-cost ratio.

2. Which of the following projects would be acceptable from a benefit-cost standpoint if the applicable discount rate is 6%?

Project	Project Life	Annual Benefits	Annual Costs	Capital Outlay
A	20	$50,000	$20,000	$300,000
B	15	$ 5,000	$ 1,000	$ 40,000
C	10	$30,000	$ 7,000	$150,000

ANSWERS

KNOW THE CONCEPTS

1. In public-sector economic analysis, the concept of marginal revenue and marginal cost can be translated into marginal social benefit and marginal social cost. It is important to recognize that while it may be difficult to achieve the demand and cost functions necessary to determine if a firm is operating at $MR = MC$, it may be next to impossible to determine the social benefits attributable to a public project, and extremely difficult to determine public cost.

2. National defense is an example of a public good, because once it is provided, no citizens in a country can be excluded from the benefits.

3. They are (1) market power, (2) externalities, (3) public goods, and (4) incomplete information.

4. Section 2(a) of the Robinson-Patman Act makes price discrimination illegal. Basically, this act helps maintain market competition. Price discrimination due to cost differences or requirements to meet competition is not illegal.

5. The basic steps taken in the construction of a cost-benefit analysis for a public-sector undertaking are as follows: (a) specify objectives and identify constraints, (b) formulate alternative means of meeting objectives, (c) estimate costs of each alternative, (d) estimate benefits attributable to each alternative, and (e) select the best alternative.

6. Public goods generate benefits to parties who do not engage in a market transaction to obtain them. These benefits are called "external benefits," or simply externalities. The market prices of privately produced goods do not reflect externalities, however, because it is difficult or impossible to force those who enjoy the externalities to pay for them.

7. The rule states that the optimal allocation of a public good is achieved when the marginal social cost of the good equals its marginal social benefit. The principle is essentially the same as the profit-maximizing principle of $MR = MC$.

PRACTICAL APPLICATION

1. The present value of the benefit is: $300,000 at 10% for 20 years = $300,000 $T4$ (10%, 20 years) = $300,000 $\times$ 8.514 = $2,554,200. B/C = 2,554,200/1,800,000 = 1.419, thus, the council should accept Henteleff's proposal because it has a B/C ratio greater than 1.

2. Project A:

PV of annual net benefits = (50,000 − 20,000) = 30,000 $\times$ 11.47 = 344,100

B/C = 344,100/300,000 = 1.147; acceptable.

Project B:

PV of annual net benefits = (5,000 − 1,000) = 4,000 $\times$ 9.712 = 38,848

B/C = 38,848/40,000 = 0.9712; not acceptable.

Project C:

PV of annual net benefits = (30,000 − 7,000) = 23,000 $\times$ 7.360 = 169,280

B/C = 169,280/150,000 = 1.129; acceptable.

APPENDIX I

SOURCES OF GENERAL ECONOMIC INFORMATION: AGGREGATE ECONOMIC DATA

Economic data are necessary for analyzing the past and forecasting future directions of the economy. Information on economic growth, inflation, employment, personal income, interest rate, money supply, and the like are important economic data that will influence business. Many business magazines carry important economic and corporate information. Useful information is also available in many publications from the government, banks, and periodicals. Below is a brief description of some of the major sources of economic and business data.

The Wall Street Journal

A business newspaper for managers who want to keep up with the economy and business environment.

- Feature articles on labor, business, economics, personal investing, technology, world events, and taxes appear regularly.

- A section called "The Market Place" providing insights into strategies used by firms to enhance sales and market penetration.

- Corporate announcements of all kinds are published.

- Trends in the economy, recent mergers and acquisitions, and government regulations are included.

- Common and preferred stock prices are organized by exchange and over-the-counter markets.

- Many other prices are printed in the *Journal*. You will find prices of government Treasury bills, notes and bonds, mutual funds, put and call prices from the option exchanges, government agency securities, foreign exchange prices, and commodities future prices.

- It publishes an educational edition that explains how to read the *Journal* and interprets some of the data presented.

Investor's Business Daily
It reports daily coverage of:

- "The Top Story"—the most important news event of the day.

- "The Economy"—sophisticated analysis of current economic topics and government economic reports.

- "National Issue/Business"—a major national and business issue of our time.

- "Leaders & Success"—profiles of successful people and companies.

- "Investor's Corner"—coverage of a wide variety of personal finance topics including investment ideas.

- "Today's News Digest"—35 to 40 brief but important news items of the day.

Further, *Investor's Business Daily* provides what it calls "Smarter Stock Tables," which feature key rankings on all 6,000 publicly-traded issues.

Barron's National Business and Financial Weekly
It contains regular features on dividends, put and call options, international stock markets, commodities, a review of the stock market, and many pages of prices and financial statistics. Barron's takes a weekly perspective and summarizes the previous week's market behavior. It also has regular analyses of several companies in its section called "Investment News and Views."

Forbes
This is a biweekly magazine featuring several company-management interviews. This management-oriented approach points out various management styles and provides a look into the qualitative factors of security analysis.

Business Week
This covers a weekly economic update on such economic variables as interest rates, electricity consumption, and market prices while also featuring articles on industries and companies. The "Corporate Strategy" section that discusses a company's future direction is first-rate. Its periodic report, "Industry Scoreboard," provides financial data and ratios for companies by industry.

Fortune
This is published biweekly and is known for its coverage of industry problems and specific company analysis. Fortune has several regular features that make interesting reading. The "Business Roundup" section usually deals with a major business concern, such as the federal budget, inflation, or productivity.

Federal Reserve Bulletin
The *Federal Reserve Bulletin* is published monthly by the Board of Governors of the Federal Reserve System, Washington, D.C. It contains the following:

1. Monetary data, such as money supply figures, interest rates, bank reserves,

2. Various statistics on commercial banks,

3. Fiscal variables, such as U.S. budget receipts and outlays and federal debt figures,

4. Data on international exchange rates and U.S. dealings with foreigners and overseas banks.

Below is a partial listing of the table of contents of the *Bulletin*. Each heading may be divided into more detailed sections that provide information for the previous month, the current year on a monthly basis, and several years of historical annual data.

Domestic Financial Statistics
Federal Reserve Banks
Monetary and Credit Aggregates
Commercial Banks
Financial Markets
Federal Finance
Securities Markets and Corporate Finance
Real Estate
Consumer Installment Credit
Domestic Non Financial Statistics
International Statistics
Securities Holdings and Transactions
Interest and Exchange Rates

Quarterly Chart Book and Annual Chart Book

These two books are also published by the Federal Reserve Board. They depict the data in the *Federal Reserve Bulletin* in graphic form.

The Report on Current Economic Conditions ("The Beige Book")

The Report, informally known as the *Beige Book*, is released about every six weeks by the Federal Reserve Board. It provides the most recent assessment of the nation's economy, with a regional emphasis. It is used to help the Fed decide on its monetary policy, such as changes in interest rates.

Monthly Newsletters and Reviews Published by Federal Reserve Banks

Each of the 12 Federal Reserve banks in the Federal Reserve System publishes its own monthly letter or review that includes economic data about its region and sometimes commentary on national issues or monetary policy. Their addresses are given in the Appendix.

U.S. Financial Data, Monetary Trends and National Economic Trends

The Federal Reserve Bank of St. Louis, publishes some of the most comprehensive economic statistics on a weekly and monthly basis.

U.S. Financial Data is published weekly and includes data on the monetary base, bank reserves, money supply, a breakdown of time deposits and demand deposits, borrowing from the Federal Reserve Banks, and business loans from the large commercial banks.

Monetary Trends, published monthly, includes charts and tables of monthly data. It covers a longer time period than *U.S. Financial Data*. The tables provide compound annual rates of change, while the graphs include the raw data with trend changes over time. Additional data are available on the federal government debt and its composition by type of holder and on the receipts and expenditures of the government.

National Economic Trends presents monthly economic data on employment, unemployment rates, consumer and producer prices, industrial production, personal income, retail sales, productivity, compensation and labor costs, the GNP implicit price deflator, the GNP and its components, disposable personal income, corporate profits, and inventories. This information is presented in graphic form and in tables showing the compounded annual rate of change on a monthly basis.

Survey of Current Business, Weekly Business Statistics, and Business Conditions Digest

The Bureau of Economic Analysis of the U.S. Department of Commerce publishes three major economic source publications: *Survey of Current Business, Weekly Business Statistics,* and *Business Conditions Digest.*

The Survey of Current Business is published monthly and contains monthly and quarterly raw data. It presents a monthly update and evaluation of the business situation, analyzing such data as GNP, business inventories, personal consumption, fixed investment, exports, labor market statistics, financial data, and much more. For example, if personal consumption expenditures are broken down into subcategories, one would find expenditures on durable goods, such as motor vehicles and parts and furniture and equipment; nondurables, such as food, energy, clothing, and shoes; and services.

Note: The Survey can be extremely helpful for industry analysis as it breaks down data into basic industries. For example, data on inventory, new plant and equipment, production, and more can be found on such specific industries as coal, tobacco, chemicals, leather products, furniture, and paper. Even within industries, such as lumber, production statistics can be found on hardwoods and softwoods right down to Douglas fir trees, southern pine, and western pine.

Weekly Business Statistics is a weekly update to the Survey. It updates the major series found in the *Survey of Current Business* and includes 27 weekly series and charts of selected series. To provide a more comprehensive view of what is available in the *Survey of Current Business* and *Weekly Business Statistics,* presented below is a list of the major series updates:

GNP
National Income
Personal Income
Industrial Production

Manufacturers' Shipments, Inventories, and Orders
Consumer Price Index
Producer Price Index
Construction Put in Place
Housing Starts and Permits
Retail Trade
Labor Force, Employment, and Earnings
Banking
Consumer Installment Credit
Stock Prices
Value of Exports and Imports
Motor Vehicles

The *Business Conditions Digest*, published monthly, provides information that differs from the other publications previously discussed in that its primary emphasis is on cyclical indicators of economic activity. The *National Bureau of Economic Research (NBER)* analyzes and selects the time-series data based on each series' ability to be identified as a leading, coincident, or lagging indicator over several decades of aggregate economic activity. Over the years, the NBER has identified the approximate dates when aggregate economic activity reached its cyclical high or low point. Each time series is related to the business cycle. Leading indicators move prior to the business cycle, coincident indicators move with the cycle, and lagging indicators follow directional changes in the business cycle.

Statistical Abstracts of the United States

Statistical Abstracts of the United States provides voluminous data on wages, the composition of the population, prices, demographics, and other valuable business information.

OTHER SOURCES OF ECONOMIC DATA

In addition to the publications discussed above, much other data is available in other publications. They are summarized below.

1. Many universities have bureaus of business research that provide statistical data on a statewide or regional basis.

2. Major banks, such as Bank of America, Citicorp, and Morgan Guaranty, publish monthly or weekly letters or economic reviews, that include raw data and analysis.

3. Several other government sources are available, such as *Economic Indicators* and the *Annual Economic Report of the President* prepared in February by the Council of Economic Advisors.

4. Moody's, Value Line's, and Standard & Poor's investment services all publish economic data along with much other market-related information.

Computer Databases and World Wide Web

Many computer databases are available for use by managers.

- FRB is published by the Board of Governors of the Federal Reserve System. It contains financial statements and supporting schedules for more than 15,000 banks. This database is updated annually and has five years' data on-line.

- Citibase From Citicorp, a database of time-series data summarizing economic and other conditions in the U.S. The database is updated quarterly.

- Dow Jones News-Retrieval (DJN/R) provides on-line access to articles carried by major wire services.

- Some of the raw economic and business data can be obtained through the Internet. For example,

  EDGAR SEC database: http://www.sec.gov
  Economic data: http://www.fedstats.gov

APPENDIX II

Table 1.   Future Value of $1.00 (Compounded Amount of $1.00)

$$(1 + i)^n = T1(i,n) = FVIF$$

PERIODS	4%	6%	8%	10%	12%	14%	20%
1	1.040	1.060	1.080	1.100	1.120	1.140	1.200
2	1.082	1.124	1.166	1.210	1.254	1.300	1.440
3	1.125	1.191	1.260	1.331	1.405	1.482	1.728
4	1.170	1.263	1.361	1.464	1.574	1.689	2.074
5	1.217	1.338	1.469	1.611	1.762	1.925	2.488
6	1.265	1.419	1.587	1.772	1.974	2.195	2.986
7	1.316	1.504	1.714	1.949	2.211	2.502	3.583
8	1.369	1.594	1.851	2.144	2.476	2.853	4.300
9	1.423	1.690	1.999	2.359	2.773	3.252	5.160
10	1.480	1.791	2.159	2.594	3.106	3.707	6.192
11	1.540	1.898	2.332	2.853	3.479	4.226	7.430
12	1.601	2.012	2.518	3.139	3.896	4.818	8.916
13	1.665	2.133	2.720	3.452	4.364	5.492	10.699
14	1.732	2.261	2.937	3.798	4.887	6.261	12.839
15	1.801	2.397	3.172	4.177	5.474	7.138	15.407
16	1.873	2.540	3.426	4.595	6.130	8.137	18.488
17	1.948	2.693	3.700	5.055	6.866	9.277	22.186
18	2.026	2.854	3.996	5.560	7.690	10.575	26.623
19	2.107	3.026	4.316	6.116	8.613	12.056	31.948
20	2.191	3.207	4.661	6.728	9.646	13.743	38.338
30	3.243	5.744	10.063	17.450	29.960	50.950	237.380
40	4.801	10.286	21.725	45.260	93.051	188.880	1469.800

Table 2.   Future Value of an Annuity of $1.00*
(Compounded Amount of an Annuity of $1.00)

$$\frac{(1 + i)^n - 1}{i} = T2(i,n) = FVIFA$$

PERIODS	4%	6%	8%	10%	12%	14%	20%
1	1.000	1.000	1.000	1.000	1.000	1.000	1.000
2	2.040	2.060	2.080	2.100	2.120	2.140	2.200
3	3.122	3.184	3.246	3.310	3.374	3.440	3.640
4	4.247	4.375	4.506	4.641	4.779	4.921	5.368
5	5.416	5.637	5.867	6.105	6.353	6.610	7.442
6	6.633	6.975	7.336	7.716	8.115	8.536	9.930
7	7.898	8.394	8.923	9.487	10.089	10.730	12.916
8	9.214	9.898	10.637	11.436	12.300	13.233	16.499
9	10.583	11.491	12.488	13.580	14.776	16.085	20.799
10	12.006	13.181	14.487	15.938	17.549	19.337	25.959
11	13.486	14.972	16.646	18.531	20.655	23.045	32.150
12	15.026	16.870	18.977	21.385	24.133	27.271	39.580
13	16.627	18.882	21.495	24.523	28.029	32.089	48.497
14	18.292	21.015	24.215	27.976	32.393	37.581	59.196
15	20.024	23.276	27.152	31.773	37.280	43.842	72.035
16	21.825	25.673	30.324	35.950	42.753	50.980	87.442
17	23.698	28.213	33.750	40.546	48.884	59.118	105.930
18	25.645	30.906	37.450	45.600	55.750	68.394	128.120
19	27.671	33.760	41.446	51.160	63.440	78.969	154.740
20	29.778	36.778	45.762	57.276	75.052	91.025	186.690
30	56.085	79.058	113.283	164.496	241.330	356.790	1181.900
40	95.026	154.762	259.057	442.597	767.090	1342.000	7343.900

* Payments (or receipts) at the *end* of each period.

Table 3. Present Value of $1.00

$$\frac{1}{(1+i)^n} = T3(i,n) = PVIF$$

Periods	4%	6%	8%	10%	12%	14%	20%
1	0.962	0.943	0.926	0.909	0.893	0.877	0.833
2	0.925	0.890	0.857	0.826	0.797	0.769	0.694
3	0.889	0.840	0.794	0.751	0.712	0.675	0.579
4	0.855	0.792	0.735	0.683	0.636	0.592	0.482
5	0.822	0.747	0.681	0.621	0.567	0.519	0.402
6	0.790	0.705	0.630	0.564	0.507	0.456	0.335
7	0.760	0.665	0.583	0.513	0.452	0.400	0.279
8	0.731	0.627	0.540	0.467	0.404	0.351	0.233
9	0.703	0.592	0.500	0.424	0.361	0.308	0.194
10	0.676	0.558	0.463	0.386	0.322	0.270	0.162
11	0.650	0.527	0.429	0.350	0.287	0.237	0.135
12	0.625	0.497	0.397	0.319	0.257	0.208	0.112
13	0.601	0.469	0.368	0.290	0.229	0.182	0.093
14	0.577	0.442	0.340	0.263	0.205	0.160	0.078
15	0.555	0.417	0.315	0.239	0.183	0.140	0.065
16	0.534	0.394	0.292	0.218	0.163	0.123	0.054
17	0.513	0.371	0.270	0.198	0.146	0.108	0.045
18	0.494	0.350	0.250	0.180	0.130	0.095	0.038
19	0.475	0.331	0.232	0.164	0.116	0.083	0.031
20	0.456	0.312	0.215	0.149	0.104	0.073	0.026
30	0.308	0.174	0.099	0.057	0.033	0.020	0.004
40	0.208	0.097	0.046	0.022	0.011	0.005	0.001

Table 4. Present Value of an Annuity of $1.00

$$= \frac{1}{i}\left(1 - \frac{1}{(Hi)}\right) = T4(i, n) = PVIFA$$

	4%	6%	8%	10%	12%	14%	16%	18%	20%	22%	24%	25%	26%	28%	30%	40%
1	.0962	0.943	0.926	0.909	0.893	0.877	0.862	.0847	0.833	0.820	0.806	0.800	0.794	0.781	0.769	0.714
2	1.886	1.833	1.783	1.736	1.690	1.647	1.605	1.566	1.528	1.492	1.457	1.440	1.424	1.392	1.361	1.224
3	2.775	2.673	2.577	2.487	2.402	2.322	2.246	2.174	2.106	2.042	1.981	1.952	1.923	1.868	1.816	1.589
4	3.630	3.465	3.312	3.170	3.037	2.914	2.798	2.690	2.589	2.494	2.404	2.362	2.320	2.241	2.166	1.849
5	4.452	4.212	3.993	3.791	3.605	3.433	3.274	3.127	2.991	2.864	2.745	2.689	2.635	2.532	2.436	2.035
6	5.242	4.917	4.623	4.355	4.111	3.889	3.685	3.498	3.326	3.167	3.020	2.951	2.885	2.759	2.643	2.168
7	6.002	5.582	5.206	4.868	4.564	4.288	4.039	3.812	3.605	3.416	3.242	3.161	3.083	2.937	2.802	2.263
8	6.733	6.210	5.747	5.335	4.968	4.639	4.344	4.078	3.837	3.619	3.421	3.329	3.241	3.076	2.925	2.331
9	7.435	6.802	6.247	5.759	5.328	4.946	4.607	4.303	4.031	3.786	3.565	3.463	3.366	3.184	3.019	2.379
10	8.111	7.360	6.710	6.145	5.650	5.216	4.833	4.494	4.192	3.923	3.682	3.571	3.465	3.269	3.092	2.414
11	8.760	7.887	7.139	6.495	5.938	5.453	5.029	4.656	4.327	4.035	3.776	3.656	3.544	3.335	3.147	2.438
12	9.385	8.384	7.536	6.814	6.194	5.660	5.197	4.793	4.439	4.127	3.851	3.725	3.606	3.387	3.190	2.456
13	9.986	8.853	7.904	7.103	6.424	5.842	5.342	4.910	4.533	4.203	3.912	3.780	3.656	3.427	3.223	2.468
14	10.563	9.295	8.244	7.367	6.628	6.002	5.468	5.008	4.611	4.265	3.962	3.824	3.695	3.459	3.249	2.477
15	11.118	9.712	8.559	7.606	6.811	6.142	5.575	5.092	4.675	4.315	4.001	3.859	3.726	3.483	3.268	2.484
16	11.652	10.106	8.851	7.824	6.974	6.265	5.669	5.162	4.730	4.357	4.033	3.887	3.751	3.503	3.283	2.489
17	12.166	10.477	9.122	8.022	7.120	6.373	5.749	5.222	4.775	4.391	4.059	3.910	3.771	3.518	3.295	2.492
18	12.659	10.828	9.372	8.201	7.250	6.467	5.818	5.273	4.812	4.419	4.080	3.928	3.786	3.529	3.304	2.494
19	13.134	11.158	9.604	8.365	7.366	6.550	5.877	5.316	4.844	4.442	4.097	3.942	3.799	3.539	3.311	2.496
20	13.590	11.470	9.818	8.514	7.469	6.623	5.929	5.353	4.870	4.460	4.110	3.954	3.808	3.546	3.316	2.497
21	14.029	11.764	10.017	8.649	7.562	6.687	5.973	5.384	4.891	4.476	4.121	3.963	3.816	3.551	3.320	2.498
22	14.451	12.042	10.201	8.772	7.645	6.743	6.011	5.410	4.909	4.488	4.130	3.970	3.822	3.556	3.323	2.498
23	14.857	12.303	10.371	8.883	7.718	6.792	6.044	5.432	4.925	4.499	4.137	3.976	3.827	3.559	3.325	2.499
24	15.247	12.550	10.529	8.985	7.784	6.835	6.073	5.451	4.937	4.507	4.143	3.981	3.831	3.562	3.327	2.499
25	15.622	12.783	10.675	9.077	7.843	6.873	6.097	5.467	4.948	4.514	4.147	3.985	3.834	3.564	3.329	2.499
26	15.983	13.003	10.810	9.161	7.896	6.906	6.118	5.480	4.956	4.520	4.151	3.988	3.837	3.566	3.330	2.500
27	16.330	13.211	10.935	9.237	7.943	6.935	6.136	5.492	4.964	4.524	4.154	3.990	3.839	3.567	3.331	2.500
28	16.663	13.406	11.051	9.307	7.984	6.961	6.152	5.502	4.970	4.528	4.157	3.992	3.840	3.568	3.331	2.500
29	16.984	13.591	11.158	9.370	8.022	6.983	6.166	5.510	4.975	4.531	4.159	3.994	3.841	3.569	3.332	2.500
30	17.292	13.765	11.258	9.427	8.055	7.003	6.177	5.517	4.979	4.534	4.160	3.995	3.842	3.569	3.332	2.500
40	19.793	15.046	11.925	9.779	8.244	7.105	6.234	5.548	4.997	4.544	4.166	3.999	3.846	3.571	3.333	2.500

*Payments (or receipts) at the *end* of each period.

Table 5. **Critical Values for the t-Statistic**

Degrees of Freedom	$t_{0.100}$	$t_{0.050}$	$t_{0.025}$	$t_{0.010}$	$t_{0.005}$
1	3.078	6.314	12.706	31.821	63.657
2	1.886	2.920	4.303	6.965	9.925
3	1.638	2.353	3.182	4.541	5.841
4	1.533	2.132	2.776	3.747	4.604
5	1.476	2.015	2.571	3.365	4.032
6	1.440	1.943	2.447	3.143	3.707
7	1.415	1.895	2.365	3.000	3.499
8	1.397	1.860	2.306	2.896	3.355
9	1.383	1.833	2.262	3.821	3.250
10	1.372	1.812	2.228	2.764	3.169
11	1.363	1.796	2.201	2.718	3.106
12	1.356	1.782	2.179	2.681	3.055
13	1.350	1.771	2.160	2.650	3.012
14	1.345	1.761	2.145	2.600	2.977
15	1.341	1.753	2.131	2.600	2.947
16	1.337	1.746	2.120	2.584	2.921
17	1.333	1.740	2.110	2.567	2.898
18	1.330	1.734	2.101	2.552	2.878
19	1.328	1.729	2.093	2.539	2.861
20	1.325	1.725	2.086	2.528	2.845
21	1.323	1.721	2.080	2.518	2.831
22	1.321	1.717	2.074	2.508	2.819
23	1.319	1.714	2.069	2.500	2.807
24	1.318	1.711	2.064	2.492	2.797
25	1.316	1.708	2.060	2.485	2.787
26	1.315	1.706	2.056	2.479	2.779
27	1.314	1.703	2.052	2.473	2.771
28	1.313	1.701	2.048	2.467	2.763
29	1.311	1.699	2.045	2.462	2.756
30	1.310	1.697	2.042	2.457	2.750
35	1.306	1.690	2.030	2.438	2.724
40	1.303	1.684	2.021	2.423	2.704
50	1.299	1.676	2.009	2.400	2.678
60	1.296	1.671	2.000	2.400	2.660
100	1.290	1.660	1.984	2.364	2.626
120	1.289	1.658	1.980	2.358	2.617

Table 6. Critical Values for the F-Statistic
Upper 5% for all light face entries
Upper 1% for all bold face entries
m_1 = degrees of freedom for numerator = k

	1	2	3	4	5	6	7	8	9	10	11	12
1	161	200	216	225	230	234	237	239	241	242	243	244
	4,052	**4,999**	**5,402**	**5,628**	**5,764**	**5,889**	**5,928**	**5,981**	**6,023**	**6,066**	**6,082**	**6,104**
2	18.51	19.00	19.16	19.25	19.30	19.33	19.36	19.37	19.38	19.39	19.40	19.41
	98.49	**99.01**	**99.17**	**99.25**	**99.30**	**99.33**	**99.34**	**99.36**	**99.38**	**99.40**	**99.41**	**99.42**
3	10.13	9.55	9.28	9.12	9.01	8.94	8.88	8.84	8.81	8.78	8.76	8.74
	34.12	**30.81**	**29.46**	**28.71**	**28.24**	**27.91**	**27.67**	**27.49**	**27.34**	**27.25**	**27.13**	**27.05**
4	7.71	6.94	6.59	6.39	6.26	6.16	6.00	6.00	6.00	5.96	5.03	5.91
	21.20	**18.00**	**14.69**	**15.98**	**15.52**	**15.21**	**14.98**	**14.80**	**14.66**	**14.54**	**14.45**	**14.37**
5	6.61	5.79	5.41	5.19	5.05	4.95	4.88	4.82	4.78	4.74	4.70	4.68
	16.34	**13.27**	**12.06**	**11.39**	**10.97**	**10.67**	**10.45**	**10.27**	**10.18**	**10.05**	**9.96**	**9.59**
6	5.99	5.14	4.76	4.53	4.39	4.28	4.21	4.15	4.10	4.06	4.03	4.00
	13.74	**10.92**	**9.78**	**9.18**	**8.76**	**8.47**	**8.26**	**8.10**	**7.98**	**7.87**	**7.73**	**7.72**
7	5.59	4.74	4.35	4.12	3.97	3.87	3.79	3.73	3.68	3.63	3.60	3.57
	12.20	**9.55**	**8.45**	**7.85**	**7.46**	**7.19**	**7.00**	**6.84**	**6.71**	**6.62**	**6.84**	**6.47**
8	5.32	4.46	4.07	3.84	3.69	3.58	3.50	3.44	3.39	3.34	3.31	3.28
	11.36	**8.65**	**7.89**	**7.01**	**6.63**	**6.37**	**6.19**	**6.08**	**5.91**	**5.82**	**6.74**	**5.67**
9	5.12	4.26	3.86	3.63	3.48	3.37	3.29	3.23	3.18	3.13	3.10	3.07
	10.56	**8.02**	**6.99**	**5.42**	**6.06**	**5.80**	**5.62**	**5.47**	**5.35**	**5.26**	**5.18**	**5.11**
10	4.96	4.10	3.71	3.48	3.33	3.22	3.14	3.07	3.02	2.97	2.94	2.91
	10.04	**7.56**	**6.86**	**5.99**	**5.64**	**5.39**	**5.21**	**5.04**	**4.98**	**4.88**	**4.78**	**4.71**
11	4.84	3.98	3.50	3.36	3.20	3.00	3.01	2.05	2.90	2.86	2.82	2.79
	9.65	**7.20**	**6.22**	**5.67**	**5.32**	**5.07**	**4.88**	**4.74**	**4.63**	**4.54**	**4.44**	**4.40**
12	4.75	3.89	3.49	3.26	3.11	3.00	2.92	2.85	2.80	2.76	2.72	2.69
	9.33	**6.93**	**5.95**	**5.41**	**5.06**	**4.82**	**4.68**	**4.50**	**4.39**	**4.30**	**4.22**	**4.16**
13	4.67	3.80	3.41	3.18	3.02	2.92	2.84	2.77	2.72	2.67	2.63	2.60
	9.07	**6.70**	**5.74**	**5.20**	**4.86**	**4.62**	**4.44**	**4.30**	**4.19**	**4.10**	**4.02**	**3.96**
14	4.60	3.74	3.34	3.11	2.96	2.85	2.77	2.70	2.65	2.60	2.54	2.53
	8.86	**6.51**	**5.56**	**5.03**	**4.69**	**4.46**	**4.28**	**4.14**	**4.03**	**3.94**	**3.86**	**3.80**
15	4.54	3.68	3.29	3.06	2.90	2.79	2.70	2.64	2.59	2.55	2.51	2.48
	8.68	**6.36**	**5.42**	**4.89**	**4.54**	**4.22**	**4.14**	**4.00**	**3.89**	**3.80**	**3.73**	**3.67**
16	4.49	3.63	3.24	3.01	2.85	2.74	2.66	2.59	2.54	2.49	2.45	2.42
	8.53	**6.23**	**5.29**	**4.77**	**4.44**	**4.20**	**4.03**	**3.89**	**3.78**	**3.69**	**3.61**	**3.58**
17	4.45	3.59	3.20	2.96	2.81	2.70	2.62	2.55	2.50	2.45	2.41	2.38
	8.40	**6.11**	**5.18**	**4.67**	**4.34**	**4.10**	**3.93**	**3.79**	**3.68**	**3.59**	**3.52**	**3.45**
18	4.41	3.55	3.16	2.93	2.77	2.68	2.58	2.51	2.48	3.41	2.37	2.34
	8.29	**6.01**	**5.09**	**4.88**	**4.25**	**4.01**	**3.88**	**3.71**	**3.60**	**3.51**	**3.44**	**3.37**
19	4.38	3.52	3.13	2.90	2.74	2.63	2.55	2.48	2.43	2.38	2.34	2.31
	8.19	**5.93**	**5.01**	**4.80**	**4.17**	**3.94**	**3.77**	**3.63**	**3.82**	**3.43**	**3.36**	**3.30**
20	4.35	3.49	3.10	2.87	2.71	2.60	2.52	2.45	2.40	2.35	2.31	2.28
	8.10	**5.85**	**4.94**	**4.43**	**4.10**	**3.87**	**3.71**	**3.56**	**3.45**	**3.37**	**3.30**	**3.23**
21	4.32	3.47	3.07	2.84	2.68	2.57	2.49	2.42	2.37	2.32	2.28	2.25
	8.02	**5.78**	**4.87**	**4.37**	**4.04**	**3.81**	**3.68**	**3.51**	**3.40**	**3.31**	**3.24**	**3.17**
22	4.30	3.44	3.05	2.82	2.66	2.55	2.47	2.40	2.35	2.30	2.26	2.23
	7.95	**5.72**	**4.82**	**4.31**	**3.99**	**3.76**	**3.89**	**3.46**	**3.38**	**3.26**	**3.18**	**3.12**
23	4.28	3.42	3.03	2.80	2.64	2.53	2.45	2.38	2.32	2.28	2.24	2.20
	7.88	**5.66**	**4.76**	**4.26**	**3.94**	**3.71**	**3.54**	**2.41**	**3.30**	**3.21**	**3.16**	**3.07**
24	4.26	3.40	3.01	2.78	2.62	2.51	2.43	2.36	2.30	2.26	2.22	2.18
	7.82	**5.61**	**4.72**	**4.22**	**3.90**	**3.67**	**3.50**	**3.36**	**3.28**	**3.17**	**3.09**	**3.03**
25	4.24	3.39	2.99	2.76	2.60	2.49	2.41	2.34	2.28	2.24	2.20	2.16
	7.77	**5.57**	**4.68**	**4.18**	**3.86**	**3.63**	**3.46**	**3.32**	**3.21**	**3.13**	**3.05**	**2.99**
26	4.22	3.37	2.98	2.74	2.50	2.47	2.39	2.32	2.27	2.22	2.18	2.15
	7.72	**5.52**	**4.64**	**4.14**	**3.82**	**3.59**	**3.42**	**3.29**	**3.17**	**3.09**	**3.02**	**2.96**

Table 7. Learning Curve Coefficients

UNIT NUMBER	70% UNIT TIME	70% TOTAL TIME	75% UNIT TIME	75% TOTAL TIME	80% UNIT TIME	80% TOTAL TIME	85% UNIT TIME	85% TOTAL TIME	90% UNIT TIME	90% TOTAL TIME
1	1.000	1.000	1.000	1.000	1.000	1.000	1.000	1.000	1.000	1.000
2	.700	1.700	.750	1.750	.800	1.800	.850	1.850	.900	1.900
3	.568	2.268	.634	2.384	.702	2.502	.773	2.623	.846	2.746
4	.490	2.758	.562	2.946	.640	3.142	.723	3.345	.810	3.556
5	.437	3.195	.513	3.459	.596	3.738	.686	4.031	.783	4.339
6	.398	3.593	.475	3.934	.562	4.299	.657	4.688	.762	5.101
7	.367	3.960	.446	4.380	.534	4.834	.634	5.322	.744	5.845
8	.343	4.303	.422	4.802	.512	5.346	.614	5.936	.729	6.574
9	.323	4.626	.402	5.204	.493	5.839	.597	6.533	.716	7.290
10	.306	4.932	.385	5.589	.477	6.315	.583	7.116	.705	7.994
11	.291	5.223	.370	5.958	.462	6.777	.570	7.686	.695	8.689
12	.278	5.501	.357	6.315	.449	7.227	.558	8.244	.685	9.374
13	.267	5.769	.345	6.660	.438	7.665	.548	8.792	.677	10.052
14	.257	6.026	.334	6.994	.428	8.092	.539	9.331	.670	10.721
15	.248	6.274	.325	7.319	.418	8.511	.530	9.861	.663	11.384
16	.240	6.514	.316	7.635	.410	8.920	.522	10.383	.656	12.040
17	.233	6.747	.309	7.944	.402	9.322	.515	10.898	.650	12.690
18	.226	6.973	.301	8.245	.394	9.716	.508	11.405	.644	13.334
19	.220	7.192	.295	8.540	.381	10.104	.501	11.907	.639	13.974
20	.214	7.407	.288	8.828	.381	10.485	.495	12.402	.634	14.608
21	.209	7.615	.283	9.111	.375	10.860	.490	12.892	.630	15.237
22	.204	7.819	.277	9.388	.370	11.230	.484	13.376	.625	15.862
23	.199	8.018	.272	9.660	.364	11.594	.479	13.856	.621	16.483
24	.195	8.213	.267	9.928	.359	11.954	.475	14.331	.617	17.100
25	.191	8.404	.263	10.191	.355	12.309	.470	14.801	.613	17.713
26	.187	8.591	.259	10.449	.350	12.659	.466	15.267	.609	18.323
27	.183	8.774	.255	10.704	.346	13.005	.462	15.728	.606	18.929
28	.180	8.954	.251	10.955	.342	13.347	.458	16.186	.603	19.531
29	.177	9.131	.247	11.202	.338	13.685	.454	16.640	.599	20.131
30	.174	9.305	.244	11.446	.335	14.020	.450	17.091	.596	20.727
31	.171	9.476	.240	11.686	.331	14.351	.447	17.538	.593	21.320
32	.168	9.644	.237	11.924	.328	14.679	.444	17.981	.590	21.911
33	.165	9.809	.234	12.158	.324	15.003	.441	18.422	.588	22.498
34	.163	9.972	.231	12.389	.321	15.324	.437	18.859	.585	23.084
35	.160	10.133	.229	12.618	.318	15.643	.434	19.294	.583	23.666
36	.158	10.291	.226	12.844	.315	15.958	.432	19.725	.580	24.246
37	.156	10.447	.223	13.067	.313	16.271	.429	20.154	.578	24.824
38	.154	10.601	.221	13.288	.310	16.581	.426	20.580	.575	25.399
39	.152	10.753	.219	13.507	.307	16.888	.424	21.004	.573	25.972
40	.150	10.902	.216	13.723	.305	17.193	.421	21.425	.571	26.543

GLOSSARY

accounting profits difference between the total revenue and the cost of producing goods or services

activity analysis evaluation involving the determination of the combination of production processes that maximizes output (or profits), subject to the restrictions on the required resources (inputs)

anti-trust policy policy encouraging fair and free trade and competition

average product total amount of output divided by the amount of the input used to produce the output

average revenue total revenue per unit of output, that is total revenue received divided by output

average variable cost total variable cost divided by the corresponding number of units of output

barometric forecasting use of economic indicators, such as leading indicators, to predict turning points in economic activity

basic feasible solutions corner point solutions of the feasible region that satisfy all the constraints simultaneously

block pricing pricing under which units of a product are sold as one package

break-even point level of sales revenue that equals the total of the variable and fixed costs for a given volume of output at a particular capacity use rate

capital budgeting process of making long-term planning and capital expenditure decisions

capital rationing situation that exists when a firm has more acceptable projects than it has funds available to invest. The projects are ranked in priority order

certainty equivalent approach approach that converts cash flows from individual projects into risk adjusted certainty equivalent cash flows

Clayton Antitrust Act one of three major antitrust laws, passed as an amendment to the Sherman Antitrust Act in 1914. It outlawed price discrimination, tying contracts and exclusive dealerships, and horizontal mergers

Cobb-Douglas production function production function that assumes some degree of substitutability among inputs. The relationship between output and the inputs is *not* linear

coefficient of determination proportion of the total variation in the dependent variable that is explained by the regression equation

coefficient of variation ratio of the standard deviation to the expected value. A relative measure of risk

commodity bundling practice of bundling several different products together and selling them at a single "bundle price"

constrained optimization optimization with the restrictions imposed on the availability of resources and other requirements. Techniques, such as linear programming (*LP*) and the Lagrangean multipliers, are used for this purpose

consumer surveys method that involves interviewing potential customers to estimate demand relations

correlation coefficient measure of the degree of correlation between the two variables

cost of capital rate of return that investors expect to receive from the firm

cost-based price widely used pricing technique that involves an appropriate cost base plus the markup—usually calculated as some percentage of the cost base

cost-benefit analysis appraisal that attempts to determine whether the favorable results of an alternative are sufficient to justify the cost of taking that alternative. This analysis is widely used in connection with capital expenditure projects in the government sector

Cournot's oligopoly model oligopoly model which assumes that each of the two firms will maximize profits assuming that its competitor's output remains constant

cross elasticity responsiveness of one product to changes in the price of some other product, holding all other factors constant

cross subsidization pricing method in which the firm may enhance profits by selling one product at or below cost and the other product above cost

decision tree graphical method of showing the sequence of possible outcomes

demand curve graph of a *demand schedule*. Price is on the vertical axis and quantity demanded is on the horizontal axis

demand function mathematical relationship showing how the quantity demanded of a good or service responds to changes in a number of economic factors, such as its own price, the prices of substitutes and complementary goods, income, and advertising

demand schedule table or tabular representation of the quantity demanded at various possible prices during a given time period, all other things remaining equal. The data from a demand schedule can be used to construct a *demand curve*

derivative instantaneous rate of change of a function at a given point or the slope of its tangent. It is a specification of the *marginal* relation in economics

discounted cash flow (DCF) techniques methods of selecting and ranking investment proposals, such as the net present value (*NPV*) and internal rate of return (*IRR*) methods where time value of money is taken into account

Durbin-Watson statistic summary measure of the amount of autocorrelation (or serial correlation) in the error terms of the regression

econometric models statistically based models where relationships among economic variables are expressed in mathematical equations, single or simultaneous in nature, and then estimated using such techniques as regression methods

econometrics branch of economics concerned with empirical testing of economic theory using various statistical methods such as *regression analysis*

economic profits difference between the total revenue and the total opportunity costs

equilibrium price price of a commodity (good and service) toward which a competitive market will move and, once there, at which it will remain

expansion path graphical device used to illustrate the amount of capital and labor that a firm will use as it expands its operations

expected utility weighted average of utilities using the probabilities as weights

expected value weighted average using the probabilities as weights

exponential smoothing forecasting technique that uses a weighted moving average of past data as the basis for a forecast

externalities positive (beneficial) or negative (harmful) effects that market exchanges have on people who do not participate directly in those exchanges

first derivative test test to locate one or more extreme (maximum or minimum) points on a function

four-firm concentration ratio fraction of total industry sales produced by the four largest firms in the industry

F-test ratio of two mean squares (variances) can often be used to test the significance of some item of interest

game theory technique that deals with competitive situations where two or more firms have conflicting objectives

goodness-of-fit degree to which a model fits the observed data

Herfindahl-Hirshman index sum of the squared market shares

homoscedasticity one of the assumptions required in a regression in order to make valid statistical inferences about population relationships, also known as *constant variance*. Homoscedasticity requires that the variance of the error terms is constant for all X

identification problem statistical problem encountered in the estimation of the parameters of one function, such as the demand function, when simultaneous relations exist

incremental (differential) costs costs associated with any managerial decision. This is equivalent to the marginal cost concept but involves multiple changes in output and discrete output choices, rather than a single-unit change

input-output analysis models concerned with the flow of goods among industries in an economy or among branches of a large organization

internal rate of return (IRR) rate earned on a proposal. It is the rate of interest that equates the initial investment with the present value of future cash inflows

iso-cost curve curve or line showing the combinations of any inputs that can be bought with a fixed sum of money

kinked demand curve "bent" or "kink" industry demand curve with a corresponding discontinuous marginal revenue curve that is found in an oligopolistic industry

Lagrangean multiplier measure of the marginal change in the value of the objective function resulting from a one-unit change in the value on the right-hand side of the equality sign in the constraint

learning curve effect reduction in labor hours as the cumulative production doubles, ranging typically from 10 percent to 20 percent

least-squares method statistical method in regression analysis aimed at finding a regression line of *best fit*

Leontief production function production function in which inputs are used in fixed proportions

Lerner index measure of the difference between price and marginal cost as a percentage of the product's price

linear production function production function that assumes a perfect linear relationship between all inputs and total output

linear programming (*LP*) mathematical technique designed to determine an optimal decision (or an optimal plan) chosen from a large number of possible decisions

linear regression regression that deals with a straight line relationship between variables

long-run average cost curve curve showing the minimum cost per unit of producing each output when all resource inputs are variable

marginal cost cost of making an additional unit of output

managerial economics branch of economics, that is economics applied in managerial decision making

marginal revenue change of total revenue with respect to quantity demanded

marginal analysis analysis that ensures that for the profit to be maximized, marginal revenues equal marginal costs

marginal product change in the quantity of output resulting from a one unit change in the quantity of input used

marginal rate of technical substitution rate that measures reduction in one input per unit increase in the other that is just sufficient to maintain a constant level of output

marginal revenue product net addition to total revenue attributable to the addition of one unit of the variable productive service

market experimentation studies of consumer behavior in actual or simulated market settings

markup on cost the profit margin expressed as a percentage of unit cost

mean squared error (*MSE*) average sum of the variations between the historical sales data and the forecast values for the corresponding periods

moving average in a time series an average that is updated as new information is received

multicollinearity condition that exists when the independent variables are highly correlated with each other

multiple regression analysis statistical procedure that attempts to assess the relationship between the dependent variable and two or more independent variables

net present value method technique widely used for evaluating investment projects. Under the net present value method, the present value (PV) of all cash inflows from the project is compared against the initial investment (I)

operating leverage measure of operating risk; the ratio of a percentage change in operating income to a percentage change in sales volume

opportunity costs net benefits forgone by rejecting the next-best use of a resource

optimal employment rule profit-maximizing rule that says that the marginal revenue product of an input is exactly equal to the input price

optimal price typically profit-maximizing price

optimization maximization or minimization of a special goal

partial derivative derivative with respect to one variable in question, holding the other variables constant

peak-load pricing pricing that charges a higher price during peak times than is charged during off-peak times

penetrating pricing pricing policy that involves setting low initial prices in order to gain quick acceptance in a broad portion of the market

perfect competition market structure possessing the following characteristics: (1) large number of small firms; (2) homogeneous products; (3) free entry and exit; and (4) perfect communication between buyers and sellers

planning (envelope) curve locus of points representing the least unit cost of producing the corresponding output

point price elasticity ratio of a percentage change in quantity demanded to a percentage change in price

present value analysis technique used widely to account for the timing of cash inflows and outflows

primal and dual problems pair of related maximization and minimization problems in linear programming

production function engineering relation that defines the maximum amount of output that can be produced with a given set of inputs

profit maximization hypothesis that the goal of a firm is to maximize its profit

public goods goods that are nonrival and nonexclusionary in consumption and, therefore, benefit persons other than those who buy the goods

r-bar squared r^2 adjusted for the degrees of freedom

regression analysis statistical procedure for estimating mathematically the average relationship between the dependent variable (sales, for example) and one or more independent variables (price and advertising, for example)

regression equation (model) forecasting model that relates the dependent variable (sales, for example) to one or more independent variables (advertising and income, for example)

relevant costs expected future costs (or revenues) which differ between decision alternatives

returns to scale increase in output arising from a proportionate increase in all inputs

risk aversion displaying a diminishing marginal utility of income or wealth

risk variability of actual cash flow around the expected cash flows

risk-adjusted discount rate riskless rate plus a risk premium

Rothschild index measure of the sensitivity to price of a product group as a whole relative to the sensitivity of the quantity demanded of a single firm to a change in its price

***r*-squared** see *coefficient of determination*

saddle point equilibrium point at which the maximum of one's own minimum gain is equal to the minimum of the opponent's maximum gain

second derivative test test to determine whether an extreme point is either a maximum or a minimum point

shadow prices implicit values or opportunity costs associated with given resources in an LP problem

Sherman Antitrust Act first law (1890) passed in the U.S. to prohibit a company's attempt to monopolize

short-run cost curves cost curves for which inputs of production are both variable and fixed

simple regression regression analysis that involves one independent variable

skimming pricing method of pricing that involves setting a high initial price for a new product, with a progressive lowering of the price as time passes, and as the market broadens and matures

standard deviation square root of the mean of the squared deviations from the expected value. An absolute measure of risk

standard error of the estimate standard deviation of the regression. The statistic can be used to gain some idea of the accuracy of our predictions

standard error of the regression coefficient measure of the amount of sampling error in a regression coefficient

statistical cost analysis empirical studies that attempt to ascertain the nature of short-run or long-run cost/output relations

sunk costs costs of resources that have already been incurred at some point in the past whose total will not be affected by any decision made now or in the future

supply function mathematical relationship showing how the quantity supplied of a good or service responds to changes in these factors

the graphical method graphical approach to solving a linear programming (*LP*) problem. It is easier to use but limited to the *LP* problems involving two (or at most three) decision variables

the simplex method linear programming algorithm, which is an iteration method of computation, to move from one corner point solution to another until it reaches the best solution

total fixed costs costs that remain constant in total regardless of changes in activity

total variable costs costs that vary in total in direct proportion to changes in activity

trend analysis statistical procedure for estimating mathematically the average relationship between the dependent variable (sales, for example) and time. Trends are the general upward or downward movements of the average over time

t-**test** test for statistical significance of the regression coefficients

two part pricing pricing that charge a per unit price that equals marginal cost, plus a fixed fee for the right to buy the good or service

unit contribution margin selling price minus average variable cost

value of game payoff at the saddle point

value of the firm *present value* of the firm's expected future cash flows or profits, discounted back to the present at an appropriate interest rate

welfare maximization stockholders value maximization, which is a long-term goal. Wealth maximization is generally preferred because it considers (1) wealth for the long term, (2) risk or uncertainty, (3) timing of returns, and (4) the stockholders' return

zero-sum game situation in which an economic gain by one company results in an economic loss by another

INDEX